Differentiating Instruction and Assessment for English Language Learners

A GUIDE FOR K–12 TEACHERS

Shelley Fairbairn

AND

Stephaney Jones-Vo

SECOND EDITION

Caslon

Philadelphia

Dedication

To Scott and Nora.
—s.f.

To Vinh.
—s.j.v.

And to our wonderful students
from around the world who
continue to teach us.

Cover photo by Tony Rocco and the Shutterbugs After School Photography Program. Courtesy Eugenio María de Hostos Charter School.

Originally published by
Caslon, Inc.
825 N. 27th St.
Philadelphia, PA 19130

Available as of April 2022 from
Paul H. Brookes Publishing Co., Inc.
Post Office Box 10624
Baltimore, Maryland 21285-0624
www.brookespublishing.com

7th printing, November 2023. Manufactured in the United States of America by Integrated Books International, Inc., Dulles, Virginia.

Library of Congress Cataloging-in-Publication Data

Names: Fairbairn, Shelley, author. | Jones-Vo, Stephaney, author.
Title: Differentiating instruction and assessment for English language learners :
    a guide for K–12 teachers / Shelley Fairbairn and Stephaney Jones-Vo.
Description: Second edition. | Philadelphia : Caslon, [2019] | Includes
    bibliographical references.
Identifiers: LCCN 2019002788 (print) | LCCN 2019004777 (ebook) | ISBN
    9781934000397 | ISBN 9781934000380 (alk. paper)
Subjects: LCSH: English language—Study and teaching—Foreign speakers. |
    Multicultural education. | Mainstreaming in education. | Language acquisition.
Classification: LCC PE1128.A2 (ebook) | LCC PE1128.A2 F245 2019 (print) |
    DDC 428.2/4—dc23
LC record available at https://lccn.loc.gov/2019002788

Foreword

The recent and continual movement toward College- and Career-Ready Standards has increased the interest in differentiating instruction for students with various needs. Many articles and books are written each year and the better ones have been helpful for increasing teachers' awareness and skillset to develop differentiated learning environments for students not well served by the mainstream school experience. Despite this increased interest and work, the topic of differentiating instruction as it pertains to language development for English language learners (ELLs) is scarcely addressed and poorly understood—at a time when the number of ELLs has surpassed 5 million in the United States.

ELLs are one of our fastest growing and most diverse populations of students and it is clear that as a nation we are not serving them adequately. Research demonstrates that ELLs, like all students, need access to the same challenging academic skills and content to maximize their opportunities to learn. However, access to grade-level content is only meaningful if teachers have the skills to recognize where ELLs are on the continuum of language development and to differentiate the instruction and assessment in ways that increase engagement and ensure understanding. This is a tall order when we consider that, for the most part, only the English-as-a-second-language (ESL) or bilingual teachers have received training that includes an extensive understanding of the needs of ELLs and effective strategies for meeting those needs. Within most language support programs, ELLs spend a fraction of the day with the ESL or bilingual teacher and most of the day in content-area classes with teachers whose pre-service program and ongoing professional development has included little or no study about meeting ELLs' needs or how to create a discourse-rich, engaging learning environment for every student.

Hence my excitement when I read Shelley Fairbairn and Stephaney Jones-Vo's guide written for all teachers who work with ELLs. Now we have the second edition of that work—even better than the first! The new edition provides more focus on and connections to College- and Career-Ready Standards, and shows teachers how to prepare ELLs to meet the increasing language demands of these standards. Teachers will learn how to use language and literacy-rich practices for ELL success, with attention to the role of home languages and cultures in learning. The second edition emphasizes the importance of gathering formative information about student progress and using that evidence to guide instruction, programming, and professional learning. This edition also prepares teachers to address the particular educational needs of long-term English language learners (LTELLs), students with limited or interrupted formal education (SLIFE), and simultaneous bilinguals in very helpful, pragmatic ways. Fairbairn and Jones-Vo understand the importance of assets-based "can-do" approaches and schoolwide collaboration among teachers to promote equity and excellence for ELLs. Thus, their second edition reflects the practices and mind sets that can make all the difference.

Differentiating Instruction and Assessment for English Language Learners, second edition, is an important resource for teachers because it provides charts and activities that are easy to understand and return to long after an initial reading. At WIDA, we talk a lot about creating an instructional framework that illustrates the linguistic pathways ELLs need to be successful in all academic subjects. This guide makes a significant contribution to recognizing and differentiating for ELLs' growth from the early levels to the more advanced levels of language proficiency. The most striking features of the book are prose that is thorough yet "readable"; the true-to-life scenarios of diverse students and teachers; the focus on classroom assessment strategies; and the connections throughout to content and English language development standards that illustrate the language demands of core content-area classrooms.

The notion that we must explicitly teach language within all academic classes is gaining ground today. Gone are the assumptions of language learning "by osmosis" or that a specialized language arts curriculum alone can provide what ELLs need. Even under the best of classroom circumstances where teachers use a variety of student-centered methods, there is still a role for developing meta-awareness of the role of language in students' learning. To engage students in this kind of intellectual work, teachers have to develop awareness of language and the ways that language is uniquely employed within their class and across differing academic subjects. This attention to academic language helps ELLs access the core school curriculum, but it also supports any learner who struggles with the discourses of school.

This guide is packed with ideas for purposeful and differentiated language instruction and assessment that can be applied in most content classrooms. It provides a guide for teachers who are eager to ensure that students are learning deeply. I predict this second edition will be as popular with teachers facing the challenges of educating ELLs as it will be in university teacher pre-service programs. As teachers read this book and make use of the strategies, they will begin to share the excitement I felt at seeing a guide that addresses language differentiation for ELLs.

Tim Boals, Ph.D.
WIDA Founder and Director
Wisconsin Center for Education Research
UW-Madison School of Education

Preface

The population of English language learners (ELLs) continues to grow in the United States and Canada, not only in number but also in terms of diverse linguistic, cultural, educational, and socioeconomic backgrounds. Using a one-size-fits-all approach to educating diverse learners simply will not work. All teachers must be able to differentiate assignments/assessments and instruction for students in their classes, particularly ELLs, so that they can engage in classroom activities, learn grade-level content, use oral and written English for academic purposes, and achieve in school.

What's New in the Second Edition?

The second edition of *Differentiating Instruction and Assessment for English Language Learners: A Guide for K–12 Teachers* by Shelley Fairbairn and Stephaney Jones-Vo builds on the success of the first edition and incorporates feedback that we have received from teachers and educators in the field. The authors have updated the book to address changes in student demographics, new learning standards, our developing understanding of how students learn to use language and literacy for school success, and innovative teacher-directed approaches to professional learning. We've also added a glossary to facilitate teachers' access to important terms used throughout the book.

For example, in response to the increasing numbers of students with limited or interrupted formal education (SLIFE) and refugees, Fairbairn and Jones-Vo emphasize strategies teachers can use to engage these students as soon as they enter school. Because new college and career-ready standards make greater language and literacy demands on all students, the second edition includes a new chapter on teaching content and language with an explicit focus on the oral and written language that students need to achieve academic success. On a practical level, the authors highlight the essential learning and language demands of each assignment in ways that facilitate differentiation. Further, the authors include new strategies that teachers can use to leverage students' home languages and literacies as resources for learning.

This edition also offers guidance that districts can use to encourage school-based professional learning, collaboration, and accountability among general education and English language development (ELD) teachers, and including literacy and special education professionals who are learning to differentiate assessment and instruction for ELLs. We emphasize the leadership role of the ELD and bilingual specialists, coaches, and mentors who can support classroom implementation. When all teachers share responsibility for educating ELLs, these students can and do achieve.

The Need for This Book

Providing equitable learning opportunities for students from unequal backgrounds requires educators to start their work with an asset orientation, meaning that they look at all students in terms of the linguistic and cultural resources they bring with them to school, with attention to what these students know and can do with content, literacy, and language. An asset orientation differs from a deficit orientation, which looks at students in terms of what they do not know and cannot do. This book encourages a very strong asset orientation.

Our classrooms include an increasing number of U.S.-born and immigrant children who speak languages other than English. Some of these students come from families who have emigrated from around the globe. In addition to specific educational, linguistic, and cultural needs, these ELLs may also have needs related to their socioeconomic status. It is important for teachers to know their students and understand how their background experiences influence learning. For example:

- Some students are the children of professionals who have come to work or study in the United States. These students are often at grade level in their home language and are ready to immediately participate in U.S. classrooms. Many have developed strong literacy skills in their home languages that support and strengthen their ELD and academic achievement.
- Other ELLs are refugees from troubled areas around the world. This group is often overlooked and in need of special consideration. Prior to their arrival, many of these displaced persons were born or living in war zones or refugee camps. Such school-age newcomers often arrive in classrooms with little or no experience regarding expectations of U.S. schools in terms of academic preparation, classroom behavior, grade-level achievement, and socialization skills.
- Some students arrive with limited or interrupted formal education (SLIFE). Most likely, these students will not have learned to read and write in their home language, or are reading below grade level. These students may also need basic literacy and numeracy instruction, as well as a cultural orientation to the norms that guide behavior in U.S. schools.
- Increasing numbers of ELLs are born in the United States and come to school with some foundation in English and cultural norms of U.S. society. Most of these students are simultaneous bilinguals who grow up

learning English and another home language at the same time. These students often sound like they are "English speakers," and unknowing teachers may not realize that they are in fact designated as ELLs. Care must be taken to provide appropriate learning opportunities so that these students don't slip through the cracks.

■ Many simultaneous bilinguals are not officially designated as ELLs and are still developing the oral and written English they need to succeed at school. Oftentimes, however, the bilingualism of these students is not seen or acknowledged. Teachers will learn strategies to leverage these students' bilingualism for learning.

■ There is increasing concern for long-term ELLs (LTELLs) who do not meet the criteria to exit their ELD program in a reasonable amount of time. Although a student may be blamed for not being able to learn English (a deficit orientation), the challenge often lies with the learning opportunities that schools provide for these students. Teachers and schools need to identify what students can do with oral and written language, in their home languages and in English, and build on that foundation so that students can acquire the English they need for academic success.

■ Another group of students that cannot be overlooked is U.S.-born home language speakers of vernacular varieties of English (e.g., African American vernacular English or AAVE, often referred to colloquially as Ebonics; regional vernaculars such as Southern American English; and Chicano English) whose use of English is not considered standard. These non-ELLs, or "standard English learners" (Freeman & Freeman, 2009), will also advance their development of oral and written English for academic purposes with appropriate instruction, differentiated according to students' linguistic needs.

The authors have developed this book in response to K–12 teachers' requests for guidance on how to differentiate instruction and assignments/assessments for the diverse ELLs in their classrooms. These teachers understand that, in accordance with Lau v. Nichols (1974), providing ELLs only with instruction identical to that designed for home language speakers of "standard" English is not sufficient. Further, such teachers realize that the key to students' understanding content and acquiring the English they need for academic success is through implementing differentiated instruction that takes into account students' ELP levels and other background factors.

The Organization of the Book

The first three chapters of this book are foundational. Chapter 1 describes what it means to differentiate assignments/assessments and instruction for ELLs, introduces the Differentiating Assignment Template that is featured throughout the book, emphasizes the need for collaboration among all teachers who work with ELLs, and shows teachers how to interpret ELP data. Chapter 2 explains the importance of and demonstrates how to become acquainted with one's students and their families. Chapter 3 begins with general guidelines for working with ELLs and explores the notion of *academic language* with an emphasis on the language acquisition and the sociocultural processes that influence how multilingual students learn to use oral and written English for academic purposes.

Chapters 4 through 8 are parallel in structure, and each chapter focuses on students at a different ELP level: Chapter 4 targets students at level 1, Chapter 5 targets students at level 2, and so on. Each of these chapters is divided into four parts. The first part introduces two scenarios of actual students who perform at the same ELP level and are in the same grade. One of the students has a strong educational foundation in the home language, while the other has experienced limited or interrupted formal education and may not have learned to read and write in their home language. By focusing on the contrasting needs of these two students, teachers learn strategies to address challenges that students face due to factors other than ELD. The second part of these chapters presents an example of a Differentiated Assignment using the template introduced in Chapter 1. The authors demonstrate how teachers choose appropriate strategies that are aligned with content area standards and appropriate for students at a given ELP level. The third and fourth part of each of these chapters takes us to lesson planning and offers a wide range of assignment/assessment and instructional strategies with concrete examples to bring this work to life.

Chapter 9 shows teachers how use the Differentiation Assignment Template for students at all five ELP levels, with examples from elementary, middle, and high school. This template provides spaces for teachers to list differentiated language-based expectations according to ELP level for any content area assignment, and to include corresponding scaffolding and support strategies for these students, ensuring that they can demonstrate their understanding of the essential learning and meet the language demands of the assignment, given consideration of students' ELP levels. This chapter also answers questions that teachers frequently ask about their most challenging cases, particularly with respect to special education considerations for ELLs.

How to Use the Book and Quick-Reference Chart

A key feature of Fairbairn and Jones-Vo's work is the quick-reference chart that accompanies the book. This popular resource includes student descriptors, assignment/assessment strategies, and instructional strategies for students at ELP levels 1–5. Teachers can use this resource to quickly identify appropriate strategies in the domains of listening, speaking, reading, and writing. All of the strategies included on the chart are illustrated in the chapters with concrete examples of classroom practice. The chart is intended to be used in classrooms as a quick reference to create appropriately differentiated assignments/assessments and lesson plans.

We encourage educators to read the book from start to finish so that they understand how to effectively implement the ideas and information presented, before using the quick-reference chart. We do, however, recognize that some teachers may elect to only read certain chapters because they work with students who represent particular ELP levels. In these cases, we recommend that readers begin with the first three foundational chapters before proceeding to the chapters that focus on the specific ELP levels. Teachers will also benefit from using the practical end-of-chapter professional learning activities and resources. These activities and resources provide teachers with opportunities, either individually or in professional learning communities, to apply what they have learned in the chapter to actual students, first to those that were highlighted in the chapter and then to their own students.

This book and the accompanying chart uniquely offer teachers detailed guidance in how to help ELLs reach high content-area standards given consideration of what they can do with oral and written English and according to other important background factors. In this way, teachers can meet students at their current level and help them use oral and written English to achieve success in the classroom and beyond.

Contents

Chapter 1

Differentiating for English Language Learners

Let us remember: One book, one pen, one child, and one teacher can change the world.

— MALALA YOUSAFZAI

All students are entitled to equal educational opportunities under the law, including students from linguistically and culturally diverse backgrounds. To understand what this means, we need to distinguish between *equality* and *equity*. Equality in education is generally understood as equal treatment. In contrast, equity in education is generally understood as equal outcomes. Educators concerned with equity in education understand that treating students from unequal backgrounds in the same way does not lead to equal outcomes. Rather, these educators hold equally high expectations for all students, and provide different educational pathways so that students from diverse backgrounds can excel (Blankstein & Noguera, 2016). Equity in education is about fairness and it is a civil right.

Differentiated instruction and assessment is a framework or philosophy for the effective teaching of diverse learners that involves providing different pathways to learning so that every student can reach equally high expectations and standards, regardless of background. Students may vary in terms of culture, socioeconomic status, language, gender, motivation, ability/disability, personal interests, and more. Teachers who differentiate start with an understanding of who their students are and what they can do, and they may differentiate in terms of content, processing, tasks, groupings, materials, and assessment so that all of their students can achieve (Tomlinson, 2014).

This book outlines what teachers and specialists need to know and be able to do to effectively differentiate instruction and assessment for the English language learners (ELLs) in their classes. This chapter introduces the concept of linguistic differentiation, and we discuss the importance of shared responsibility among all teachers with language learners in their classes, including general education, English as a second language (ESL), literacy, bilingual education, and special education teachers and specialists. Next we consider how teachers can use their state-mandated English language development data to understand what ELLs can be expected to do with listening, speaking, reading, and writing in content-area instruction. Then we introduce a differentiation template that teachers can use as a guide when selecting appropriate assessment and instruction strategies for the ELLs in their classes. The chapter ends with a description of the process of differentiating instruction for ELLs in any K–12 classroom and for any content area.

We use the term *general education teacher* to refer to elementary classroom and secondary content-area teachers who use English to teach grade-level content in the general education classroom. We use the term *English language development* (ELD) teacher to refer to language education specialists who teach English as a second or new language at school. We use the term *bilingual education teacher* for all teachers who use two languages for instructional purposes in transitional bilingual programs and dual language programs.

All educational programs that include ELLs (in general education, bilingual education, special education, and talented and gifted programs) are required to offer a coherent ELD component taught by competent ELD teachers. Literacy and special education teachers and specialists need to work closely with general education, bilingual education, and ELD teachers to ensure coherent implementation of differentiation strategies for ELLs throughout the instructional day.

Our focus in this book is on differentiating instruction and assessment for students who are officially designated as ELLs. We refer to all other students as non-ELLs (instead of English-speakers) and remind teachers that the non-ELLs category is very broad. Some non-ELLs may be monolingual speakers of English and some may speak vernacular or regional varieties of English. Other non-ELLs may speak languages other than English at home in addition to English, and there is a wide range of expertise in oral and written home languages among these multilingual learners. Some non-ELLs may be former ELLs who have been exited from ELL status. These former ELLs are still learning to use oral and written English for academic purposes, although they are no longer officially designated as ELLs. Teachers will find that the instructional and assessment strategies that we recommend for ELLs will also serve diverse groups of non-ELLs in the general education classroom. After all, every student in the classroom is learning to use English for academic purposes—non-ELLs and ELLs alike.

What Does It Mean to Differentiate for English Language Learners?

Teacher Scenarios

Ms. Harris is a first-year teacher who was surprised to learn that she will have four English language learners (ELLs) in her classroom. Her teacher education program did not require her to take a course on working with ELLs, so she is feeling somewhat nervous. A friend who has also just begun teaching reminds her that they were both taught about the concept of differentiation. The friend assures Ms. Harris that she will be fine if she simply applies those concepts.

Mrs. Turner is not new to teaching, or to working with diverse learners. She feels comfortable about her work with a colleague in special education. This collaboration has served her special needs students well in the past few years, but she is troubled with how to best meet the needs of the ELLs in her classroom. Although she has served one or two very studious ELLs in the past, this year she has six students from a variety of educational, cultural, and linguistic backgrounds in her classroom. At times, she feels overwhelmed by the challenge of working with these students and disheartened because she is unsure of how to best meet their needs.

The notion of differentiated instruction has gained currency and credibility as an effective and powerful means to meet the needs of diverse learners in today's classrooms. This approach allows content-area teachers to take into consideration the readiness of each learner while facilitating instruction and assessment using the same content standards for all students. According to Tomlinson (2014),

> Teachers in differentiated classrooms use time flexibly, call upon a range of instructional strategies, and become partners with their students so that both what is learned and the learning environment are shaped to support the learner and learning. They do not force-fit learners into a standard mold; these teachers are students of their students (p. 4).

Many differentiated assessment and instruction professional learning opportunities to date have focused on addressing the needs of special education students, with little attention to ELLs.

Differentiating instruction and assessment for ELLs is not the same as differentiating for special education students. Differentiating for ELLs involves considering how these students' English language proficiency (ELP) levels in listening, speaking, reading, and writing influence what individual students can be expected to do with content. Differentiating for ELLs also involves knowing how student background factors, including prior schooling, home language literacy, cultural orientation, immigration and refugee status, and other difficult experiences influence their learning in grade-level classes. Although some of the instructional and assessment strategies that teachers use with special education students and ELLs might be similar, the reasons for using these strategies are different.

Furthermore, differentiating instruction and assessment for ELLs is not the same as sheltered instruction, an approach that teachers use to make complex content comprehensible to these students while promoting their development of academic English. The sheltered instruction observation protocol (SIOP) model (Echevarria, Vogt, & Short, 2016) is fundamentally a lesson planning framework that teachers can use when planning and implementing content-area instruction in classes that include ELLs. While the SIOP model highlights important features of effective instruction for ELLs, it does not show teachers how to use students' ELP levels to select differentiation strategies. This book shows teachers how to understand and use information about their ELLs' strengths and needs to ensure that they have equal access to learning opportunities all day, every day.

Creating Classrooms That Are Accessible to All Learners

Teachers can draw on universal design to create classroom practices that are accessible to all students from the start (Meyer, Rose, & Gordon, 2014). Mimicking the idea of universal design for architecture, which creates an environment accessible to all individuals regardless of abilities (CAST, 2011), universal design for learning helps teachers create classroom environments and activities that are accessible to diverse learners. Rather than attempt to retrofit unsuitable instructional design for diverse learners, universal design for learning begins with the needs of diverse learners in mind.

With universal design for learning, variations in student needs are anticipated and planned for, rather than perceived as aberrations or problems. Therefore, teachers, whether novice or veteran, must know how to make the curriculum accessible according to the student's current level of content knowledge and skills, and with an understanding of each student's ELP level, as well as information about the student's prior schooling, literacy, language, cultural background, and any other relevant factors. This means that general education teachers, such as Ms. Harris and Mrs. Turner, can work together to plan content lessons that address the needs of all of their students, including ELLs. ELD and bilingual education teachers can also tailor their instruction and assessment to the needs of students at different levels of language and literacy development across the two languages. Likewise, ELD teachers can work with general education teachers to provide appropriate instruction and assessment for linguistically and culturally diverse learners in all of their classes. This type of collaborative work on behalf of ELL students is the ideal approach, merging the expertise of different kinds of teachers to ensure that diverse learners receive high-quality instruction and assessment that is responsive to their linguistic and cultural needs.

This merging of teacher expertise requires that teachers work together to build an atmosphere that fosters the sharing of pedagogical insight and skills. For instance, many ELD teachers may not be experts in all content areas. Likewise, many general education teachers, such as Ms. Harris and Mrs. Turner, have not received training to deepen their expertise in the issues associated with teaching ELLs. Teachers need cross-training, which we define as professional learning opportunities in which teachers with one kind of expertise (e.g., content teachers) gain expertise about another area (e.g., language learning and teaching strategies). To maximize the efficacy of both content-area teachers and ELD teachers, we advocate that these teachers partner and share expertise for the benefit of all of their students (Jones-Vo et al., 2007).

Sharing Responsibility for English Language Learner Achievement

To ensure that diverse learners enjoy equal access to the curriculum and equal opportunity to realize their educational potential, every teacher must embrace responsibility for the learning of each of the students in her or his classroom. More specifically, ELLs are the shared responsibility of all teachers, including general education, ELD, and bilingual education teachers, as well as literacy, special education, and talented and gifted specialists, who have these students in their classes. Together, these teachers are responsible for ensuring that the ELLs in their classes can comprehend and engage with standards-based content and texts. ELD teachers are responsible for ensuring that ELLs acquire the oral and written academic language they need to perform in the content-area classroom. All teachers need to tailor their instruction and assessment so it is accessible for the diverse students in their classes, and teachers need to collaborate with each other. Through purposeful collaboration, teachers can ensure comprehensible instruction that promotes English language development throughout the school day.

This collaborative approach stands in contrast to traditional approaches for educating ELLs, in which the ELD teacher is primarily responsible for ELL achievement, despite the fact that these students generally spend much less time with their ELD teachers than with their general education teachers. Increasingly, we find that districts are elevating the status of ELD teachers, who are taking on more leadership and capacity-building roles in the district.

We urge teachers to enter into collaborative relationships, or reciprocal mentoring (Jones-Vo et al., 2007), while learning about differentiating instruction and when implementing this approach in the classroom. There are many ways that districts can do this. For example, some districts create professional learning communities (PLCs) of ELL educators, with the goal of equipping these teachers to become ELL coaches or teacher leaders who support the learning of general education teachers. Other districts may form PLCs by content areas, with groups of science teachers, for example, working together to develop a differentiated science curriculum that is appropriate for linguistically and culturally diverse learners. Districts may include ELL teachers, coaches, or teacher leaders who can support the linguistic differentiation work of the science teachers as they roll out their differentiated science curriculum to the larger school community in the PLCs. The curriculum work done by the science team could then serve as a launching point for developing the next differentiated content-area curriculum, for example, in social studies. Another possibility is that interdisciplinary teams of teachers work together to develop a theme-based differentiated curriculum that aligns with cross-curricular standards.

Such mutually beneficial partnerships can expand and enrich teaching capacity, resulting in improved instructional and assessment practices that better serve all students in the classroom. Through purposeful collaboration, teachers can seamlessly blend appropriate strategies for instruction and assessment and set the stage for increased academic achievement for students from diverse backgrounds.

General Education Teacher Role

ELLs spend the majority of their instructional time in general education classrooms. General education teachers, therefore, need to know how to differentiate content-area instruction and assessment for these students, a reality that Ms. Harris will soon discover, and one of which Mrs. Turner is already keenly aware. Without specific knowledge related to language development, even the most willing and eager teacher will struggle needlessly with understanding how to differentiate instruction and assessment for ELLs. Knowing how important educational, cultural, and linguistic factors can profoundly and predictably affect each student's learning and language development will provide a lifeline for Ms. Harris, Mrs. Turner, and other teachers in similar situations. General education teachers who know how to differentiate for ELLs will enable every ELL student to participate equitably in content-area instruction and to achieve.

The general education teacher is primarily responsible for teaching standards-aligned content to all students in the classroom, including ELLs. Because general education teachers use language as a vehicle for content-area instruction and assessment, they are responsible for teaching and assessing both content and language. General education teachers do not need to be language specialists, but they do need to know how to differentiate content-area instruction in ways that build on what students know and can do with language. Their primary responsibility is for teaching and assessing content, using language for academic purposes and according to students' ELP levels and other factors. Ultimately general education teachers need to ensure that ELLs can demonstrate content mastery while still developing English.

English Language Development Teacher Role

Like general education teachers, the ELD teacher is responsible for teaching content and language. However, the ELD teacher focuses primarily on ensuring that students learn the language they need to participate and achieve in content-area classes and succeed academically. As general education teachers assume responsibility for the ELLs in their classes, ELD teachers can take on more of a leadership and capacity-building role in the general education program. This leadership role can include a wide range of practices, with the ELD teacher or specialist taking on one or more of the following:

- Introducing general education teachers to the specific ELLs in their classes, with attention to their ELP level, home language literacy, prior schooling, cultural background, and other important factors they need to consider as they teach and assess these students.
- Sharing instruction and assessment strategies that general education teachers can use with ELLs at different ELP levels.
- Creating demonstration lessons for general education teachers that illustrate differentiation strategies in action.
- Developing ELL portfolios that illustrate student growth over time.
- Team teaching with general education teachers.
- Collaborating with content-area teachers to develop differentiated math, science, social studies, and language arts curricula that will engage ELLs from diverse backgrounds.
- Working in teams to develop a content-based ELD curriculum with a scope and sequence that aligns with all content areas and includes formative assessments.
- Documenting model lessons for a professional learning library that teachers can use for professional development.

Equity for all students is an important focus of these and other innovative collaborations that we increasingly find in schools and districts today.

Structures for Collaboration

There are a variety of ways that teachers with a common vision can team up to address the content, language, literacy, and learning needs of all students, particularly ELLs, while considering the resources and needs of the district. Here are a few specific examples of collaborative structures commonly found in districts and schools today.

Pull-out. Pull-out ELD instruction means that ELLs are pulled out of the general education classroom for dedicated ELD instruction. In terms of collaboration, pull-out ELD instruction can be a useful delivery model, particularly during the early levels of students' ELD. During pull-out sessions, the ELD teacher can focus on targeted instruction for small groups of specific ELLs to build their oral and written competence in English. The general education teacher can collaborate with the ELD teacher to choose topics, projects, and themes for their shared students. As such, the pull-out time can be utilized to thematically support language development in ways that are linked to curricular topics. Interdisciplinary integrated thematic instruction provides a strong foundation for students' continued development of oral and written English for academic purposes.

Pull-out ELD classes should not be used indefinitely because they tend to isolate ELLs from their non-ELL peers, who provide modeling and authentic opportunities to interact and use language. Integrating ELLs into general education classes benefits the student learning English and enriches the classroom environment for everyone.

Push-in. In this model a trained professional joins the general education teacher in the classroom and provides support for the ELLs in the class. The professional who pushes in could be an ELD specialist, a bilingual content teacher, an experienced paraprofessional, or even a volunteer. A bilingual push-in teacher can use the students' home language to clarify instruction and support ELLs as they complete assignments. The push-in model works well when the classroom teacher and the push-in teacher or paraprofessional work closely to align their planning and focus on student achievement of the content and language standards and objectives. This expanded support can ensure that ELLs comprehend the curriculum content and are producing oral and written English for academic purposes.

Teacher Leader. In this model, a classroom teacher takes on additional leadership responsibilities; works with other teachers; and provides demonstration lessons, coaching, and mentoring. A teacher leader may be an experienced mathematics teacher, knowledgeable in the grade-level curriculum, and experienced in teaching ELLs. The teacher leader might design weekly instructional units based on the curriculum, identify essential vocabulary, and create differentiated assignments/assessments, and instructional strategies. The teacher leader may also design and procure manipulatives, games, and other classroom materials. Further, at weekly grade-level planning meetings with the other classroom mathematics teachers, the teacher leader shares differentiation strategies used in the math unit for ELLs at different ELP levels.

This approach ensures that all students receive consistent content-area instruction and the same high-quality materials to enhance student learning. Further, through the teacher leader model, linguistically differentiated mathematics instruction is consistently linked to the district's curriculum. If teachers notice that a student is falling behind or has difficulty with a math concept, the pull-out model can be implemented for enrichment and further instruction.

When implementing a collaboration structure such as the teacher leader model, it is incumbent on districts to allocate dedicated planning time for teachers in the school day on a regular and sustained basis.

Collaborative Lesson Planning. Another way to collaborate and build capacity is to use dedicated time for weekly meetings where general education and ELD teachers co-plan lessons. In this model, the classroom and ELD teachers meet to choose assignments, set clear goals, develop content and language objectives, select important vocabulary, and identify differentiated instruction and assessment strategies that meet learner needs. The ELD teacher enhances language instruction through actual classroom content material, making language learning authentic and meaningful. Both teachers share and exchange their expertise and apply it in the classroom. As a result, classroom teachers can learn to use recommended linguistic differentiation strategies and ELD teachers become more familiar with the classroom material and support content learning in the classroom. These combined efforts are likely to result in increased student learning, and can be adapted and spread to other classrooms.

Co-teaching. In this model, two experts with different backgrounds, such as an ELD teacher and a 3rd-grade content teacher, teach a class together and share responsibility for all students. When observing this type of partnership, one might not recognize which teacher is actually the "teacher of record." Through co-planning and co-delivering the content, students receive the benefit of both teacher perspectives and types of expertise. The co-teachers require dedicated planning time and are mutually responsible for the learning of all students in the class.

While we have offered a brief overview of a few collaborative models here, teachers are reminded that there are numerous ways to collaborate (Honigsfeld & Dove, 2017). We encourage teachers to engage in conversations and develop collaborative models that best suit their own instructional contexts.

Using English Language Proficiency Data

Teachers need to understand and be able to use data on students' ELP levels, which are readily available in U.S. public schools. All students who are officially designated as ELLs must take annual state-mandated ELP tests. Most states belong to the WIDA Consortium, which administers the ACCESS for ELLs test. Other states belong to the ELPA21 Consortium, which administers the ELPA21 test. New York, California, and Texas have each developed their own state-approved standards and assessment systems. Teachers are encouraged to draw on their state ELD frameworks because they constitute an important part of their state accountability system. All of these systems provide data about what ELLs can do overall with English, and, specifically, in the domains of reading, writing, listening, and speaking every year. These data can be used to monitor ELL growth over time.

Consistent with the WIDA standards framework, we distinguish between ELD and ELP. ELD refers to movement along a continuum of language development over time and can be made explicit through appropriate formative assessment. ELP is a snapshot of performance at one moment in time and is identified using state-mandated ELP tests.

There are similarities and differences, as well as pros and cons, among the different state ELD systems. For example, WIDA, ELPA21, and New York all divide the ELD continuum into five levels, while Texas uses four levels and California uses three. New York has also created bilingual Common Core progressions for language arts that teachers can use to identify English and home language development levels relative to state language arts standards. We encourage teachers to relate the five ELD levels used in this book to the levels used in their state, and to draw on other systems as appropriate. ELD and bilingual teachers can help general education, literacy, special education, and talented and gifted teachers and specialists understand the language development systems used in their context. Because WIDA is used by most states, this book aligns most closely with their system and uses five ELP levels.

Teachers can turn to their state-mandated ELP data and identify what each of their ELLs at different ELP levels can do with reading, writing, listening, and speaking in English. When teachers know what their ELLs can do with oral and written English, they can choose appropriate instruction and assessment strategies for these students. To support teachers in this work, WIDA has created the Can-Do descriptors (www.wida.us/standards/CAN_DOs), which are general indicators of what students at a particular ELP level can do with English in the domains of listening, speaking, reading, and writing at different grade levels and across content areas. We refer to these indicators, presented in Table 1.1, as "student descriptors." Teachers can also find the student descriptors on the top row of the quick-reference chart included with this book. These student descriptors reflect an assets-based perspective on language that draws attention to what students can do with their developing language, rather than defining them in terms of language limitations or deficits.

To illustrate the kinds of variation we find among ELLs, we look at profiles of five 5th-grade students. Each profile begins with the student's composite or overall ELP level, followed by information about the student's background and then his or her levels in the domains of listening, speaking, reading, and writing. Readers are encouraged to consult Table 1-1 to identify what each student can do with listening, speaking, reading, and writing.

- **Julia:** composite ELP level 3. Julia was born in the United States to a Mexican family that speaks mostly Spanish at home and in the neighborhood. She has attended school in the United States since kindergarten. There is no bilingual program at her school, and Julia has not learned to read and write in Spanish. According to the state ELP test, Julia has reached level 5 in listening, level 4 in speaking, level 3 in reading, and level 2 in writing.

- **Ko Than Nu:** composite ELP level 3. Ko Than Nu is a refugee from Myanmar who speaks Karen and who has been in the United States for two years. Prior to coming to the United States, he had no formal schooling and had not learned to read or write. When Ko Than Nu arrived, he was placed in a newcomer class that focused on literacy and numeracy development, with attention to the cultural norms of U.S. schools and society. According to the state ELP test, Ko Than Nu has attained level 4 in listening and speaking and level 2 in reading and writing in English.

- **Amitabh:** composite ELP level 3. Amitabh is from India, speaks Gujarati, and arrived in the United States in the middle of last year. He has a strong educational background that included English instruction every year in India. However, Amitabh's English class gave him very little opportunity to speak English, and he had little exposure to American English prior to his arrival. According to the state ELP test, Amitabh has attained level 2 in listening, level 1 in speaking, level 5 in reading, and level 4 in writing.

- **Marco:** composite ELP level 1. He was born in Brazil and speaks Brazilian Portuguese. Marco attended school in Brazil up to 4th grade, and he can read and write in Portuguese. Marco's family moved to the United States earlier this year for work. According to the state ELP placement test, Marco is at ELP level 1 in all four domains.

- **Aurelio:** composite ELP level 4. Aurelio is from Columbia where he attended a strong Spanish–English bilingual elementary school before coming to the United States two years ago. Aurelio speaks mostly Spanish at home. According to the state ELP test, Aurelio has attained level 5 in listening, level 4 in speaking, and level 3 in reading and writing.

These profiles illustrate the need to look beyond a student's composite or overall ELP score or level to target needed language instruction. Let's start with Julia, Ko Than Nu, and Amitabh, who have all attained composite ELP level 3. Notice, however, that their levels vary when we look at the domains of listening, speaking, reading, and writing. This variation can be explained when we consider these students' language, literacy, cultural, and educational backgrounds (Field, 2015).

Julia represents a large number of ELLs who score higher in listening and speaking than in reading and writing in English. Julia can use English to converse with her friends, tell them what she did the night before, joke with them,

Table 1-1   Student Descriptors by English Language Proficiency Levels

Level 1	Level 2	Level 3	Level 4	Level 5
LISTENING				
Begins to recognize often-heard words and phrases that are supported contextually; requires frequent restatement or paraphrasing; begins to develop awareness of the sound system of English.	Develops ability to respond to frequently heard language with continued dependence on context, paraphrasing, and repetition; begins to build content and academic vocabulary.	Interprets meaning of sentence-level communication in social and general academic contexts; understands main ideas of more complex oral discourse, particularly when supported visually; continues to build repertoire of content and academic vocabulary and sentence structures.	Understands social and academic discourse of differing lengths and levels of complexity; comprehends a wide variety of social and content/academic vocabulary related to both concrete and abstract concepts, particularly with visual or contextual support.	Comprehends a broad spectrum of social and academic discourse, attends to language with an increasing amount of linguistic complexity, understands most grade-level content/academic vocabulary, approaches the range of grade-level performance exhibited by non-ELLs.
SPEAKING				
Possibly silent; produces often-heard words, memorized phrases, or self-generated language to express meaning or ask questions; supports communication with nonverbal cues; begins to produce the range of sounds of English.	Uses phrases and simple sentences, likely omitting key words, to communicate about common experiences and situations; begins to produce content and academic vocabulary; errors often inhibit communication.	Generates simple sentences with minimal errors, though more complex sentences contain errors that may inhibit communication; may appear fluent because of near mastery of social language, whereas content and academic language continues to develop related to concrete and abstract concepts; uses more precise and specific content and academic vocabulary and increasingly complex grammatical structures.	Generates grammatically varied speech in a wide variety of social and academic contexts using content/academic vocabulary related to concrete and abstract concepts; errors do not typically obstruct meaning.	Produces a broad spectrum of extended discourse with increasing linguistic complexity and vocabulary mastery; approaches the range of grade-level performance exhibited by non-ELLs.

Level 1	Level 2	Level 3	Level 4	Level 5
READING				
Gains meaning primarily from visual support; if literate in the first language, may start to transfer those skills to English when provided with high-quality, visually supported reading instruction.	May recognize and read words and phrases frequently encountered; gains meaning from simple and familiar text with visual support.	Derives meaning from increasingly complex sentence- and paragraph-level text, but requires visual and teacher support; draws on background knowledge and previous experiences to make sense of longer text.	Comprehends increasingly complex text on known topics, while unknown topics continue to require visual or contextual support.	Comprehends text of increasing linguistic complexity and vocabulary related to a variety of grade-appropriate subjects and genres; approaches the range of grade-level performance exhibited by non-ELLs.
WRITING				
May draw, copy written text, or write or dictate individual letters, words, or phrases (or approximations thereof) to convey meaning.	Dictates phrases and simple sentences with occasional content and academic vocabulary when supported; errors often obstruct meaning.	Writes increasingly complex sentences with a wide social vocabulary and a developing range of content and academic vocabulary related to concrete and abstract concepts; errors sometimes obstruct meaning.	Produces social and academic text using increasingly precise content/academic vocabulary and increasingly complex grammar and mechanics related to concrete and abstract concepts; errors do not typically obstruct meaning.	Writes text varying in length, complexity, vocabulary mastery, and level of academic discourse; approaches the range of grade-level performance exhibited by non-ELLs.

and argue about who is the fastest runner. Julia can also use Spanish to talk with her parents and grandparents about what she did at school and to keep them apprised of her after-school plans, but she has not learned how to read and write in Spanish. As the most advanced English speaker in her household, Julia takes on responsibilities as a language and cultural interpreter by answering phones, negotiating health and social service appointments for her parents and grandparents, and moving fluidly between Spanish and English as needed. Julia has a strong foundation in oral Spanish and English, but she is still developing the ways of using oral and written English in school settings to summarize a reading, demonstrate her understanding of a text with sufficient detail, and produce a strong, evidence-based argument in writing. Students like Julia are sometimes referred to as long-term ELLs (LTELLs) (Menken & Kleyn, 2010).

Ko Than Nu also scores higher on the state ELP test in listening and speaking than he does in reading and writing. He participates enthusiastically in everyday conversations in English with his peers and eagerly contributes orally in class discussions about topics that he knows something about. However, Ko Than Nu had not had attended school before he came to the United States. He spent nearly ten years at a refugee camp in Thailand, and he understands Thai in addition to Karen. He and his family now regularly attend a local Baptist church where English, Karen, and other languages from Myanmar are used. Ko Than Nu has not had the opportunity to learn to read and write in his home language, and he is far below grade level. He is unsuccessful when the teacher asks him to read grade-level texts independently, and he struggles with colloquial English (e.g., "The boy was in a pickle" in a children's story). Because the cultural norms at school are new to Ko Than Nu, sometimes teachers think he has behavior problems. Ko Than Nu represents a group referred to as students with limited or interrupted former education (SLIFE). These students need intensive and comprehensive support for literacy and numeracy development, with attention to the cultural norms of U.S. schools and society (DeCapua & Marshall, 2011).

We find students like Amitabh less frequently in U.S. schools, but his profile helps us avoid overgeneralizations and stereotypes about intermediate ELLs. Amitabh's prior schooling provides him with a strong foundation for literacy and academic success in English and in Gujarati. Amitabh's family travels internationally every year to visit their relatives, and this year he will spend the summer break in India and England. Because Amitabh's English instruction in India focused on grammar, reading, and writing, he is just beginning to develop oral American English. Because it is uncommon for ELLs to have stronger reading and writing skills than listening and speaking skills, teachers may not recognize Amitabh's content-area expertise or literacy strengths, and they may treat him more like a beginning ELL in all domains.

Let's turn now to Marco, who scores as a level 1 ELL in all domains. Many general education teachers get apprehensive when they find students like Marco in their classes because Marco's English is just emerging. Marco is beginning to recognize words that he has heard before, but he probably needs a considerable amount of paraphrasing and repetition to support comprehension. Marco may not speak in English at first, or he may simply be able to produce high-frequency words, formulaic expressions, or memorized phrases. To derive meaning from print, Marco will need to rely on visuals and on his home language. Marco's writing will consist primarily of drawings, or copied written texts. Marco will benefit from teachers who are welcoming and open to all of his efforts to communicate, in English and in his home language. Marco will also really benefit from a buddy, especially one who speaks his home language.

We conclude this section with a closer look at what Aurelio can do with listening, speaking, reading, and writing, using the student descriptors for guidance. Recall that Aurelio has attained a composite ELP level 4, with level 5 in listening, level 4 in speaking, level 3 in reading, and level 3 in writing. As we can see from the student descriptors in Table 1-1,

- *Level 5 listening* means that Aurelio can independently comprehend a broad spectrum of social and academic discourse; attend to language with an increasing amount of linguistic complexity; understand most grade-level, content-specific, and general academic vocabulary; and approach grade-level performance in English.
- *Level 4 speaking* means that Aurelio can independently generate grammatically varied speech in a wide range of social and academic contexts and use academic vocabulary related to concrete and abstract concepts. Errors do not typically obstruct meaning.

A major challenge for general education teachers is to understand that students who are at relatively advanced levels of listening and speaking may have attained lower levels in reading and writing. That is, students like Aurelio sound like they can speak English, but their literacy levels are not as advanced. Because literacy is associated with academic success on standardized achievement tests, teachers need to pay particular attention to literacy development.

- Aurelio has reached *level 3 in reading*. At this level, Aurelio can be expected to comprehend increasingly complex text on known topics. Unknown topics continue to require visual or contextual support.
- Aurelio has attained *level 3 in writing*. Teachers can assume that Aurelio will write increasingly complex sentences, use a wide range of social vocabulary, and a developing range of content and academic vocabulary related to concrete and abstract concepts. Errors sometimes obstruct meaning.

Teachers can draw on Aurelio's strengths in listening, speaking, and reading to support his writing development. Because Aurelio is literate in Spanish and English, teachers can also apply his Spanish literacy to further English literacy development.

This book shows teachers how to select differentiation strategies that help students advance from their independent level (i.e., what students can do with language independently) to the next higher ELP level, given appropriate instructional scaffolding and support. Educators are reminded that these levels are broad and that a student whose test data lists one level may actually be on the cusp of the next level and should be pushed toward that level. Alternately, a given student may be at the lower end of the continuum for his or her particular ELP level and may struggle to meet the assignment demands for that level. The micro-differentiation necessary for these students is, of course, at the discretion of the teacher and is part of the art of teaching. Sorting out when and how to perform micro-differentiation can be achieved through reciprocal mentoring, in which content and language teachers and paraeducators collaborate to share their expertise and insights.

Teachers can also draw on students' home language—oracy and literacy—to support content, literacy, and language learning in English. With strategic language differentiation, ELLs across the continuum of language development can engage with grade-level content-area instruction in all of their content and language classes. With linguistically mindful pedagogy, ELLs benefit from learning content and language simultaneously, and they are afforded parity in terms of access to the curriculum. Developing the skills necessary for data-based linguistic differentiation of instruction and assessment is a necessity for teachers like Ms. Harris and Mrs. Turner, and all other teachers with ELLs in their classes.

Differentiating Assignment Template

This book shows teachers how to differentiate content-area assignments/assessments and instruction for ELLs at any level of language development, grade level, and content area. Teachers need to begin by understanding which parts of an assignment can be differentiated. Any assignment can be divided into three parts:

1. Standards-based content or topic from the curriculum
2. Language-based expectations
3. Scaffolding and support

In most cases, the standards-based content or topic will remain the same for students at all ELP levels. This ensures that all students are focused on the same content, which is aligned with state content-area standards. The language-based expectations and the scaffolding and support are the aspects of the assignment that are differentiated according to students' ELP levels in listening, speaking, reading, and writing.

For the sake of illustration, Table 1-2 presents a generic differentiated assignment template for an unspecified ELP level. For any given ELP level, the assignment is rewritten and read vertically, from the standards-based content

Table 1-2   Differentiated Assignment Template, Unspecified English Language Proficiency Level

Standards-Based Content or Topic (from the curriculum)*

Language-Based Expectations†

Scaffolding and Support†

*Same for all ELP levels.
†Differentiated by ELP level.

or topic from the curriculum, to the language-based expectations for ELLs at the focal ELP level, to the scaffolding and support that students at the focal ELP level need to be successful in the assignment.

We use the same example assignment to illustrate how teachers differentiate for students across ELP levels throughout the book. This assignment asks all non-ELL students in the general education classroom to:

Write a set of instructions using an introduction, sequential organization, detailed description using appropriate grade-level vocabulary, sentence structures, transition words, and a conclusion for a self-selected content-based process.

The standards-based content or topic taken from the curriculum is indicated in the plain font above, and the language-based expectations are in italics. The scaffolds and supports that teachers use with non-ELLs in the general education classroom include an example assignment to model the writing product that is expected, a teacher demonstration of the task using a think-aloud, a sequential graphic organizer for planning writing, a language wall with sequencing words and key sentence structures, and feedback designed to push students to reach grade-level English language arts writing standards. Note that this assignment can be aligned with any content area for students at any grade level. For example, the assignment could be part of planning for a content-based task in science or social studies or a more reflective summary of a completed task. Students are encouraged to choose the task for which they write instructions, allowing them to draw on a content-based process that they know something about or are interested in learning.

As teachers prepare to differentiate their assignments for the ELLs in their classes, they need to ask themselves three important questions. First, what is the essential learning of the assignment? The essential learning can be understood as the focus of the assignment that is tied to the standards and curriculum. For this assignment, the essential learning is *clarity in communicating steps in a content-based process, effective use of transition words, and logical sequencing.* The essential learning clarifies the instructional goals of the assignment and is the same for all students. Identifying the essential learning of a lesson, with attention to what all students—regardless of ELP level—need to know and be able to do with content, provides guidance regarding how to differentiate expectations for students at different ELP levels.

Second, what are the language demands of this assignment? That is, how will students need to use oral and written language in this assignment? For example, does the assignment ask students to use listening, speaking, reading, or writing to *describe, interpret, explain, summarize, recount, argue, sequence, synthesize, compare, contrast, persuade, agree, disagree* (to name a few important language functions used at school)? For our example assignment, students need to use writing to *describe* each step in a process, *sequence* those steps, and *explain* how following these steps leads to the completion of the process.

Third, how will teachers gather valid and reliable evidence of student performance in terms of both content and language? Teachers should use the same differentiation strategies for assessments as they use for assignments because they rely on the same process of linguistic differentiation. This approach also reflects the backward design of Wiggins and McTighe (2005), because teachers are to start with the end in mind. Thus, teachers would differentiate a writing assignment and writing assessment using the same strategies for students at the same ELP level. We use the term *assignment/assessment* to remind teachers to use the same differentiation strategies in assignments and assessments for students at different ELP levels. Introducing a new type of assessment that is completely untethered to the instructional strategies used in the lesson is unfair, and it will not yield reliable data that measure what the student has learned.

Each of the level-specific chapters (4–8) illustrates a portion of the differentiation template in action, with attention to

- How the assignment is designed for non-ELLs in the general education classroom
- The language-based expectations and the scaffolding and support needed for ELLs at the focal level of the chapter
- The language-based expectations and scaffolding and support needed for ELLs to move toward the next higher ELP level

Our approach demonstrates how we start with the end in mind (i.e., what non-ELLs are expected to do in the general education classroom) and continuously push students toward higher ELP levels. Table 1-3 shows how we use the differentiation template to present our example assignment for non-ELLs in the general education classroom. We show teachers how to fill in the language-based expectations and scaffolding and support for ELLs at different ELP levels throughout the book.

Table 1-3   Differentiation Template with Completed Example Assignment for Non–English Language Learners

. . . .

Assignment: *Write a set of instructions using an introduction, sequential organization, detailed description (using appropriate grade-level vocabulary, sentence structures, transition words), and a conclusion for a self-selected content-based process.*

Standards-Based Content or Topic (from the curriculum)		
For a content-based process		

Non-ELL	Independent ELP Level	Next ELP Level
Language-Based Expectations		

Write a set of instructions using
 	
■ *An introduction*
■ *Sequential organization*
■ *Detailed description using*
  ○ *appropriate grade-level vocabulary*
  ○ *grade-level sentence structures*
  ○ *appropriate and varied transition words*
■ *Conclusion*		

Scaffolding and Support		
Using ■ *Model assignment* ■ *Teacher demonstration of the task using a think-aloud* ■ *Sequential graphic organizer for planning writing* ■ *Language wall with sequencing words and key sentence structures* ■ *Feedback designed to push students to produce accurate grade-level writing*		

Essential Learning: *Clarity in communicating steps in a content-based process, effective use of transition words, and logical sequencing.*

Language Demands: *Use writing to describe each step in a process, sequence those steps, and explain how following these steps leads to the completion of the process.*

Our use of the same example assignment for students at different ELP levels helps teachers accomplish the following:

■ Learn how a single assignment might be differentiated for students at different language development levels as they read the level-specific chapters.

■ Consider some of the level-specific assignment/assessment and instructional strategies discussed in each chapter.

■ Recognize and internalize the importance of pushing students to the next higher level of language development by thinking about those expectations as they consider their work with students at a given ELP level.

Teachers can use the differentiation template to plan assignments/assessments and instruction for ELLs at any grade level, in any content area.

Steps for Differentiating for English Language Learners

There are a variety of perspectives on differentiation. While content, process, and product are all areas for consideration (Tomlinson, 2014), when focusing on ELLs, we emphasize the need for teachers to make changes to process and product based on students' language development levels. At times content must also be differentiated, with prominence given to essential learning that has enduring value beyond the classroom and is a prerequisite to future classroom-based learning. For instance, many ELLs do not have the understanding of American history that students who have grown up attending U.S. schools may have. So in some cases their learning will need to focus on more foundational information rather than on the extensive detail associated with extension activities for non-ELLs in the class.

When differentiating assignments for diverse learners, teachers can draw on a three-stage framework that Wiggins and McTighe (2005) call understanding by design. First, teachers clearly define the desired results of instruction, or the essential learning, that they want all students to know and be able to do. Second, teachers decide what counts as acceptable evidence of student learning and identify assessments, such as a formative assessment of student performance in activities, tasks, projects, and presentations, that will yield such evidence. Third, teachers plan learning experiences and instruction that lead to strong student performance. By designing assignments and differentiating assessments for students at different levels of language development before creating lesson plans, teachers can focus on differentiating instruction that leads to student learning. Wiggins and McTighe (2005) refer to this process as backward design.

This book shows teachers how to implement differentiated instruction and assessment for ELLs using backward lesson design, according to the following steps:

Gather Important Information about Your Students. Teachers begin their lesson planning by collecting the ELP levels of each ELL in listening, speaking, reading, and writing, as well as data about prior schooling and home language literacy, cultural background, immigrant and refugee status, special needs of students pertaining to giftedness and cognitive or behavioral disabilities, and student interests. When teachers understand these factors, they can design instruction that matches students' needs and that facilitates learning. Assessments that take these factors into account allow students to fully reflect their knowledge and skills in the content areas.

Determine Long-Range Learning Goals and Set Corresponding Content and Language Objectives. Once teachers have identified the essential learning of an assignment for all students, they create standards-based content objectives in clear, specific, and measurable terms for the units of instruction they develop. Teachers also identify the language demands of the assignment and articulate language objectives for each activity that focus attention on how students use language to achieve the content objectives (Echevarria, Vogt, & Short, 2016). Language objectives can be drawn from the oral and written language that is explicit or implicit in the standards-based content objectives.

The student descriptors show teachers how to differentiate language objectives and set reasonable language-based expectations for students at five ELP levels. When teachers differentiate language objectives according to ELP levels and use content objectives that are the same for all students, they enhance students' simultaneous development of language and content-area knowledge and skills.

Design and Differentiate Assignments/Assessments. Measures of student achievement should yield evidence of student performance relative to the content and language objectives set forth for a given lesson, set of lessons, unit, or longer period of instruction. The assessments must account for a range of student factors that influence learning, such as prior schooling and home language literacy, ELP level, cultural background, and special needs. Teachers also need to include accommodations that prevent those factors from confounding assessment. For example, students' differing background knowledge can hinder their achievement on a reading comprehension test because they are not familiar with the topic. Further, the scoring criteria for these assignments/assessments must take into account students' ELP levels so that the expectations for students at different levels are in keeping with the test data for each student. Differentiated tests can be provided.

Design Lesson Plans. Lesson plans should be designed to enable students to learn the content and language necessary to achieve the instructional objectives of the lesson. Differentiated instructional and assignment/assessment strategies appropriate for the students' levels of language proficiency are selected to align with the lesson's content and language objectives. In this way, ELLs will be able to demonstrate their learning on the predesigned assignments using differentiated assessments. Teachers must not think of this sort of planning as "teaching to the test" in its negative connotation. Rather, this constitutes high-quality instruction that is focused on the precise knowledge and skills that the standards require from all students. Thus, teachers set ELLs up for success in achieving the objectives of each lesson, thereby providing access to the curriculum.

Teach, Assess, and Adjust. Teachers implement their differentiated lesson plans, with attention to their differentiated instructional and assessment strategies for students at different ELP levels. Information gleaned from the assessment process should be used to inform future instruction. Teachers can use differentiated rubrics to assess student performance, document growth, and identify targets for instruction.

Conclusion

This chapter introduced the notion of differentiating instruction and assessment for ELLs and helps all teachers and specialists work together to ensure that these students can reach parity with their non-ELL peers. We discussed what it means to create classrooms that are accessible to all learners and focused on the roles of general education and ELD teachers and specialists in this process. There is no one-size-fits-all way to do this work, so we offered suggestions for how teachers can collaborate within the context of the learning configurations that we find in many districts. Throughout this discussion, we highlighted the leadership role of the ELD professional.

After introducing the roles and responsibilities of content and language teachers in different contexts, we focused on how all teachers can use state ELP data to make decisions about assignments/assessments and instruction for ELLs. We encouraged teachers to go beyond the composite ELP level and look at student descriptors that tell them what students at each ELP level can do with listening, speaking, reading, and writing. We presented a simple template that teachers can use to differentiate for ELLs at any grade level, in any content area, so that all students attain the essential learning necessary to move along the ELD continuum. We used the differentiation template to introduce an example assignment that we differentiate for students at five ELP levels throughout the book. Teachers are encouraged to use this template to differentiate other assignments, with a focus on appropriate instruction and assessment for all students, particularly ELL students, in their classes.

Professional Learning Activities

1. **Sharing responsibility for the ELLs in your context**

   a. Who is responsible for educating ELLs at your school? Place an X next to your primary role and a check next to all other educators who work with ELLs in your context.

   _____ Elementary general education teacher

   _____ Secondary content teacher

   _____ ELD teacher

   _____ Bilingual educator

   _____ Literacy specialist

   _____ Talented and gifted teacher

   _____ Special education teacher

   _____ Paraprofessional

   _____ Coach

   _____ Administrator

   _____ Other

   b. What collaboration structures do you have in place for teachers who share responsibility for the same ELLs?

   c. How do collaborating teachers and specialists use data on students' ELP levels to support their collaboration?

   d. What are the strengths and challenges of this collaborative approach?

   e. What new approaches might you consider implementing in your school or district?

2. **Identifying what your ELLs can do in English**

   a. Select five ELLs who you (and a partner) currently work with, have worked with, or expect to work with in the future. Fill out the following information about each student's ELP level.

Student Name	Overall	Listening	Speaking	Reading	Writing
_____	_____	_____	_____	_____	_____
_____	_____	_____	_____	_____	_____
_____	_____	_____	_____	_____	_____
_____	_____	_____	_____	_____	_____
_____	_____	_____	_____	_____	_____

   b. Using Table 1-1, place your students with the student descriptors according to their levels in listening, speaking, reading, and writing.

   c. Share the information of several of your students with another partnership, explaining what each student can be expected to do with English in listening, speaking, reading, and writing.

   d. When you look at these students in terms of what they can be expected to do with English, what do you notice? How might you use this information?

Chapter 2

Exploring Diversity among English Language Learners

Striving for social justice is the most valuable thing to do in life.
—ALBERT EINSTEIN

Teaching English language learners (ELLs) is about much more than English language development (ELD), although helping students progress along the ELD continuum is certainly an important part. Teachers create learning opportunities for all students—including ELLs—when they purposefully use differentiated assignment/assessment and instruction strategies that respond to variation in student background, with attention to the student's ELP level, as well as to his or her prior schooling, home language literacy, cultural orientation, immigrant or refugee status, prior difficult experiences, and special needs. It is important to emphasize that effective teachers view what students know and can do as assets or resources to build on, and not as deficits to overcome.

Teachers who know how to differentiate according to ELLs' needs help level the playing field because these students are afforded equal opportunities to learn content, reach grade-level standards, and graduate. Teachers who differentiate for the diverse learners in their classes position all students, including ELLs, to succeed. When these students see themselves as integral parts of the classroom and school community, they can and do realize their academic potential.

Prior Schooling, Literacy, and Students with Limited or Interrupted Formal Education

Student Scenarios   **Kho Than Nu** is from Myanmar and arrives at high school with little formal education. He is unable to read or write in his home language and is unfamiliar with school protocols, such as sitting in a desk or holding a pencil. His teachers mistakenly assume that this is evidence of cognitive impairment, though it is the result of no formal classroom experience.

Svetlana, a student from Ukraine, arrives at the same high school having consistently attended school in Kiev through 11th grade. Her skills are on grade level in her home language, and she can immediately participate in some classes because of her strong language and education background.

Increasingly, U.S. schools are welcoming students from a wide variety of educational backgrounds and experiences. While some ELLs arrive with solid educational backgrounds, others arrive with little to no former schooling—students with limited or interrupted former education (SLIFE). There are many reasons that a student may not have attended school in his or her home country, including political unrest, poor economic conditions, racial and ethnic discrimination, and sexism. Some students may have been migrants who moved frequently, resulting in inconsistent schooling and below-grade-level performance. Other students may have studied in places where the curriculum or teaching methods are so different from the expectations in U.S. schools that students arrive behind U.S. grade-level expectations. Still others, like Ko Than Nu, may have never had the benefit of any formal education. Because students' prior educational experiences influence content, language, and literacy learning at school, teachers need to learn about the educational and literacy background of each their students.

One way teachers can address the content, language, and literacy needs of students from diverse backgrounds is to identify and build on student, household and community "funds of knowledge" (González, Moll, & Amanti, 2005). The concept of funds of knowledge is based on a simple premise: People are competent and knowledgeable and they develop their competence through their life experiences. Teachers can visit households and communities to identify local knowledge and skills, and teachers can draw on those practices for pedagogical purposes. For example, a student who lives in a household that has access to a garden—in the backyard, part of a community garden, in the home country—may have developed funds of knowledge about gardening that teachers can connect to and build on in instructional units on life cycles, growth, and nutrition. Although some household and community knowledge, such as local ways of storytelling, may not carry as much currency as the official curriculum in traditional K–12 classrooms, teachers are encouraged to find creative ways to leverage funds of knowledge as rich resources for learning and teaching.

When general education teachers see ELLs who are seemingly challenged with English, they may mistake limited or interrupted formal schooling for a learning disability. It is important for educators to ensure that ELLs are never placed in special education programming without careful evaluation. For explicit guidance on the process of determining when special education programming is warranted, see Hamayan, Marler, Sanchez-Lopez, and Damico (2013).

In contrast, some ELLs like Svetlana arrive with grade-level content knowledge and literacy in their home language. These students may be accompanying parents who are enrolled at institutions of higher education or working in professional contexts. Just as with the SLIFE group, these students benefit from instructional practices that acknowledge and capitalize on their home cultures and languages. Teachers are encouraged to tap into the knowledge and expertise that their ELLs bring to the classroom, regardless of their educational backgrounds.

All students need to learn how to use oral and written English for academic purposes in all K–12 schools. When teachers know what students can do with oracy (listening and speaking) and literacy (reading and writing) in their home languages and in English, they can select strategies that leverage languages, literacies, content, and culture as resources for learning. Cummins (2001) maintains that academic language knowledge and skills can transfer from one language to another, meaning that concepts and skills learned in one language do not need to be relearned in another language. This can explain differences in the challenges faced by Ko Than Nu and Svetlana. Students like Svetlana who have a strong educational background are likely to transfer previous learning to English language contexts, while students like Ko Than Nu have fewer formal language and literacy resources to draw on. Students in the SLIFE group face a much bigger task in learning academic language and content than their peers with uninterrupted schooling. Teachers need to recognize that limited formal education is in no way indicative of cognitive deficit.

The educational advantage for ELLs who have developed literacy skills prior to learning English cannot be overstated. Such a foundation provides a reference point that can accelerate language learning. Having once learned basic tenets of literacy, such as the relationship between sounds and print, directionality, and features of text, the language learner with prior schooling is in a position to transfer home language and literacy skills to English. ELLs, particularly older students in higher grades who have not learned to read and write in their home language, or who are reading well below grade level in English, will require sustained and developmentally appropriate instruction in early reading skills.

To understand the educational benefit of home language literacy development, imagine an ELL whose home language is Arabic. This student arrives in his 3rd-grade classroom already reading at a 3rd-grade level in Arabic. He will need to learn that books in English are read from left to right and that what he considers to be the front of a book is the back of a book written in English. Through literacy instruction, he learns that both English and Arabic print depend on word order and progression for meaning and that letters and words in both languages represent sounds (although the student may not have heard or articulated some of the sounds in English). Further, this student will more easily grasp that written language is represented by words and governed by a system of grammar than his counterpart who has not had the opportunity to develop formal literacy in any language. Because this student has already developed a systematic understanding of fundamental reading concepts, he will likely be able to derive meaning from English text with relative ease.

In contrast, imagine that a Rohingya student from a refugee camp in Bangladesh has appeared in the same 3rd-grade classroom. This newcomer has never experienced formal schooling and has not had the opportunity to develop literacy in his home language, a tribal language rich in oral tradition. This prior experience means that it will take more time for him to learn about concepts of the written word in English in U.S. schools. This sort of difference in language development does not indicate that the student is lacking cognitive ability or other communication skills. Neither does it necessarily indicate a need for special education, as some teachers suspected in the case of Ko Than Nu. Educators and other constituents need to understand that neither limited prior schooling nor obvious cultural differences are themselves indicators that identify a student as a candidate for special education.

While the Rohingya student would benefit from literacy instruction in his home language to lay the groundwork for the development of literacy in English, pragmatic concerns often dictate the efficiency of instructing students from multiple language backgrounds using English as the common instructional medium. In cases like this, an ELD program is frequently the choice for economic and other reasons. Teachers and administrators need to remember, however, that ELD in isolation is not an effective means of providing equal access to learning opportunities at school. Rather, all of the general education teachers must share responsibility for ELLs' education and be trained to differentiate instruction for these students.

Regardless of the ELD model used, students with and without strong home language reading and writing skills must be provided with rigorous, comprehensible, and meaningful literacy instruction that will enable them to gain access to the content curriculum. U.S. school districts would do well to follow the lead of our neighbors to the north regarding ELL placement and services. In Ontario, Canada, students who have not yet developed literacy in the home language are afforded instruction that meets them at their home language literacy level, thus providing an improved opportunity for the development of literacy in English and access to the general education curriculum. Students who know how to read and write in their home languages are provided different instruction that is appropriate to their needs (Ontario Education, 2007).

Unfortunately, ELLs in the United States with and without home language literacy are frequently not distinguished from one another for placement and service purposes. As a result, many of these students are at risk of being instructed by teachers who might not recognize their different underlying instructional needs or know how to address them. Students who are in the beginning stages of literacy development and who do not receive developmentally appropriate reading instruction are less likely to reach grade-level achievement, graduate, or otherwise reach their greatest potential. Such outcomes are patently unacceptable, yet, unfortunately, not uncommon.

Cultural Orientation

Student Scenarios

> ***Brigitta,*** a student from Germany, exhibits many behaviors similar to those of her U.S.-born counterparts. She has a strong sense of personal identity and is not afraid of competition. Further, she shows initiative in individual class projects.
>
> ***María,*** a student from Ecuador, is quite different from Brigitta in her cultural orientation. She consistently strives to work with others and shies away from individual recognition. Some teachers have misinterpreted her checking her work against peers as cheating. María lives with her extended family of 13 people.

The more teachers know about their students' cultural backgrounds, the better equipped they are to interact in meaningful and productive ways with these students and their families. Teachers must remember that their job is not to make students become similar to them, but to respectfully facilitate their students' negotiation of cultural differences so they can be successful in different cultural contexts. For example, María complains that she feels pressure from her parents to maintain her heritage culture. Yet, at the same time, she feels the tension of peer pressure calling on her to be an "American" teenager. Culturally responsive teachers can help students like María negotiate this difficult time by respecting her home culture while informing her about the new culture (Herrera, 2016).

Although there are many definitions of culture, it is important to remember that it is much more than visible external trappings like attire, food, and music. Culture is about deeper, underlying ways of thinking, believing, and interacting that are reflected in what people say and do in their everyday activities. Culture can be defined as "a learned meaning system that consists of patterns of traditions, beliefs, values, norms, meanings, and symbols that are passed on from one generation to the next and are shared to varying degrees by interacting members of a community" (Ting-Toomey & Chung, 2012, p. 16).

Cultural competence can be understood as the ability to maintain one's own cultural stance while respecting the perspectives of another (Moule, 2012). No one needs to abandon his or her cultural beliefs and practices. Rather, a culturally competent person becomes informed about and sensitive to the belief systems, experiences, and practices of other cultures as well as their own. Culturally responsive teachers can apply cultural knowledge and skills to understand, encourage, and support all students, particularly those who are least able to ask for assistance. Culturally responsive teachers also provide opportunities for all students to develop cultural competence, including intercultural communication skills.

Cultural Differences

Effective intercultural communication requires participants to be open to new ways of thinking, believing, and interacting. There are many ways to describe cultural differences; here we focus on the continuum from individualism to collectivism (Hofstede, 2010; Ting-Toomey & Chung, 2012). Members of more individual cultures tend to regard the interests of the individual over the group, while members of more collective cultures tend to regard the interests of the group over the individual.

While all cultures fall somewhere along this individual–collective continuum, some nations, such as Germany where Brigitta is from, are noted for more individualistic practices. Brigitta is not especially interested in cooperative group work; she generally prefers individual academic tasks. Brigitta seeks personal recognition for her individual efforts and takes pride in her accomplishments and achievements. Some teachers may notice that students from more individualistic backgrounds tend to emphasize "self-efficiency, individual responsibilities, and personal autonomy" and that their personal identity, rights, and needs take precedence over those of the group (Ting-Toomey & Chung, 2012, p. 44).

Other nations, such as Ecuador, Maria's country of origin, tend toward more collective practices. María prefers working as part of a group and receiving recognition for group-based achievements. Members of collective cultures tend to emphasize group-based identity, rights, and needs, and they value "relational interdependence, in-group harmony, and in-group collaborative spirit" (Ting-Toomey & Chung, 2012, p. 45). For example, educators may have recognized differences in the living arrangements of families from different countries, in which larger numbers of extended family members often live under one roof. Such practices may be explained, at least in part, by the individualism–collectivism continuum. Extended family relations provide important social and safety networks for new arrivals, and for negotiating life in U.S. society.

According to Hofstede's extensive research on six cultural dimensions in 76 countries, the majority of the people of our world live in societies where the interests of the group prevail over the interests of the individual. Table 2-1 draws from this work, listing the top ten most individual countries on the left and the top ten most collective countries on the right.

While most people in the world come from more collective countries, the United States exemplifies an individual culture (Ting-Toomey & Chung, 2012).

Table 2-1   Individual and Collective Countries

Most Individual Countries*	Most Collective Countries*
United States	Guatemala
Australia	Ecuador
Great Britain	Panama
Canada	Venezuela
Hungary	Colombia
The Netherlands	Pakistan
New Zealand	Indonesia
Belgium	Costa Rica
Italy	Trinidad
Denmark	Peru

*In descending order.
Adapted from Hofstede, 2010.

Cross-cultural differences along the individualism–collectivism continuum may help explain cultural misunderstanding and conflict at school and in the larger community. An understanding of cultural differences also helps educators and students become more interculturally competent.

When teachers observe students in classroom interaction, they may notice variation in student preferences for individual or collective practices. For example, some of María's teachers may misinterpret her working with other students (a collective practice) as cheating (an individual interpretation of María's behavior). When teachers understand cross-cultural differences like these, they can minimize miscommunication and maximize learning.

Acculturation and Language Learning

Early work on acculturation and language learning, known as the acculturation model, draws attention to the influence of language, social, and psychological distance on language learning, and these insights are useful today. According to the acculturation model, the smaller the language, social, or psychological distance between an ELLs' home language and culture and English, the easier it is for that learner to acquire English (Schumann, 1978).

Language distance is defined as the extent to which languages differ from each other. Table 2-2 indicates the language distance between English and various other languages (Chiswick & Miller, 2005).

From this table, teachers can see that students who speak languages with smaller linguistic difference indices, such as Afrikaans and Norwegian, will likely learn English more easily than students who speak languages, such as Japanese and Korean, with larger linguistic difference indices.

Table 2-2   Language Distance Index Showing Language Difficulty Relative to English

Language Distance Index								
.33	.36	.4	.44	.5	.57	.67	.8	1.0

Level of Language Difficulty

Easy to learn ◄———————————————————————————————————► Difficult to learn
(Similar to English)   (Different from English)

Language								
Afrikaans	Dutch	French	Danish	Indonesian	Bengali	Lao	Cantonese	Japanese
Norwegian	Malay	Italian	German	Amharic	Burmese	Vietnamese		Korean
Rumanian	Swahili	Portuguese	Spanish	Bulgarian	Greek	Arabic		
Swedish			Russian	Czech	Hindi	Mandarin		
				Dari	Nepali			
				Farsi	Sinhala			
					Finnish			
					Hebrew			
					Hungarian			
					Cambodian			
					Mongolian			
					Polish			
					Serbocroatian			
					Tagalog			
					Thai			
					Turkish			

Adapted from Chiswick and Miller, 2005.

Social distance also influences language learning, with a small social distance between ELLs and non-ELLs facilitating language acquisition. By small social distance, Schumann (1978) means that ELLs

- Are on equal footing with monolingual English speakers
- Set assimilation or acculturation as a goal
- Integrate readily with non-ELLs across contexts
- Do not focus on intragroup cohesiveness
- Are small in number
- Share cultural similarities with English speakers
- View English speakers in a positive light (and vice versa)
- Intend to stay in the United States for a long time

Examination of these aspects of social distance may assist teachers in understanding the cultural preferences and language learning patterns of their students. For example, ELLs who live in enclave communities (and, as such, are more socially distant from English speakers) are likely to take longer to learn English than their counterparts who are more fully integrated with English speakers outside of school.

Psychological distance refers to the reasons and ways a person responds to new learning situations. Though Schumann's research in this area focused primarily on adults rather than school-age children, his work provides insight for teachers in the K–12 setting. Schumann (1978) lists language shock, culture shock, culture stress, and integrative versus instrumental motivation as key aspects of psychological distance. These factors may resonate with K–12 educators working with ELLs.

Language shock is associated with feelings of discomfort stemming from an inability to conceptualize and use the new language and a fear of appearing ignorant. Culture shock is "a stressful transitional period when individuals move from a familiar environment to an unfamiliar one," wherein "the individual's identity appears to be stripped of all protection" (Ting-Toomey & Chung, 2012, p. 93). Culture stress refers to the long-term impact of dealing with cultural differences. Both culture shock and culture stress can hinder the language learning process, for example, when the language learner rejects the new country and its people, and even her- or himself and her or his heritage culture (Schumann, 1978). What a student experiencing culture shock or culture stress needs is the support of a small community of sympathetic people who can help her or him understand her or his new cultural context. The school community should fill this role as it welcomes and supports ELLs and their families.

Relationships between motivation and language learning were a central concern of early second-language researchers. Schumann (1978) argues that individuals with integrative motivation generally desire to get to know speakers of the new language and this desire motivates them to learn the new language. In contrast, individuals with instrumental motivation generally desire to learn the language for personal gains, like getting a job or getting a degree. Individuals with integrative motivation are more likely to feel psychologically connected to English speakers and are more likely to learn English at a faster pace than their otherwise-motivated counterparts. Ting-Toomey and Chung (2012) echo the importance of motivation and highlight the role of personal expectations to the process of adjusting to the new cultural context. Educators who understand the psychological distance that ELLs perceive between themselves and English speakers can better understand the pace of ELLs' language learning and support them in making the transition to a life in the United States.

Language, Identity, and Power

By the end of the 20th century, second-language-acquisition research and practice began to emphasize sociocultural considerations and interdisciplinary approaches, which Block (2003) called the social turn in second language acquisition. At this time, relationships among language, identity, and power gained prominence. Norton (2013) helps us understand these relationships, with attention to language learning. Drawing on case studies of Canadian immigrant women, she developed three important concepts—*investment*, *identity*, and *imagined communities*— that are useful for K–12 educators with ELLs in their classes.

Norton's notion of investment goes beyond the traditional idea of motivation in acculturation theory and second language acquisition discussed earlier and accentuates the role of human agency and choice. According to Norton, language learners who choose to *invest* in their own language learning actively look for or create opportunities to use language for the purposes they need, and they take ownership of and responsibility for their learning. In other words, these learners demonstrate their agency. Over time, as these language learners use the new language for a wide range of purposes, they construct new *identities* as, for example, "English speakers," "good students," "bilinguals," "cultural brokers," and "integral members of the school community."

Identity is understood here as dynamic and multiple, rather than static and unitary. That is, the identities of, for example, ELLs, Mexicans, Muslims, and girls should not be looked at as the identities of monolithic groups whose beliefs and practices are more or less the same. Rather, a dynamic notion of identity sees intersections among different aspects of identity, including language, gender, race, ethnicity, religion, and socioeconomic status, to name a few. According to Norton (2013), as students, teachers, administrators, families, and community members co-construct new identities through the ways they use language in different contexts, they create *imagined communities* that can open new positions, roles, and possibilities for all community members. Ideally, new identities, empowering narratives, and imagined communities make space for linguistically and culturally diverse students to have equal access to learning opportunities at school.

Educators need to remember, however, that power relations at school and in society often constrain the identity options that are available to different groups of students. For example, at the time of this writing, it is not unusual to find ELLs of any background marginalized in general education classes in U.S. schools. Furthermore, anti-immigrant rhetoric is not uncommon, especially in relation to Mexican immigrants and Muslim refugees. In such contexts, ELLs can find it difficult to position themselves as engaged, integral members of the school community—regardless of their current ELD levels. Unsurprisingly, general education classes that marginalize or exclude ELL participation are not conducive environments for language learning or academic achievement.

Moreover, English is the language of power in the United States and home languages other than English (e.g., Spanish, Arabic, Haitian Creole, Gujarati) generally have lower status attributed to them, especially when they are used by low-income ELLs (Wardhaugh & Fuller, 2015). When teachers, schools, and society implicitly or explicitly stigmatize the home languages of low-income students and the speakers themselves, many ELLs choose to reject their home language and cultural practices in an effort to assimilate into an English-speaking environment. However, these students may not be fully accepted into the English-speaking environment either, which can restrict language and content learning. As we saw earlier, literacy in the home language is associated with stronger literacy in English and with higher academic achievement. Students who are negatively positioned at school may feel pressure to abandon their home languages in favor of English.

Because U.S. schools generally operate within the framework of the mainstream culture, students often need explicit instruction about how to function within the dominant school power culture. In her classic book *Other People's Children*, Delpit (2006) takes a close look at power relations at school, and she argues that: 1. Issues of power are enacted in classrooms. 2. There are codes or unspoken rules for participating in power; that is, there is a "culture of power." 3. The rules of the culture of power are a reflection of the cultural rules of those who have power. 4. If you are not already a participant in the culture of power, being told explicitly the rules of that culture makes acquiring power easier. 5. Those with power are frequently least aware of—or least willing to acknowledge—its existence. Those with less power are often most aware of its existence (2006, p. 24).

Although Delpit's work focuses on African American and white relationships in U.S. schools, her discussion of power in the classroom can be extended to relationships among ELLs and non-ELLs at school, with attention to the identities that matter in particular schools and communities. When teachers recognize how power relationships structure classroom interaction and shape identity options and opportunities for ELLs, they can take action. Teachers and administrators can choose to speak and act in ways that position all students as more or less equal. As Delpit (2006) emphasizes, teachers can also explicitly teach minority students how to participate and achieve in the culture of power at school, for example, how to ask questions, agree and disagree, and offer opinions. As minority students, including ELLs, gain experience seeing themselves as, for example, students who have the right to speak in the general education classroom, they are likely to become more invested in content and language learning, leading to higher achievement.

Immigrant and Refugee Status

Student Scenarios

Juan, the son of a professional multinational company employee, enrolls in middle school in 8th grade. His father's company in Venezuela has transferred the family to the United States. The family resides in a wealthy suburb.

David, an unaccompanied minor from Liberia, enrolls in 8th grade in the same middle school. As a child, he witnessed the brutalization of his grandmother during a war. He still has nightmares about that event.

Schools cannot deny access to a basic education for any student residing in the state, whether present in the United States legally or otherwise (*Plyler v. Doe,* 1982). This court ruling clarified that districts cannot require legal documentation when enrolling ELLs or any other students into school. This stance positions schools to educate children. Nevertheless, knowing details about each student's background contributes to the quality and appropriateness of the education and support provided to individual students and their families.

The term *immigrant* refers to individuals who have permanently relocated to a new country of their own accord. Juan, described in the scenario above, and his family are easily identified as immigrants. The term *refugee* is defined by the United Nations High Commissioner for Refugees (UNHCR) as:

> a person who is outside his or her country of nationality or habitual residence; has a well-founded fear of persecution because of his or her race, religion, nationality, membership of a particular social group or political opinion; and is unable or unwilling to avail himself or herself of the protection of that country, or to return there, for fear of persecution. (UNHCR, 2007, p. 6)

Although many immigrant families face incredible challenges, refugees, by definition, have often experienced extreme situations, including separation, loss, and trauma that require teachers to exercise the utmost awareness and sensitivity toward these students and their families. Students such as David, in the scenario above, would be designated as refugee. When teachers make the necessary effort to learn about their individual students, many issues that inform instruction and best support for (both immigrant and refugee) students and families can come to light.

Prior Difficult Experiences

Student Scenarios

Laura, a student from Mexico, shares with her class that she arrived in the United States with her mother after a long separation from her father and brother, who came to the United States first. She describes the abject poverty in her hometown that precipitated the family's move.

Dariou, a student from Sudan, experienced significant, life-altering trauma when his right arm was amputated by rebel soldiers prior to arriving in the United States. In addition, he does not know what happened to members of his immediate family and is living here with an uncle.

Laura came to the United States unwillingly. She left behind a network of friends and her grandmother with whom she was very close. She cries nearly every night because she misses her grandmother so much. Laura continues to blame her parents for uprooting her and has displayed a poor attitude at school.

Her teachers struggle with how to help her to become motivated to engage in school activities.

Though Dariou's injury was sustained years earlier, he is still traumatized by mental health symptoms associated with post-traumatic stress disorder. These issues, together with his physical impairment, family situation, academic challenges because of interrupted schooling, and emerging academic language skills, frame his extensive needs as a learner.

The prior difficult experiences of students like these are likely to have significant and often negative effects on students' abilities to adjust to their new culture, language, and schooling. Culturally responsive teachers who make concerted efforts to understand these students will be well positioned to address their sociocultural and educational needs. These efforts can include working with other school professionals like guidance counselors and school psychologists, as well as advocating for the additional resources needed to ensure academic learning opportunities for diverse learners. School professionals can also connect students and their families with community agencies that provide support like mentoring programs and medical care. Just making appointments and arranging the transportation can make the difference between a student receiving health care or not.

In the absence of formal programs for immigrant families, teachers can work to forge relationships with community and faith-based organizations to support student and family needs. We have found that making this extra effort can be vital for students and families and essential for positioning students for academic success. In addition, providing this type of support can be very rewarding personally. Teachers must ask themselves, "If I don't do this for my student, who will?"

Special Programming for English Language Learners

In some countries, children with disabilities are not afforded educational access and are instead kept at home. There are a variety of reasons for this, including lack of the availability of appropriate services and resources to serve potential special education students or cultural attitudes about disabilities that cause family embarrassment. Regardless of the reason for limited formal schooling, ELLs with special needs must be given the same access to educational opportunities as their non-ELL peers in U.S. schools.

We find a considerable amount of confusion about ELLs and special education in many U.S. schools. Teachers must recognize that neither lack of exposure to education nor differences in language and culture are intrinsic indicators for special education. Further, teachers must be cognizant that students who qualify for both special education and ELD services are entitled to both streams of service.

Teachers are reminded that, in general, the percentage of ELLs for whom special education is appropriate is similar to that of non-ELL students. Given that some districts report disproportionality in the numbers of ELLs receiving special education services, we recommend that identification for such programming be carefully scrutinized and potential placements carefully weighed.

Similarly, other district programs that require an identification process, such as those for talented and gifted students, should make use of appropriate identification processes for ELLs (other than language-dependent standardized assessments) to include a representative number of these students for participation in those programs. At this time, we find disproportionately low representation of ELLs in talented and gifted programs, a challenge that districts need to address (Beisser, personal communication). Once ELLs are identified for special programming, including talented and gifted programs or special education programs, the principles and strategies laid out in this book should be applied to serve them, as appropriate, in such programs.

Gathering Information about Your Students

Teachers must not underestimate the importance of becoming familiar with the background of each of their ELLs prior to beginning classroom instruction. Teachers are encouraged to learn about each of their student's ELP levels in listening, speaking, reading, and writing, as well as their prior schooling, home language and literacy practices, cultural orientation, immigration and refugee status, and any difficult experiences that may influence learning at school. Gathering this information is an important prerequisite to lesson planning that helps teachers set realistic goals for student performance and provide differentiated instruction that is responsive to each student's needs.

Understanding the student's background, recognizing its role in the learning process, and tailoring instruction to meet the student's needs helps the student feel comfortable in the new setting. The positive interaction provided by a welcoming and supportive teacher and a comfortable student promotes language development and learning (Fig. 2-1).

Building positive, reciprocal, and productive relationships can be one of the most rewarding parts of working with ELLs and their families. These relationships enable students, families, and communities to engage with teachers in the educational process in mutually beneficial ways. Further, positive and reciprocal relationships move everyone along the continuum of cultural understanding.

Teachers can learn about their students in many ways, including reviewing their students' cumulative folders; using multiple measures of student learning and achievement; communicating directly with students, teachers, and para-

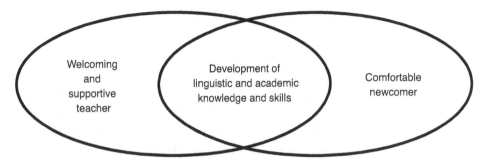

Figure 2-1 Key components in facilitating ELL learning.

educators; and conducting home visits. When teachers gather data about their students from a range of sources, they are better able to address their students' educational needs.

Review the Cumulative Folder

The cumulative folders of ELLs are an often underutilized resource that teachers should regularly consult for information to guide their instruction and assessment. English language proficiency (ELP) test results, information about prior schooling and literacy, and other background information should all be kept in a student's cumulative folder. Schools may also include information about students' content knowledge and skills based on a formative assessment of student work and samples of student performance. Most of this information can be kept electronically for easy reference by general education, ELD, and bilingual teachers and literacy, gifted, and special education specialists. Teachers can use these data to guide their individual and collaborative work with ELLs.

Use Multiple Measures of Students' Knowledge and Skills

While individual data points, such as standardized test scores, can provide a glimpse of a student's knowledge and skills, the importance of using multiple measures for ELLs should not be understated. Because of their linguistic and cultural demands, large-scale standardized academic achievement tests are often an ineffective means of gaining an understanding about what ELLs know and can do (Fairbairn & Fox, 2009).

Teachers are encouraged to use a variety of alternative assessments to gauge the learning of ELLs. For instance, some schools maintain collections of student work in portfolios. These collections can include a range of differentiated assignments and assessments that allow students to demonstrate content-area learning as they learn to use English for academic purposes. Teachers are urged to design a range of authentic, culturally, and linguistically appropriate assessments of student learning that demonstrate what students can do with content and language, as well as their advancement over time.

Seek Input from Students and Colleagues

Teachers must not forget to ask students themselves about their prior schooling and literacy, cultural practices, background knowledge, interests, activities, and so on. Asking such questions may require the assistance of a bilingual paraeducator, but who better to inform you about students than the students themselves? These conversations should be conducted on enrollment and can be part of the ongoing and developing relationship between the student and teacher. This relationship can reduce student anxiety and increase student confidence, and the resulting information can serve as a springboard for a range of instruction and assessment opportunities.

A variety of school personnel can share insights regarding the best ways to work with an individual student. For instance, a teacher, or group of teachers, may have worked with students from a particular country and have experience with the group's cultural and educational backgrounds. Bilingual personnel may be able to share linguistic and cultural insights. Teachers are urged to make connections with others in the school and community to gain a better understanding of who their students are and how to best serve them.

Make Home Visits

Another productive way to learn about students and their families is through home visits. DeOliviera and Athanases (2007) point out that home visits are a key form of advocacy on the part of teachers, both novice and expert. These visits provide a means of building relationships with students and their families and for promoting educational parity for families unfamiliar with how U.S. schools work. During home visits, teachers can encourage family engagement with the school. In addition, home visits for family events like the birth of a child, celebration of citizenship, illness, death in the family, and other occasions should be considered. This kind of teacher involvement acknowledges the family culture while helping to reduce the cultural distance between family and school.

Intercultural Communication. There are numerous factors to remember when visiting the home of a student whose culture is different from one's own. For instance, giving gifts is an expectation in some cultures. As the visitor, you can learn about these expectations from your students, community leaders, school personnel, and other cultural brokers in the community. One author (Jones-Vo) took coffee beans and chocolate to the home of a grieving Eastern European family that had experienced a death in the family. She learned of the necessity of these particular gifts from a bilingual paraeducator familiar with the community. While living in Indonesia, the other author (Fairbairn) provided coconut milk to an Indonesian acquaintance after a car accident. She learned of this traditional expectation from local colleagues and friends. In addition to expectations for specific situations, a small token might be appropriate during an initial home visit to convey the teacher's good intentions. It is important to know what constitutes an appropriate gift in this context. For example, while yellow flowers might indicate positive intentions and friendship to some born in the United States, this same gift is likely to be construed as a symbol of ill will by some Middle Eastern individuals (Dresser, 2005).

After arriving at a student's home, a teacher can avoid many cultural missteps through simple observation. For example, knowing whether or not to remove your shoes can be determined by noting if your host is wearing shoes in the home. If you are unsure, err on the side of caution and leave your shoes with the other shoes near the door. Follow your host's lead regarding where to sit during the visit. This precaution can prevent an embarrassing faux pas such as sitting in the position reserved for the head of the home.

Refreshments are often served at these home visits. Watch others to learn the protocol for eating or drinking your serving, and take sparing portions of new foods to prevent waste and in case you do not care for them. It is, of course, important to respectfully eat at least a portion of what you are served. In addition, hospitality in some cultures requires that hosts are extremely generous with food; sometimes three refusals are needed before the host can stop offering additional portions. Consider the fact that a flat refusal of any food or drink offered may indicate a lack of openness to the culture and, therefore, to the family. While living in Asia, Fairbairn recalls a situation wherein she prepared a meal of typical U.S. foods for her students. She was dismayed when one student could not even bear to try his apple crisp; she found herself thinking, "It's just apples, sugar, butter, and oatmeal!" She later realized that this must have been the same reaction of an Asian host who had served her tripe soup, which she struggled even to appear to eat. That host must have been considering the familiar ingredients of the dish, thinking, "It's only tripe, vegetables, water, and spices!" Put yourself in the situation of your hosts when partaking of refreshments and recall that your goal is to build connections with families.

Consider the purpose of your visit when planning the length of your stay, bearing in mind that a 10-minute quick-and-to-the-point first visit may be viewed as rude. If the purpose is to meet the family members and invite their participation in the educational process, plan accordingly and take along materials for some meaningful activities and discussions. Together, Jones-Vo and a district paraeducator routinely visited new families prior to their children's enrollment in school. Together, they delivered a welcoming message and pertinent school materials like registration forms and immunization requirements. Further, because of relationships built with civic and community organizations, they provided each new student with grade-level-appropriate school supplies tucked into a new backpack. As a result, students were outfitted and ready for the first day of school. In addition, the relationship between home and school was established and phone numbers were exchanged between family members and the bilingual paraeducator, setting up a mechanism for successful home-language communication between home and school.

During home visits, you may encounter long pauses in the discussion or periods of silence. These may not indicate a problem or a desire for the visit to end. Again, observe your hosts to understand the meaning of these pauses; sometimes, these transitions prompt further and deeper engagement. Jones-Vo recalls an experience when attending a wake for the father of a student from Afghanistan. After removing her shoes and entering the home, she was greeted and informed that the men seated on the floor needed to finish reading the Qur'an. Her student's son received the basket of fruit that she offered and served her a drink. Observing the environment, she sat on the sofa and noted that there was no conversation. The point seemed to be that all those gathered were expressing their sympathy and communal grief simply by being present and sharing the moment. She sensed the privilege in being accepted into this circle and remained in silence until the reading of the prayers was completed. This particular home visit proved especially valuable in strengthening the relationship between teacher and student; she could never have learned as much by simply hearing or reading about Afghan traditions. She came away with a broader understanding that could be applied to a wide variety of cultural contexts.

While extended periods of silence can be viewed as an environmental distraction, many normal home activities can also be seen as distractions to a visitor. It is possible that the television may be turned on or that other children may interrupt the discussions and activities planned by the teacher. These distractions may not indicate that the home visit is over or unwelcomed by the hosts. A productive visit may still be possible, particularly if your hosts do not seem distracted by the activity. As the guest, it is important not to take offense at distractions or allow them to disrupt your visit.

As might be expected, the communication style of people from collective cultures is often very different from the style found in individual cultures. Speakers from collective cultures tend to focus on the needs of the group and use an indirect style of speech that may "camouflage the speaker's actual intentions . . . [using] a softer tone" (Ting-Toomey & Chung, 2012, p. 125). Speakers from individual cultures strive to be clear, direct, and linear in their communication; speakers communicate their intent and get to the point (Ting-Toomey & Chung, 2012). When individuals from each end of this spectrum interact, there are possibilities for miscommunication; these differences in style must be considered when interacting with those from different cultural and language backgrounds. Educators also benefit from understanding that communication with individuals with a less direct style may also need interpretation, as when a parent's seemingly casual comment about not having a car may be a request for a ride to a school event. Examples of individual and collective approaches to communication are shown in Table 2.3.

Table 2-3   Individual and Collective Approaches to Communication

Direct Approach (more individualistic)	Indirect Approach (more collective)
I'm glad you made it. We need to discuss five aspects of your child's learning today. (The teacher has been charged with following a specific format for conferences and is under a limited timeframe.)	*Welcome to my classroom . . .* (followed by a bit of small talk). *Some parents have questions or concerns about their students' school performance.* (Gauge next statement or question based on parental response—this approach is likely to open the door for a question or comment by the parent that will direct the conversation.)
What problems is your child experiencing in school? (The teacher is attempting to broaden her or his understanding of the challenges of being a newcomer in the school.)	*Some parents say that their children have problems in school.* (Gauge next statement or question based on parental response—this approach is likely to open the door for a question or comment by the parent that will direct the conversation.)
Does your family need assistance in finding community resources? (The teacher has noted that the student comes to school in the same clothes every day.)	*Some families like to learn more about community resources. Here is some information about a few that may be helpful.*

As teachers remember that they are guests during home visits, they must also show similar respect and sensitivity when interviewing parents. It can be useful to soften direct speech, particularly when asking for, or about, personal information. This softening may be needed not only to accommodate a collective culture but because of cultural expectations regarding what are considered appropriate topics to be discussed with a teacher. For example, direct questions about family, student cognitive development, and student deportment may not be considered appropriate (Trumbull, Rothstein-Fisch, Greenfield, & Quiroz, 2001). Taking into account cultural differences and interaction styles, it can be more effective to abandon a strict adherence to either a collective or individual style and adopt a give-and-take approach. In this approach, speakers move along the continuum and constantly adjust their communication between more collective and individual interactional practices in an effort to start and maintain respectful communication between the family and the school. Building these kinds of relationships helps to reduce the cultural distance and ease the family's adjustment to the new culture.

Home Environment. During a home visit, take the opportunity to conduct an informal environmental scan to better understand the realities of your students' context at home. Notice the general surroundings and cultural artifacts, such as religious symbols and items, handmade textiles, pictures from the home country, and so on. Also notice the reading or print materials in the home, like books, magazines, and lists on the refrigerator. Are these materials in English or the home language? Observations like these can assist you in gaining insight into the importance of reading in the family's daily activities, and in what languages. Notice whether the student has a dedicated quiet space in which to study with adequate light. If the space seems inadequate, this may be because private space is valued differently across cultures. We can see these cross-cultural differences reflected in Chinese and Arabic. For instance, in Chinese "the words that are closest in meaning to privacy are secretive or selfishness" (Ting-Toomey, 1999, p. 134) and the "best synonym for privacy in Arabic is loneliness" (Nydell, 1996, p. 29, as cited in Ting-Toomey, 1999, p. 134).

Another point to consider is the number of individuals living in the home; it is not uncommon in many cultures for extended families to live in one home. You may also have an opportunity to learn about the family power structure. This can be ascertained by paying attention to which family member assumes a lead role during your visit, who participates in the meeting, and who remains silent in the background. Some teachers mistakenly assume that it is appropriate to direct conversation equally to both parents, whereas the culture may be patriarchal or matriarchal, rather than egalitarian, in this respect. Understanding the importance and visible indicators of cultural values within a family will assist you in meeting your student within his or her context.

Conducting Business. Home visits can be a productive time for completing necessary tasks prior to a student starting school. When visiting the home, teachers and bilingual paraeducators should consider the efficiency of collecting as much information as possible at the earliest opportunity. As always, this effort calls for cultural sensitivity. Also, it is very helpful to have forms translated into the appropriate languages. Examples of the types of information that could be collected include the following:

- Accurate and detailed contact information
- Enrollment forms, including registration forms and immunization documentation
- Free or reduced-cost lunch application forms
- Information on students' previous schooling, home language literacy practices
- Information about household structure and home environment

Consider providing grade-level-appropriate school supplies for the student. Many community and civic organizations may be interested in providing support by making donations of needed items. Local civic and religious groups, like the Lioness Club, United Methodist Women, Rotary International, Kiwanis, and the Optimist Club, may be interested in developing opportunities to collaborate and help ELLs and their families adapt to their new home.

Another essential consideration when communicating with students' families is that educators must not insist, or recommend, that parents speak English to their children. Doing so can cause breakdowns in family communication when children learn to speak English more quickly than their parents, leaving parents at a distinct disadvantage when interacting with their children (Wong-Fillmore, 2000). Wong-Fillmore points out that, taken to the extreme, this practice can result in a total breakdown of communication within the family. Instead, teachers must encourage students and their families to maintain their home languages and cultures, thus supporting appropriate dynamics in parent–child interactions. Further, maintaining the home language is an important resource in content and literacy learning in English for ELLs.

Conclusion

This chapter explored diversity among ELLs. We started by addressing the important background variable of prior schooling, including literacy development and the realities faced by the SLIFE group. Next, cultural orientation was discussed, highlighting cultural differences; acculturation and language learning; and language, identity, and power. Next, we considered immigrant and refugee status and prior difficult experiences, followed by an examination of special programming for ELLs. Gathering student information was the topic of the remainder of the chapter, with emphasis on various sources of information, including the cumulative folder, multiple measures of students' knowledge and skills, input from students and colleagues, and detailed guidance on conducting home visits.

Professional Learning Activities

1. **Application of Student Background Factors**

   Using information from the chapter, make notes about each student factor for an ELL in your class. Hypothesize how each factor is likely to influence your student's learning.

Student Name _____ Photo

Student Factor	Notes	Hypothesized Influence on Learning
Prior Schooling ■ What kind of schooling? ■ Where? ■ How long? ■ SLIFE: Yes ____ No ____		
Home Language and Literacy ■ What language(s) is/are used at home? ■ What can student do with literacy in the home language?		
Cultural Differences ■ What country is the student from? ■ Using Table 2.1 as a guide, identify what type of a cultural orientation characterizes people from this country. ■ Place student on the continuum with an X.	**Individual** **Collective** ◄───────────────►	
Language Distance ■ What language(s) does the student speak? ■ Using Table 2.2 as a guide, identify the distance between student's home language and English. ■ Place student on the continuum with an X.	**Small** **Large** ◄───────────────►	

Social Distance		
■ How does the student relate socially to students, school, and community members? ■ Identify the social distance between the student's social group and non-ELLs. ■ Place student on the continuum with an X.	**Small** **Large** ◄─────────────────────►	
Psychological Distance		
■ How does the student respond to new learning situations? ■ Identify the psychological distance between student and non-ELLs. ■ Place student on the continuum with an X.	**Small** **Large** ◄─────────────────────►	
Power Relations		
■ Is student's sociocultural group stigmatized by school and society? ■ Does student position him- or herself as stigmatized by others at school and in society?	**Lower Status** **Higher Status** ◄─────────────────────►	
Immigrant or Refugee Status Immigrant _____ Refugee _____	Country of origin: _____ Prior country or countries of domicile _____	
Prior Difficult Experiences (e.g., civil war, religious persecution, gang violence)	**Minimal** **Extreme** ◄─────────────────────►	
Special Programming Does the student receive special services? Talented and gifted _____ Special needs _____		

2. **Using the Student Data Collection Checklist**
   Complete the following checklist about one of your ELLs. Then complete the questions at the end of the checklist.

CUMULATIVE FOLDER

Student Name _____ Photo

Standardized Testing Results					
English language proficiency test results	Overall	Listening	Speaking	Reading	Writing
Academic achievement test results	Language Arts		Mathematics		

Information about Previous Schooling	
Schooling in Non-U.S. Schools	
Number of years completed?	Primary _____ Secondary _____
Literacy in home language?	Yes _____ No _____
Are transcripts from previous schools available?	Yes _____ No _____
Do transcripts need to be translated?	Yes _____ No _____
Are report cards from previous schools available?	Yes _____ No _____
Do report cards need to be translated?	Yes _____ No _____
Do parents have other information about non-U.S. schooling?	

Schooling in U.S. Schools	
No, of years completed?	Primary _____ Secondary _____
Literacy in home language?	Yes _____ No _____
Are transcripts available?	Yes _____ No _____
Are report cards from U.S. schools available?	Yes _____ No _____
Are immunization records available?	Yes _____ No _____
Is information about program placement and services received available?	Yes _____ No _____
Do parents have other information about previous U.S. schooling?	
Formative assessments (list those used)	

Conversations with the Student

Teacher and Paraeducator Input

Other Relevant Information about the Student
(e.g., linguistic or cultural background information, family information, special needs)

Home Visit

Date(s) of home visit(s):

Informal Environmental Scan	*Notes*
Dedicated study space	Yes _____ No _____
Literacy materials in the home ■ What language(s)?	Yes _____ No _____
Family situation ■ Number of family members in the home? ■ Do extended family members live in the home?	Yes _____ No _____
Environmental realities ■ Cultural norms, artifacts, etc.	
Family power structure ■ Who is doing the talking during the visit?	

Contact Information
Home/cell phone number/Email address
Home address
Work phone number
Work address

Forms to be Filled Out

■ School registration
■ Immunization records
■ Free or reduced-cost lunch forms (in the appropriate language)
■ Other forms

Materials to be Given to the Family or Student

Think in terms of what the student needs on the first day of school.

■ Backpack
■ Grade-level-appropriate school supplies
■ Other items

Additional Notes on the Home Visit

3. **Questions**

   a. Why is it important to collect this information?

   b. How can this information inform your teaching?

   c. Who can help you collect this information?

   d. What are potential barriers to collecting this information?

   e. How can you overcome these barriers?

   f. What is the name of the first student for whom you will collect this information? Why?

Chapter 3

Teaching Content and Language to Diverse Learners

What is equity? It is the quality of citizens of a given society to relate to each other in fairness and impartiality.

—SUNDAY ADELAJA

Like all students, English language learners (ELLs) need to be in classes with high expectations, fair assessment, and strong instruction. According to Goldenberg (2006), good instruction for ELLs is similar to good instruction for all students, but with a strong focus on English language development (ELD), home language literacy, and culture. Teachers who have ELLs in their classes need to understand some basic principles for educating these students, with attention to promoting the development of oral and written language for academic purposes in culturally responsive classrooms. Equipped with this foundation, teachers can select appropriate assignment/assessment and instruction strategies that advance ELLs along the continuum of language development and prepare them to succeed in general education classes and beyond.

Getting Started

Teacher Scenarios

Mr. Tate is in his third year of teaching but is new to serving ELLs, as is his school district. In fact, since the district does not have a plan for serving these students, it enrolled an 11-year-old ELL in his 2nd-grade classroom, claiming that this placement would support the child's early language development. Mr. Tate recognizes that a number of his students (not only the ELLs) have gaps in their content understanding, but he is not sure how to fill in those gaps without deviating from the district's required curriculum. Further, he is afraid to ask for help or to implement some of the innovative teaching practices that he has learned about through his own professional reading because he is still in his probationary period as a new teacher.

Mrs. Allen is a veteran teacher who was taught to "aim for the middle" in her teaching. She is struggling with the changing clientele in her school, yet she firmly believes that "good teaching is good teaching" and that the needs of all students should be met if she uses a variety of activities and assignment types. Further, she senses that strict routines with swift consequences for infractions will provide her increasingly diverse students with the structure that they need. She has an English-only rule in her classroom as a way of encouraging her ELLs to strengthen their English.

This section introduces five guidelines—borne of research and best practice—that teachers can follow when they are getting started in their work educating ELLs. Grade-level placement, reducing student anxiety, student-centered assessment and instruction, gradual and incremental scaffolding, and using the home language in the classroom are fundamental practices that help ELLs get off to a good start at school.

Place Students in Age-Appropriate Grade Levels

An important first step in effectively meeting ELLs' needs is to ensure appropriate grade placement. Even when older students are just beginning to read and write, districts must resist the urge to place them in inappropriately low grade levels to shore up these skills, as Mr. Tate's district chose to do. It is recommended that these students be placed in a grade with those of the same age, or within two years of that grade level when justifiable. For example, one parent advocated for placing her adopted 12-year-old daughter who arrived mid-year in 5th grade rather than 6th grade. Her reasoning was that finishing the school year at the elementary level would support early language and social skills development, allowing her daughter to start at the middle school the next school year with a social network and basic communication skills in place.

Older students who arrive at high school with incomplete transcripts or no transcripts should be enrolled in 9th grade so that they have time to earn the credits they need for graduation as they learn English. However, much older students can feel demeaned by a designation of "freshman." Districts can and should exercise sensitivity in designating the level of new enrollees. For example, one 18-year-old student who subsequently graduated at the age of 21 (as the law allowed) was initially enrolled as a sophomore. Since earning credits is more important than the designation of freshman or sophomore, this student remained a "sophomore" for two years as she accumulated credits, affording her some dignity according to her age.

Put Students at Ease

It is important for teachers to create environments that help newcomers feel at ease so that they can acquire the linguistic and academic knowledge and skills

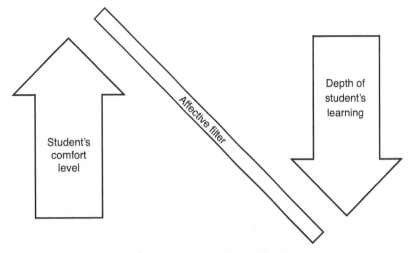

Figure 3-1 Relationship between the affective filter and the depth of student learning.

that they need to be successful in school. Krashen (1982) introduced the notion of an *affective filter* to account for the influence of affective factors such as motivation, self-confidence, and anxiety in second language acquisition. According to Krashen's affective filter hypothesis, affective variables such as fear, nervousness, boredom, and resistance to change influence language acquisition by facilitating or preventing comprehensible input. When the affective filter is lowered, students are better able to comprehend input and acquire a new language. Positive attitudes and a welcoming environment help lower this filter, allowing students to attend to the input that they are receiving and to ultimately learn content as they acquire the new language. The relationship between the student's comfort level and depth of learning as affected by the affective filter in the classroom is shown in Figure 3-1. Teachers who work to ensure that students feel comfortable in the classroom set these students up for success in this regard.

We can also think about putting students at ease from a sociocultural perspective in terms of social identity construction (Norton, 2013). When teachers use language and create activities that position all ELLs—from beginners to advanced—as full participants in the classroom community, these learners become much more at ease. They can take advantage of opportunities to learn grade-level content as they acquire English. In contrast, when teachers position ELLs as students who do not know enough English to engage with classroom content or interact with non-ELLs, their learning opportunities are severely diminished.

Mrs. Allen's strict routines and swift consequences for infractions may work against creating a comfort level among newcomers, who may struggle to make sense of classroom routines. While routines are certainly helpful for ELLs, teachers are cautioned to provide students with clear guidance regarding how to participate in such routines and to allow students time to understand and practice them before imposing consequences for infractions. This is particularly true for students with limited or interrupted formal education (SLIFE) who may require extra time to understand and internalize school routines, not having had the opportunity to do so prior to their arrival in the United States.

Create Student-Centered Assessment and Instruction

One of the most effective ways for teachers to provide differentiation is by developing assignments/assessments that are sensitive to the needs of their students. In the case of ELLs, teachers must apply an understanding of what students can be expected to do with language at different ELP levels, and they must take into account the cultural backgrounds of these students to get the best "read" on their knowledge and skills. The assessment tool itself should not prevent students from demonstrating what they know and can do.

Instead, teachers must ensure that the tools that they use to gather information on content learning allow students to best demonstrate their content knowledge and skills, taking ELP levels into consideration. Teachers (including Mr. Tate) should not be afraid to use innovative practices in their classrooms. Rather, teachers are encouraged to think creatively when using performance-based assessments. Such creative thinking affords students the opportunity to show what they know and can do in the content areas without being hindered by varying levels of language development or lack of familiarity with assessment formats.

A content assessment for an ELL should seek to separate conceptual understanding from language development—as long as the language of the content area is not part of what is being assessed. Teachers must realize that test results for these students are often confounded because of the influence of students' levels of language development. For example, a standardized science test given in English is also a test of English, and is inappropriate for ELLs. Accordingly, teachers need to do their best to strip assessments of any unnecessary language load, thereby allowing students to show in a variety of ways that they are learning.

Creative instruction goes hand-in-hand with the development and use of innovative assignment/assessments. Once teachers have developed procedures for ascertaining ELLs' content knowledge and skills without extensive reliance on language, they must craft instruction that facilitates learning of predetermined content and language objectives taking into consideration students' ELP levels. This type of instruction goes beyond the one-size-fits-all approach characterized by some curricula. Teachers, such as Mr. Tate, should not be afraid to seek assistance in formulating plans for differentiated teaching, which will facilitate learning for students with diverse needs.

Use Gradual, Incremental Scaffolding

In the field of education, the term *scaffolding* refers to a process in which teachers break a challenging task or problem into smaller pieces that students can manage when provided with appropriate supports. First, teachers model or demonstrate how to solve a problem or complete a task. They then provide instructional supports such as visuals, graphic organizers, and home language resources to individual students and to small groups in an effort to meet students where they are and help them perform pieces of the task or solve portions of the problem one step at a time. As students are working with each other using the supports provided by the teacher or other students, teachers step back and observe student progress. Teachers incrementally add or reduce the amount of scaffolding and support as students demonstrate what they know and can do in collaboration with their peers and independently.

Teachers must provide gradual and incremental scaffolding so that the ELLs in their classes can engage with grade-level content-area instruction. When ELLs are provided with appropriate scaffolding and supports, they can interact with their more competent peers and reach higher levels of content, language, and cultural development than they could if they were working independently (Gibbons, 2015; Van Lier & Walqui, 2010). This definition of scaffolding reflects Vygotsky's (1978) notion of the zone of proximal development.

Teachers can organize students and their peers into groups and include paraeducators or volunteers as needed to provide classroom support for ELLs. Teachers can also design language- and literacy-rich activities that require students to use oral and written language to engage with complex content and texts and participate in academic conversations (Zwiers, 2011). In general, teachers should scaffold students' oral language to support their development of reading and writing. As students gain independence, teachers remove scaffolding and focus on facilitating student achievement at a slightly higher level of language development, providing different types of scaffolding that continue to support learning.

The specific kinds of scaffolding can vary according to student background and needs. For example, students in the SLIFE group need far more reading and writing support than their counterparts who are at grade level in the home language. These students will likely need extensive comprehension-based vocabulary and oral language development as they are likely reading below grade level. Based on reading assessments developed for ELLs, SLIFE of any age require targeted reading instruction as part of their ELD curriculum. We emphasize that reading instruction for these students should be comprehension-based, rather than focusing on elements like phonics that are less critical for initial ELL reading development. According to Cloud, Genesee, and Hamayan (2009, p. 31), "effective teachers focus on top-down processing (building concepts, background knowledge) before building bottom-up reading and writing skills."

Teachers who use gradual, incremental scaffolding gather evidence of what students can do with content and language, and they are mindful of students' developing oral and written language use over time. Teachers should never allow students to stagnate at a certain language development level, as is the case with ELLs who get stuck around the intermediate level, with higher levels in listening and speaking and lower levels in reading and writing. Rather, these teachers always push students to the next level, which requires vigilance and finesse. Teachers select assignment/assessment and instructional strategies that build on what students know and can do and that scaffold and support content, literacy, and language learning.

Leverage Students' Home Languages and Cultures for Learning

When teachers see languages other than English as resources for learning, they can use students' home languages to strategically and purposefully support content, literacy, and language learning in the classroom. Support for a student's home language also contributes to the student's sense of pride in his or her heritage, an important part of bilingual and multicultural identity development. Furthermore, schools are encouraged to support biliteracy development to the greatest degree possible for ELLs because biliteracy is associated with high levels of academic achievement (Escamilla, 2014). Even when schools cannot implement biliteracy programs, we recommend that they encourage the maintenance and development of their students' home languages whenever possible. This view of languages other than English as assets stands in contrast with the English-only rule in Mrs. Allen's class.

Teachers do not have to know how to communicate in a student's home language to emphasize its value. For instance, monolingual teachers can use the home languages of their students to welcome families and community members to the school and teachers can provide interpreters as needed. Teachers can encourage parents to continue to use the home language at home and in other contexts in the community to support students' development of oral and written skills in that language. Teachers and students can display community languages in the school, and invite parents—and their languages—into the classroom. Monolingual teachers can also point out cognates, words that are virtually the same in two languages (e.g., *language* and *lenguaje*), thus contributing to students' vocabulary development. Teachers can provide multilingual, multicultural books for students to take home for family literacy activities, and they can design activities to connect homes, schools, and communities. Schools that create multilingual, multicultural learning environments and celebrate the diversity of their student population enrich the learning experiences of all students at school.

When the focus of instruction is content, using the home language can be a far more efficient strategy to explain or clarify a concept than using extensive charades, drawings, and explanations in simplified English. Teachers can also use the home language as a springboard for grade-level assignments by allowing students to discuss content or an assignment using a common home language. For example, a student with strong home language literacy who is at the early stages of reading and writing development in English is likely to produce much better writing in English when encouraged to prepare for writing in the home language (García et al., 2016). Teachers can also ask bilingual paraeducators to provide clarification about concepts or expectations to a student. In short, rather than forbidding students to use their home languages in the classroom, teachers are urged to support students in using this all-important resource to facilitate their learning.

Sharing Responsibility for Content and Language Teaching

Elementary and secondary content teachers can learn to shelter instruction, making complex content-area instruction comprehensible to ELLs, while teaching these students how to use language for academic purposes. There is no one-size-fits-all way to shelter instruction. One common approach is the sheltered instruction observation protocol (SIOP) model (Echevarria, Vogt, & Short, 2016), which helps content-area teachers plan and deliver lessons for ELLs using sheltered instruction strategies. The SIOP model has eight components: preparation, building background, comprehensible input, strategies, interaction, practice/application, lesson delivery, and review/assessment. Teachers who use the SIOP model learn to develop content and language objectives to guide their assessment and instruction. Content objectives are about the big ideas or essential learning and are more or less the same for all students. Language objectives focus on the oral and written language that all students need to engage with and achieve in content-area instruction. The SIOP model does not explicitly demonstrate how to use students' ELP levels and other factors to linguistically differentiate instruction and assessment. This book addresses that gap.

All teachers are responsible for teaching students who are learning English how to use the oral and written language they need for academic success. But what does this mean for elementary and secondary content teachers; literacy, special education, and talented and gifted specialists; and ELD teachers and specialists? When educators understand who is responsible for teaching the ELLs in their classes and assessing their content and language, collaboration possibilities clearly emerge.

Let's start with elementary and secondary general education teachers because ELLs spend the majority of their time in general education classes. These content teachers are first and foremost responsible for preparing linguistically and culturally diverse learners to reach the same high standards in all content areas as non-ELLs. Because these content teachers use English to teach and assess content, they are also responsible for ensuring that all of their students, including ELLs, can use the oral and written English they need to participate and achieve in the general education classroom. Specifically, the math teacher is largely responsible for teaching students how to use oral and written language for math purposes, the science teacher is largely responsible for teaching students to use language for science purposes, and likewise for the social studies and language arts teachers. English language arts teachers also have primary responsibility for teaching all students, including ELLs, how to read and write across the curriculum. In other words, elementary and secondary general education teachers focus on content and use language as a vehicle for content-area assessment and instruction. Literacy, math, special education, and talented and gifted specialists provide important instruction and support for students who would benefit from additional resources.

ELD teachers work with and complement the roles of the general education content, literacy, special education, and talented and gifted professionals with respect to ELLs. ELLs generally spend much less time in ELD classes than in general education classes, which means that ELD teachers cannot be held exclusively responsible for the achievement of these students. ELD teachers are primarily responsible for ensuring that ELLs acquire the oral (listening and speaking) and written (reading and writing) academic language they need in all content areas, and for monitoring their progress along the ELD continuum toward proficiency. As such, ELD teachers focus on language development and use content as a vehicle for language assessment and instruction.

The roles of the elementary and secondary content teachers; the literacy, special education, and talented and gifted specialists; and the ELD teachers come together in service of student learning. ELD teachers are also increasingly being invited to take on a leadership role in districts across the country as they help build capacity in language teaching and learning among all staff. We see an increasing number of ELD or multilingual coaches and teacher leaders who can support the professional learning opportunities of general education teachers and specialists. We also see ELD or multilingual mentor teachers in demonstration classrooms modeling how they use ELL strategies.

What Do We Mean by Academic Language?

Language educators have called administrators' and teachers' attention to the importance of *academic language* for decades, although we are still learning exactly what this term means. This section briefly reviews what we do know about academic language, and focuses on helping all teachers support students' development of the oral and written language that all students, particularly ELLs, need to be successful in content-area classrooms.

In the 1980s, Jim Cummins distinguished between what he called "basic interpersonal communicative skills" (BICS) and "cognitive/academic language proficiency" (CALP) to explain why ELLs who could speak conversational English after one to three years were not performing well on written academic achievement tests until five or more years of English instruction. More recently, Cummins (2012) refers to these two types of language as "conversational fluency," the language people use in everyday communication, and "academic language proficiency," the language people use for school success. Students develop conversational fluency primarily through conversation and academic language proficiency primarily through reading academic texts.

Although this relatively simple distinction masks considerable complexity, the notions of conversational fluency and academic language proficiency have provided an important entry point for teachers and administrators who ask how long it takes for ELLs to acquire English at school (Wright, 2015). For example, the distinction between social and academic language can help educators begin to understand why ELLs who sound like they speak English are often slower to develop reading and writing for academic purposes. We see this pattern reflected in current ELP data, with many students' scoring higher in listening and speaking and lower in reading and writing (Cook, 2012).

Language education research and practice reflect a complex understanding of academic language. According to Bailey, academic language involves knowing and being able to

> use general and content-specific vocabulary, specialized or complex grammatical structures, and multifarious language functions and discourse structures—all for the purpose of acquiring new knowledge and skills, interacting about a topic, or imparting information to others. (2007, pp. 10–11)

The focus here is on using language at the word, sentence, and discourse levels for a wide range of academic purposes. We can see this broader orientation in contemporary state content standards, which place a much higher language demand on all students, particularly ELLs, than previous state standards (Valdés, Menken, & Castro, 2015). For example, students need to be able to describe, interpret, explain, compare, contrast, summarize, and synthesize content-area concepts, and they need to demonstrate these competencies using oral and written language.

It can be helpful to think about these kinds of language demands from the students' perspective, with a focus on language functions or language use. For example, WIDA (2012) organizes its five ELD standards according to the different ways students need to use oral and written language at the sentence, word, and discourse levels across content areas.

1. Language for social and instructional purposes
2. Language for language arts purposes
3. Language for math purposes
4. Language for science purposes
5. Language for social studies purposes

Reflecting the cross-cutting relationship among social and academic language use, WIDA emphasizes that all content teachers are responsible for addressing Standard 1, the language for social and instructional purposes. Content teachers are also responsible for teaching students how to use the language associated with their content areas. We have found, however, that many content teachers do not realize that they are responsible for teaching, for example, language for science, math, social studies, or language arts purposes. We also find that many content teachers have a much narrower notion of academic language, assuming it means only academic vocabulary.

WIDA's (2012) *Amplification of the English Language Development Standards* identifies four overarching communicative purposes or key uses for language in core content standards: recount, explain, argue, and discuss. WIDA organizes its Can-Do descriptors around these four key uses to demonstrate how students at different ELP levels can be expected to use language to recount, explain, argue, and discuss for language arts purposes (Standard 2), math purposes (Standard 3), science purposes (Standard 4) and social studies purposes (Standard 5). Although the specifics of the other state ELD frameworks vary, we see a focus on language use, language functions, or language practices in each framework.

Of course, what it means to *explain* varies across content areas. What it means to explain orally and in writing for math purposes, is linguistically different from what it means to explain orally and in writing for language arts purposes, and is linguistically different from what it means to explain orally and in writing for science purposes. Content and language teachers need to provide opportunities for all students, to *use* the oral and written academic language required for school achievement, as well as for college and career readiness. Content teachers need to remember that academic language includes, but is not limited to, academic vocabulary. And language teachers need to remember that teaching students to use language for academic purposes includes, but is not limited to, grammar instruction.

We encourage teachers to think carefully and broadly about how students need to use oral and written language for social and academic purposes, first in the classroom and later in larger academic and professional communities. For example, students may need to use language to describe, interpret, explain, recount, argue, sequence, synthesize, compare, contrast, persuade, justify, and so on to succeed in content-area classrooms. When teachers look at the content standards that they teach, and think about the activities they structure in the classroom, they can identify exactly how students need to use language. Teachers can then teach students how to use language for those purposes.

Teaching Students to Use Language for Academic Purposes

Teachers can feel overwhelmed working with students who are beginning to acquire English. These educators may suffer anxiety resulting from beliefs borne of previous training, experience, or both. They may think that all students must work toward the academic standards in exactly (or nearly) the same way, using the same or very similar instructional materials and assessments. This anxiety is exacerbated when students' ELD rates seem slower than expected. This section provides a general understanding of how to teach students to use English for academic purposes, and it is intended to alleviate this anxiety.

First, teachers can use the student descriptors on the quick-reference chart that accompanies this book to identify what ELLs at different ELP levels can be expected to do with language in the domains of listening, speaking, reading, and writing. These descriptors reflect an understanding of language development as incremental, taking place over time in somewhat predictable stages (Lightbown & Spada, 2013). Research further bears out two claims: (1) students learn English more quickly at lower ELP levels and more slowly at higher ELP levels, and (2) younger students advance more quickly in their ELD than do older students (Cook, 2008). Cook refers to these claims in the phrase "lower faster, higher slower."

Next, teachers need to provide language and literacy-rich learning environments so that all students, particularly ELLs, have opportunities to learn. We know that students learn more content, language, and literacy at school when they have structured opportunities to use oral and written language for a wide range of academic purposes. Teachers can use the reading workshop format wherein students work in small groups on different activities while the teacher meets with a small group, as a structure that supports differentiating content-area reading instruction. Teachers can design learning-centered activities, tasks, and projects that require students to use oral and written language to, for example, seek information, inform, compare, order, classify, analyze, infer, justify, persuade, solve problems, synthesize, and evaluate. Teachers can provide students with opportunities to read and write narrative and expository text—in English and in their home languages—in genres that cut across content areas, such as descriptive accounts, opinion pieces, and persuasive essays, as well as those associated with different content areas, such as math word problems, scientific reports, and poetry. Using visual supports—including pictures, realia, graphs, maps, and other visual aids—and home language supports as appropriate, teachers can scaffold and support learning as students read, write, and talk about increasingly complex content and texts. As students work in groups and independently, teachers are encouraged to observe and document student performance using formative assessments, with attention to content, language, and literacy learning. Teachers can then use evidence of what students can do with content, literacy, and language to inform instruction. This approach benefits all students in the class, including ELLs.

Learning to Read in English is Imperative. Teachers often report an increasing number of middle- and high-school-age students who have not learned to read and write in their home language, or whose data demonstrate that they are reading well below grade level in English. Administrators must assign accountability for the systematic teaching of reading to these students, and they must ensure that formative and summative assessments provide evidence of students' ongoing improvement in reading. The authors recommend a developmentally appropriate balanced literary approach provided by qualified reading teachers who understand the process of new language development and emphasize oral language as a foundation for literacy.

Perspectives on Literacy Instruction for English Language Learners. While principles of language learning and teaching drive our work, specific discussion of literacy instruction is warranted in a book that addresses the needs of SLIFE ELLs. Within the context of our work, literacy is defined as reading and writing, with oral language (listening and speaking) playing a fundamental role.

We recognize that different genres affect literacy development in different ways. For instance, storytelling is a culturally bound activity; speakers from some cultures tell stories in a more linear or topic-centered style, whereas others construct narratives that are more episodic or topic-associated in nature (Garcia, 2008). An ELL's understanding and production of stories may therefore appear to be less comprehensible when she or he uses culturally bound narrative styles that contrast with the more linear style of traditional Western narratives. For these students, instruction in both reading and writing development will need to include specific attention to culturally bound styles of writing, including guidance in how to construct narratives according to U.S. school assumptions and expectations.

In addition to the organizational style of stories in English, topics and vocabulary may pose a challenge for students from different backgrounds. For instance, many children's stories focus on castles and knights. Such topics may be entirely unfamiliar to students from other narrative traditions, resulting in the need for additional conceptual and vocabulary instruction. Further, certain grammatical structures common to narratives, such as "once upon a time," may warrant explanation.

Narratives are not the only genre that may be challenging for ELLs; other genres may also require extra attention. For instance, the direct style of communication often seen in persuasive or argumentative writing in English may be somewhat shocking to a student whose culture indicates that an indirect style is more suitable. Students may require assistance in understanding how to appropriately construct and support arguments that are in keeping with more individual U.S. school expectations.

Reading instruction, like all ELL instruction, must focus on comprehension. For many ELLs, nonfiction instructional text may be easier to grasp than other genres because of the many supports that often accompany text materials, including headings, pictures, and captions. However, ELLs, just like non-ELLs, must be taught how to interpret and take advantage of these text features.

Facilitating reading development for students across the five levels of proficiency requires graduated, incremental scaffolding. The specific kinds of scaffolding vary according to student background; SLIFE ELLs need far more support than their counterparts who are at grade level in the home language. For both groups, teachers can use best practice in reading instruction for non-

ELLs as a starting point, broadening these practices to focus on essential cultural and linguistic issues throughout the process. For example, ELLs may need supplemental instruction to add to their background knowledge, and they will most certainly require a wide variety of supports for making sense of text, including special attention to vocabulary development.

Home language knowledge and life experiences can serve as a springboard for meaningful literacy instruction that focuses on vocabulary development and comprehension for students who have not learned to read and write in any language, as well as for students who can read and write in their home language. Monolingual content and language teachers can build on the home languages of their students by respecting and welcoming the use of those languages by students in the classroom, pointing out cognates (words that are virtually the same in two languages) where possible, inviting parents into the classroom, providing multilingual multicultural books for students to take home for family literacy activities, and other relevant and innovative bridge-building activities that facilitate interlanguage connections.

Administrators and teachers are strongly encouraged to support home-language literacy instruction whenever possible. However, if this is not an option, developing oral language in English should be emphasized as a foundation for literacy in English. ELLs need opportunities to hear the sounds of English and to develop phonemic awareness, which can be accomplished within the context of meaningful ELD instruction. As ELLs develop phonemic awareness in English, they can learn and apply the alphabetic principle. Teachers of older students who are not literate in their home language must realize the importance of these building blocks for literacy development and make certain to address student needs for oral and aural development as they provide reading instruction.

In literacy classrooms where ELLs are served, the importance of visual support through the use of pictures, realia, graphs, maps, and other visual aids cannot be overemphasized. If activities do not focus on vocabulary and comprehension, the activities are not useful for ELLs. In addition, the use of such visual materials benefits all students, not only ELLs.

Language experience stories, in which the teacher acts as a scribe as students describe shared experiences, can be a means to bridging the oral–written language divide. Students are at an advantage when asked to read print that was written based on their own oral language production. Appreciation of reading and motivation to engage in the learning of reading skills can also be facilitated by reading books of interest to students. Teaching thematic literature-based units that focus on themes relevant to students' lives engages them in content and language instruction and fosters vocabulary development through the natural recycling of vocabulary that occurs in thematic studies.

We also support the creation of a print-rich environment in which students regularly see reading and writing used in real-life contexts, in keeping with recommendations found in the educational literature (e.g., Peregoy & Boyle,

2016). The use of big books; word, language, and concept walls accompanied with pictures; and other displays of meaningful print can foster the process of literacy emergence. Though this strategy is often thought of as one for elementary teachers, educators at all levels will do well to make increasing amounts of meaningful print available to students as a resource.

Explicit reading development must be part of the ELD program and constitutes core instruction for ELLs of all ages. Teachers are encouraged to implement a balanced, meaning-based approach that moves from whole to part to whole. After considering students' ELP levels, teachers begin instruction with a whole text that will be meaningful to all students. Teachers then help students engage with and comprehend the text using instructional strategies appropriate for their ELP levels. Once students comprehend the text, teachers can move to text analysis of, for example, a particular aspect of content or to a feature of language use at the discourse, sentence, or word level. Equipped with a holistic understanding of the text and a focused understanding of an aspect of the text, teachers can invite students to move back to the meaningful whole and produce their own texts for academic purposes (Fountas & Pinnell, 2016).

Students also benefit from explicit instruction, for example, to learn how to use content, language, and literacy strategies, and they need opportunities to practice. Once students comprehend a text or produce a draft, teachers can focus on form. That is, teachers can teach discrete aspects of language, including pronunciation, grammar, and spelling, within the context of meaningful oral and written communication. This is not to say that language teaching takes a backseat to content and literacy instruction; rather, language teaching is embedded in meaningful literacy instruction, which in turn is embedded in meaningful content instruction (Peregoy & Boyle, 2016).

This balanced approach to reading development can be used with ELLs at all levels, as long as teachers choose texts that can be made comprehensible to the learners they are working with. Factors to consider include students' ELP levels, especially in reading, as well as their background knowledge, interests, home language literacy, prior schooling, and cultural orientation. With scaffolding and support, students at more advanced reading and writing ELP levels may be able to produce written texts that meet grade-level expectations. However, students at lower ELP levels, and especially those in the SLIFE category, cannot be expected to produce grade-level writing. At all times, however, teachers should expect growth, and they should continually push their students to achieve higher levels of writing development.

Grading English Language Learners Equitably

Of necessity and in fairness, the scoring of differentiated assignments/assessments must take into consideration students' language development levels. Based on students' ELP levels, with attention to the student descriptors for each level, teachers understand where language learners fall along the continuum of language development. This knowledge allows educators to design appropriate assignments/assessments for individual students who have not yet met local requirements to be designated proficient in English. As students strive to meet expectations set according to their levels of language development, teachers must assign grades accordingly.

For example, if a student at level 3 in writing has met all the expectations set forth by the teacher, the student should be graded bearing in mind those differentiated expectations. That is, students at each ELP level should be able to achieve success and corresponding good grades. Further, these students should be graded in terms of the extent to which they have met the expectations set by the teacher, rather than in comparison to non-ELLs. It should be possible for both types of student to receive top grades, though an ELL's report card may include a notation clarifying that data-driven accommodations were used in adapting curriculum.

Developing a Differentiated Scoring Rubric. The process of creating a rubric that differentiates expectations according to students' language development needs is similar to rubric creation for other contexts. The additional step is the adjustment of expectations for students at different levels of language proficiency, and teachers can use the student descriptors to ensure that expectations are appropriate.

Differentiated rubrics require specific details rather than global descriptions. Rather than using more general holistic rubrics, teachers must break down each level into discrete and specific benchmarks. In so doing, teachers and students have a clear understanding of the overall expectations and student progress toward success. The steps for developing this type of detailed analytic rubric that is differentiated for students at different ELP levels are as follows:

1. Determine what criteria, such as content, organization, or grammar and mechanics, will be graded. It is recommended that three to five criteria be selected; choosing a greater number results in a cumbersome grading process. If many criteria must be graded, perhaps some can be merged under umbrella terms, such as *mechanics*, rather than divided into separate categories of capitalization, punctuation, and spelling.
2. Determine what performance levels, such as below basic, basic, proficient, or advanced, will be incorporated. Note that three to six levels are recommended; when using more levels, differentiating between the performance levels can become difficult. For example, it is challenging to distinguish between a 5 and a 6 in a 10-level scale.
3. Set up a seven-column table (Table 3-1), with the ELP levels listed across the top and the performance levels listed down the side.

Table 3-1   Rubric Layout

	Level 1	Level 2	Level 3	Level 4	Level 5	Non-ELL
Advanced						
Proficient						
Basic						
Below Basic						

4. Copy this table for each of the criteria, such as content, organization, grammar, and mechanics, to be graded. Label the tables accordingly (e.g., one for content, one for organization). Further, note that the criteria can be weighted differently. For example, content may be afforded twice the value of grammar in a science term paper. Make decisions about weighting according to the emphasis on each criterion in the classroom and in real life.

5. Using the student descriptors as a guide, write appropriately differentiated descriptions of performance expectations in each cell. Teachers may determine that some criteria are not be extensively differentiated across language development levels if they are not language-related, such as volume in an oral presentation.

6. Employ parallel language for aspects of a given criterion, such as sentence structure within grammar, across performance levels.

7. Use positive language to the extent possible.

8. Ensure that expectations in the cells differ across ELP levels.

Though this sounds like considerable effort, it is an essential aspect of the use of differentiated assignments/assessments. After all, why should teachers differentiate expectations and then grade all assignments using the same set of expectations? To minimize the demands on their time, and to assist students in internalizing requirements, we recommend that teachers create a few standard rubrics that are used consistently throughout the year, such as one for essay writing and one for presentations. To tailor such rubrics to specific assignments, teachers might add a criterion or two for scoring. In this way, teachers are consistent in their expectations and students are able to internalize these expectations, rather than working throughout the year to meet the moving target of expectations that differ for each assignment. Further, teachers do not have to invest extensive time in creating scoring schemes for each assignment. This is a win-win solution to the grading conundrum.

As with the development and differentiation of assignments/assessments, there is no one perfect way to create a differentiated rubric. Teachers must rely on their own expertise to determine what criteria are included. The key is to ensure that the language demands of the assignment/assessment are scored or graded in accordance with reasonable expectations for students at the various ELP levels.

Table 3-2 is an example of a differentiated rubric designed for scoring or grading content-based writing. It is not meant to be a perfect representation of how to grade ELLs across ELP levels; rather, it is meant to provide insight and to serve as a starting place for teachers to develop their own differentiated rubrics. Readers may notice that some language-related criteria are either not graded at all for students at lower ELP levels or are graded more "gently." For example, as a general rule, no Ds or Fs are issued to students at level 1 because their language development does not allow much production; there are data-based reasons for not requiring level 1 or 2 students to produce grammatical work.

Classroom Strategies

This section provides a plethora of classroom strategies that teachers can use with ELLs at any ELP level, and they reflect the fundamentals of teaching and assessing ELLs discussed in the preceding sections. Modeling after Wiggins and McTighe (2006), we encourage teachers to begin their work with linguistically and culturally diverse learners with the end in mind, and design the assignments/assessments first. When teachers have a clear understanding of how to differentiate assignments/assessments for the ELLs in their classes, they are prepared to plan instruction. Reflecting this orientation, we begin with general assignment/assessment strategies for students at all ELP levels, and follow with instructional strategies that teachers can use to support all the ELLs in their classes.

Assignment/Assessment Strategies for All English Language Proficiency Levels

ELLs at all ELP levels are capable of engaging in both lower-order, knowledge- and comprehension-based, thinking skills and higher-order thinking skills, including application, analysis, synthesis, creation, and evaluation. To effectively assess what students know and can do with content, teachers must incorporate differentiated, authentic, and culturally and linguistically appropriate assignments/assessments for ELLs into their practice. Effective assignments/assessments therefore require that teachers consistently apply their own creativity in developing and implementing ways that students can demonstrate higher-order thinking, regardless of ELP level and other relevant student factors like prior schooling, home language literacy, and cultural orientation. The interrelationship of ELP level, relevant student factors, and essential learning based on state content standards and district curricula is illustrated in Figure 3-2.

Table 3-2 Example of a Differentiated Writing Rubric with Three Parts: Content, Organization, and Grammar and Mechanics

	Level 1	Level 2	Level 3	Level 4	Level 5	Non-ELLs
For Content						
A	3–4 big ideas	4 big ideas	4 big ideas	4 big ideas	4 big ideas	4 big ideas
B	2	3	3	3	3	3
C	0–1	2	2	2	2	2
D	N/A	0–1	1	1	1	1
F	N/A	N/A	0	0	0	0
For Organization						
A	Ideas in sequence	Ideas in sequence	Ideas in sequence with some connectors used	Logical organization with good use of basic connectors	Strong organization facilitated by use of a wide variety of connectors (a few minor errors may be present)	Exemplary organization facilitated by use of a wide variety of connectors
B	Ideas generally in sequence	Ideas generally in sequence	Some sequence and/or connector problems	Logical organization with some use of connectors	Well organized with a number of connectors	Strong organization facilitated by a wide variety of connectors (a few minor errors may be present)
C	Out of sequence	Out of sequence	Significant sequence and/or connector problems	Some breakdowns in organization and use of connectors	A few breakdowns in organization and use of connectors	Noticeable problems in organization and use of connectors
D	N/A	N/A	Serious problems	Significant breakdowns in organization and use of connectors	Noticeable breakdowns in organization and use of connectors	Serious problems in organization and use of connectors
F	N/A	N/A	N/A	Serious breakdowns in organization and use of connectors	Serious breakdowns in organization and use of connectors	Lack of organization

	Level 1	Level 2	Level 3	Level 4	Level 5	Non-ELLs
For Grammar and Mechanics						
A	N/A	N/A	Basic subject-verb agreement and mechanics in place; correct use of simple tenses	A range of grammatical tenses used with minor errors, mechanics generally strong after revision	Few errors in use of grammar; complex sentence structures used; strong mechanics	Grade-level expectations in use of grammar, sentence structure, and mechanics
B	N/A	N/A	Some subject-verb agreement and mechanics in place; some correct use of simple tenses	Some problems with subject-verb agreement, mechanics, and/or tense	Some problems in use of grammar, sentence structures, and/or mechanics	Few errors in use of grammar; complex sentence structures used; strong mechanics
C	N/A	N/A	Minimal subject-verb agreement, mechanics, and simple tenses in place	Significant problems with subject-verb agreement, mechanics, and/or a tense	Significant problems in use of grammar, sentence structures, and/or mechanics	Some problems in use of grammar, sentence structures, and/or mechanics
D	N/A	N/A	N/A	Serious problems with subject-verb agreement, mechanics, and/or a tense	Serious problems in use of grammar, sentence structures, and/or mechanics	Significant problems in use of grammar, sentence structures, and/or mechanics
F	N/A	N/A	N/A	N/A	N/A	Serious problems in use of grammar, sentence structures, and/or mechanics

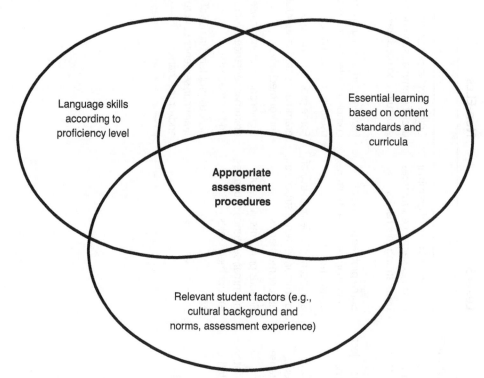

Figure 3-2 Factors that inform appropriate English language learner assessment.
● ● ● ● ● ●

In the next sections, we focus on general assignment/assessment practices that teachers are encouraged to use with ELLs at any ELP level.

Focus on the Same Content Standards for ELLs and non-ELLs. For the sake of academic parity, teachers must ensure that instruction for all students in the classroom is aligned with the same content standards. That is, ELLs cannot focus on alternate content because of their language development levels. This imperative calls for intentional linguistic differentiation of both instruction and assessment. For instance, if the assignment is for students to create group presentations, ELLs at lower ELP levels must be allowed to contribute to the presentation verbally according to their linguistic abilities. While a student at level 2 might speak a few sentences, a student at level 1 might simply pronounce key words for the audience with visual accompaniment.

Differentiate Assignments/Assessments according to Students' ELP Levels. In as much as students at any ELP level can produce predictable amounts and kinds of language in English, assessment instruments must draw on and match those specific levels when measuring learning. For example, rather than expecting a five-paragraph compare-contrast essay from a student at level 2 in writing, a teacher might assign the creation of a Venn diagram or T-chart that would require the student to correctly place words and phrases accompanied by pictures on the graphic organizer. In this way, students at all ELP levels can exhibit higher-order thinking skills differentiated according to their individual language development levels.

Provide Clear Directions and Check for Student Understanding. Students whose school experiences may not be commensurate with U.S. classroom practices need explicit instruction in for completing assignments/assessments. Teachers are urged to incorporate sensory supports, such as manipulatives, modeling, and work examples, to ensure understanding. When giving directions, teachers might consider incorporating the skills of a bilingual paraeducator to confirm that students understand directions and can follow the specified protocol. Teachers can also ascertain whether students understand directions for assignments/ assessments by asking for indications of comprehension that go beyond a simple yes. For example, teachers can have students demonstrate understanding nonverbally or restate the directions.

Match Scoring Rubrics to Students' ELP Levels. Differentiated assessments call for differentiated scoring. Teachers can support students by scaffolding their simultaneous learning of language and content when they emphasize content understanding over language mastery for ELLs at lower levels of language proficiency. Multiple representations of conceptual learning, including posters, dioramas, and labeled charts, must be accepted and fully credited as legitimate demonstrations of content mastery, unless, of course, the content standards require high levels of language production. Meanwhile, linguistic conventions such as grammar, spelling, paragraph, and text, are given appropriate weight with expectations aligned to students' individual language proficiency levels in cases where language is not part of what is being assessed. For example, linguistic conventions might not be graded at all for students at levels 1 and 2.

Provide Differentiated Rubrics along with Assignments. Best instructional practice demands that teachers share grading expectations with students in advance of the completion of an assignment/assessment. This assures that students clearly understand the learning targets throughout the learning and assessment cycle. Further, knowing the expectations in advance empowers students to actively aim for and meet achievement criteria. For students at lower ELP levels, teachers can present their expectations in the form of differentiated rubrics and can support understanding by showing students example assignments. This assessment practice applies to ELLs and non-ELLs alike.

Use the Same Supports in Instruction and Assessment. Good assessment is a reflection of instruction. That is, supports that are provided to students during instruction should also be available during the assessment process. For example, if pictures are used during instruction to support learning, pictures should also be included as part of the assessment process whenever possible. If a word bank is provided on an assignment/assessment, icons or clip art can be used. Similarly, if particular supports are used in one part of the teaching-assessment cycle, they should be used consistently throughout the cycle.

Allow the Demonstration of Content Learning through Performance-Based Assessments. Teachers should feel free to use their imaginations and creativity when designing assessment tools and procedures, such as demonstrations, dioramas, collages, journals, art projects, maps, models, and posters, to gauge the learning of ELLs. In fact, using innovative assessments is the only way to gain accurate insight into the knowledge and skills of many students, particularly those at lower ELP levels. All students, including ELLs who are just beginning to learn English, are capable of sophisticated thoughts and complex ideas. Teachers who know their students and their content well are best equipped to develop meaningful and imaginative assessments that reflect their students' content knowledge and skills matched to individual language development levels. For example, one family and consumer science teacher allowed students to demonstrate understanding of the components of a balanced meal based on the food pyramid with a nontraditional test. This assessment took the form of displaying a specified number of food groups on a paper plate by cutting out, affixing, and labeling magazine pictures on the plate. The resulting artifact is an excellent example of a creative way to support students in demonstrating content knowledge without relying on language.

Permit Student Choice in Assignments to Draw on Background Knowledge and Enhance Motivation. ELLs bring deep funds of knowledge with them to the classroom. Permitting students to make assignment-related selections that allow them to capitalize on this knowledge can pay significant dividends in terms of student motivation and academic performance. For instance, a teacher could allow a student to do a project about her or his country of origin rather than about a randomly assigned country.

Match Traditional Paper-and-Pencil Tests to Students' ELP levels. While content standards and curricula must not be watered down for ELLs, teachers need to acknowledge the incremental process of learning content in a new language. This process will likely take longer for students with lower language proficiency levels than for their peers at higher levels of language proficiency. Teachers must focus on the most critical aspects of each lesson during instruction and create appropriate assessments to scaffold the individual learner toward the next ELP level. During this process, care must be taken to ensure that all students are assessed on the same content objectives while not burdening ELLs with unreasonable linguistic demands. For example, teachers might create a new version of a paper-and-pencil assessment to be used for intermediate-level

ELLs; this test could be written in simplified English and incorporate supplementary icons and pictures (Fairbairn, 2006).

Use Multiple Assessment Methods for the Most Accurate Picture of Student Learning. This strategy applies equally to ELLs and non-ELLs. Some students tend to perform better on certain test formats than on others. In addition, some formats, such as multiple-choice tests, are typically more language intensive than other formats like demonstrations. By using a range of assessment procedures, teachers can obtain a broader sample of student work and, as a result, get a more accurate picture of what students know and can do.

Focus Error Correction on Specific Aspects of Language. When assisting ELLs in strengthening their language skills, educators must be careful not to overwhelm students with an inordinate number of corrections. Rather, teachers must focus their efforts on specific types of errors that are appropriate to the student's level of language proficiency. For instance, if a teacher is grading the writing of a student at level 3, he or she may focus on particularly meaningful aspects of language, such as the correct use of commonly used verb tenses, rather than on less critical facets of the student's writing that are inaccurate, such as the spelling of infrequently used words.

Grade Students Relative to Standards for Success That Align with ELP Data. In today's standards-based environment, students must be graded against standards rather than against each other. Comparing ELLs to their non-ELL peers is not equitable. Rather, teachers must compare all students' accomplishments to specified content standards and benchmarks. Given that the purpose of grading is to provide meaningful information about student achievement to students and their families or guardians, it is crucial that the grade reflect the simultaneous acquisition of content and language knowledge and skills. Because the learning curve for ELLs follows a different trajectory than for non-ELLs, the best information about student achievement relates specifically to each student's progress in comparison with standards (both content and ELD standards). When differentiated grading is used, school districts can determine whether such grades are flagged to indicate the use of differentiation. This consideration may be particularly important when high school students' grade point averages are compared for computing class rank. Districts should develop a comprehensive grade reporting policy that addresses such needs.

When students ask how they are doing in comparison with the rest of the class—as they sometimes do—providing an undifferentiated grade using scoring schemes devised for non-ELLs can offer the kind of standards-based information that students seek, informing them of where they stand in reference to the range of performance expected of their non-ELL peers.

Give Students Enough Time to Complete Assessments. Most tests, including many large-scale standardized achievement tests, focus on measuring students' knowledge and skills without factoring in time pressure. Extra time is certainly an appropriate accommodation for ELLs on these tests because it gives them a greater opportunity to process the language demands of the test. This can result in a more accurate picture of what students know and can do.

Match Accommodations with ELP Levels. ELLs are certainly deserving of accommodations, such as a word-to-word dictionary or receiving directions in their home language, when taking tests that have challenging language demands. However, these accommodations should be provided in alignment with a student's individual linguistic needs, rather than in a one-size-fits-all approach (Fairbairn, 2007).

For Large-Scale Tests, Only Use Accommodations That Are Approved by Test Developers and Familiar to Students. It is inappropriate to introduce new accommodations to students while large-scale standardized tests are being administered. In fact, the use of such accommodations can actually hinder student progress on such a test. For example, a student who is unaccustomed to using a bilingual dictionary may spend more time trying to figure out how to use the dictionary than on the test items. Further, only certain accommodations are appropriate for these high-stakes tests; lists of such accommodations can be found in the technical manual or other guidance documents that accompany the tests. Deviating from these approved accommodations can endanger the validity of the interpretations made of students' test scores, meaning that the unapproved accommodations can undermine what is tested and result in inaccurate scores.

Prepare Students with Test-Taking Strategies. Some students may be unfamiliar with important skills and strategies needed for success on traditional classroom and large-scale standardized tests. For instance, ELLs may not know how to negotiate a "bubble sheet" when answering questions. Further, they may not realize that referring to a reading passage is generally acceptable when taking a reading comprehension test. For detailed guidance on issues that may need to be addressed, refer to Fairbairn (2007).

Do Not Rely Solely on Standardized Tests to Identify ELLs for Talented and Gifted Programming. Early levels of ELP should not preclude ELLs from participating in talented and gifted classes. However, the typical measures used in identifying students for such programming may not reveal an ELL's giftedness because of the confounding factor of (lower) language proficiency level. For this reason, teachers must innovate to create assessment procedures that can accurately reveal the student's giftedness to qualify them for talented and gifted programming. After identification, talented and gifted ELLs must be instructed according to their individual language proficiency levels (Castellano & Diaz, 2001; Iowa Department of Education, 2008).

Use Appropriate Assessments to Identify ELLs for Special Education Services. A lower level of language proficiency is not, in and of itself, a reason for referral to special education programming. Nor are lower levels of academic achievement because of limited or interrupted formal schooling experiences indicative of a cognitive impairment. However, to separate issues of language from those of disability, particular care must be taken. Assessment procedures that may be appropriate for non-ELLs can incorrectly recommend ELLs for special education services. Such a recommendation, however, is unlikely to benefit students who do not have disabilities or who have distinct needs related to their ELD when compared to non-ELLs. For example, many teachers who specialize in this area often have inadequate educational backgrounds in serving students who are still acquiring English. For excellent guidance on how to determine if ELLs need special education services, see Hamayan, Marler, Sánchez-López, and Damico (2013).

Instructional Strategies for All English Language Proficiency Levels

Instructional strategies must be designed and implemented in such a way that they support student learning and the demonstration of that learning. When planning instruction, teachers must remember the specific types of data that are acceptable as evidence of student learning (Wiggins & McTighe, 2006). This instruction must also take into account the language development levels, content knowledge, and skills of the students. Four principles guide effective instruction of students at all ELP levels (Kaufmann, 2007):

1. Increase comprehensibility
2. Increase student-to-student interaction
3. Increase higher-order thinking and the use of learning strategies
4. Make connections to students' background knowledge

The first task of teachers during instruction is to ensure that their teaching is accessible to all the students in the classroom. To enhance comprehensibility, teachers can incorporate visual supports, highlight vocabulary, employ multimedia, and use other teaching strategies designed to support learning for students acquiring English. Interaction between and among ELLs and non-ELLs can be facilitated by creating opportunities for students to talk about the lesson, such as think-pair-share and small group discussions. Higher-order thinking can be incorporated using graphic organizers and with the explicit teaching and practice of strategies for students. Making connections to students' background knowledge is possible when teachers know their students. Teachers are encouraged to keep these principles in mind as they select from the following instructional strategies for ELLs at any ELP level. These principles also enhance the teaching of all students in the general education classroom.

Welcome All Students by Visually Representing Their Cultures. It is essential that newcomers to your classroom and school feel a sense of belonging; this will facilitate a level of comfort that allows students to settle into the learning process. One way to accomplish this purpose is to display and incorporate various cultural artifacts, such as pictures, flags, and other memorabilia from different countries, in your room and in your teaching. For example, teachers might display international items that were purchased during travel or received as gifts from students across the globe. There might also be a special place in the classroom or school where students of all nationalities can exhibit cultural items relevant to the curriculum. The display of cultural artifacts representing the students' cultural backgrounds acknowledges and honors these cultures and helps to establish a comfortable space for learning. In addition, posters depicting diverse achievers can inspire students of all backgrounds to reach their full potential.

Build Relationships by Learning Key Words and Phrases in Students' Home Languages. Students can gain a sense of belonging in a new school when they hear their teachers using their home languages. Such a simple thing as morning greetings in students' home languages can mean the difference between students wondering if they will ever fit in and their beginning to feel at home. Learning a few basic words, such as *listen*, *sit down*, *please*, and *thank you*, in various languages enables teachers to heighten attention by giving instructions in home languages. Far more than validating the importance of each student's language, such comprehensive inclusion of all of the languages represented in the classroom serves as a model to all students of the value and worth of languages other than English and of respect for all cultures and languages.

Engage ELLs in All Classroom Activities by Using Visual, Sensory, and Graphic Supports. All instruction must be accessible to all students. Rather than creating separate lessons for ELLs, teachers must assist those students in understanding and taking part in the standards-based lessons that they create by using, for example, realia, pictures, diagrams, models, demonstrations, graphic organizers, nonverbal communication, videos, and computer-assisted instruction. Authentic realia are effective in achieving this end. For example, a high-school biology teacher brought in a cow's heart for a lesson on the heart and the circulatory system. This teacher was able to show students the parts of the heart and demonstrate the flow of blood by referring to the heart. Students were able to learn content vocabulary and then retell the path of blood circulation using academic language.

Use the Same Content Standards for ELLs and non-ELLs. Because ELLs are generally accountable for learning the same content as non-ELLs, teachers must ensure that they target the same instructional goals for both sets of learners. Although ELLs at lower ELP levels may have more difficulty in accessing content instruction, teachers must create ways for them to do so. For instance, rather than excuse ELLs from a unit on mitosis and meiosis because it seems too complex and language intensive, a teacher might require students to demonstrate the processes through the manipulation of concrete objects. This calls to mind a wonderful example focusing on this very topic, in which ELLs outperformed non-ELLs in explaining cell division as a result of their practice in demonstrating the process with plastic forks and spoons, pipe cleaners, and other hands-on materials in the ELD classroom. The science teacher in this case creatively and capably exemplified the strategy of maintaining the same content standards for all students by employing this activity. The hands-on work meant that ELLs could meet the standard, and it was helpful to non-ELLs, as well.

Integrate Content and Language Teaching Using Visual Support and Contextualized Examples. In the current standards-based environment, ELLs no longer have the luxury of concentrating on language development before focusing on content learning; the two processes must occur simultaneously. It is possible to achieve this only when teachers ensure that students are able to learn the language needed to function in school and associated with the curricular content that is the focus of instruction. For instance, teachers can explicitly teach academic language by modeling its meaning through the use of graphic organizers, as in the use of a Venn diagram or T-chart to teach the functions of words (e.g., compare and contrast).

Write Daily Content and Language Objectives and Share Them with Students. Students will benefit from using content and language objectives to keep them informed about exactly where each lesson is going. Content objectives are aligned with the content standards, focus on the big ideas or essential learning of a unit or lesson, and are more or less the same for all students. Language objectives help both teachers and students focus on ways to use language to achieve content objectives. In developing language objectives and sharing them with students, teachers will be able to differentiate expectations for classroom participation according to students' ELP levels. We advocate that objectives be explicitly shared with students both orally and in writing—that is, written on the board, discussed at the beginning of the lesson, and reviewed at the end of the lesson, in keeping with the SIOP model (Echevarria, Short, & Vogt, 2016). When students know the objectives, they learn to be accountable for achieving them. In addition, they may enjoy holding the teacher accountable for addressing all the objectives, as one of our colleagues shared with us.

Match Instruction to Student ELP Levels. The student descriptors that we introduced in Chapter 1 specify what students at each of the five ELP levels can be expected to do with language independently in the domains of listening, speaking, reading, and writing. Teachers need to remember that students may be able to do more with listening and speaking in English than they can do with reading and writing, as reflected in higher ELP levels in listening and speaking and lower ELP levels in reading and writing. Teachers can use these ELP levels and corresponding student descriptors to select appropriate assignments/assessments and instructional strategies. When teachers match their instruction and assessment to what students can do with language independently and with instructional support, they encourage ELLs' progress along the ELD continuum.

Provide Clear Directions and Check for Student Understanding. Students must understand the directions for all instructional activities. Teachers must remember that the general academic language used in directions, such as asking students to summarize, infer, or compare may be unfamiliar to ELLs. Teachers need to do more than simply ask, "Do you understand?" Students may say "yes" just to please the teacher or for other cultural reasons. Rather, checks for understanding are more productive when they require students to actively demonstrate their comprehension of expectations. The few moments that are required to carefully clarify directions and check for understanding pay worthwhile dividends in student achievement. For example, if students are to first create an outline and then write an essay based on it, teachers might ask students to explain the steps for the assignment rather than asking a yes or no question to check for understanding.

Provide Directions Both Orally and in Writing. All students, and particularly ELLs, benefit when information is shared in more than one modality. Oral directions accompanied by written directions—especially those that also use pictures or icons—are more comprehensible to students who are still learning the language. Teachers should consider posting templates for assignments used regularly in their content areas, such as a sample format for a lab report in science class.

Incorporate ELLs' Interests and Prior Knowledge into Instruction. ELLs do not enter U.S. classrooms as blank slates; they bring with them a wealth of knowledge and skills. Teachers who appreciate and draw on these funds of knowledge foster more rapid learning of language and content. For instance, high school ELLs from Myanmar can serve as social studies class panelists, addressing the realities of the Rohingya people from the Myanmar conflict because they have firsthand knowledge of the situation.

Activate ELLs' Interests and Prior Knowledge. Interest is a form of intrinsic motivation (Ormrod, 2012), while prior knowledge serves as "mental Velcro" to which students can attach new knowledge. ELLs are well served by teachers who intentionally capitalize on their individual interests and make connections to their prior knowledge, just as non-ELLs are. Teachers should therefore allow students to focus assigned projects on topics that interest them. For example, teachers could tailor a health assignment on forms of recreation to focus on soccer because many ELLs come from countries where soccer is played.

Highlight ELLs' Home Languages and Cultures. An important part of making students feel welcome and of priming them for learning is valuing what they bring with them to the classroom. The knowledge and skills that ELLs possess are not liabilities; rather, they can serve as classroom resources. Honoring this expertise can be as simple as letting students teach each other phrases in various languages or asking ELLs to share about different climates where they have lived. All students benefit from such exchanges in terms of increased understanding across linguistic and cultural groups and within the curricular content. Another example of honoring students' home languages is to grant them world language credit toward graduation for their home language oracy and literacy, in the same way that non-ELLs are awarded credit for learning a new language.

Use Students' Home Languages to Support Content Learning. While the implementation of bilingual or dual language education is impossible for speakers of all languages in all school districts, teachers are encouraged to allow ELLs to capitalize on the language or languages that they bring with them to facilitate classroom learning. Students might use bilingual dictionaries if they are literate in the home language; they might work with a bilingual paraeducator; or they might work with other students who share the same home language, to name just three examples. While ELD programming aims to teach English through the medium of English, this generalization does not preclude the use of a student's home language to enhance learning. Clearly, the home language is a significant asset, not a problem to be overcome or extinguished.

Create and Use Identity Texts. Students create identity texts when they bring in parts of their personal stories or histories. Encouraging students to create identity texts, and using those texts for instructional purposes, can be an extremely motivating approach. Honoring students' personal stories and histories supports students in preserving, maintaining, and developing their personal identities and voice while they acquire English. According to Cummins and Early,

> Students invest their identities in the creation of these texts, which can be spoken, signed, visual, musical, dramatic, or combinations in multimodal form. The identity text then holds a mirror up to students in which their identities are reflected in a positive light (2011, p. 3).

Students' experiences provide the perfect vehicle for authentic writing, vocabulary building, and self-expression. In one such example, Jones-Vo's K–12 ELLs each contributed a personal immigration story to a bound volume titled *Kaleidoscope of True Stories*. This inspirational collection of stories spanned all ELP levels with contributions ranging from 1st-grade drawings that included falling bombs to high school multipage essays recounting details of refugee camps. Housed in each district building's media center, the book became a sought-after resource for teachers, administrators, and others. Teachers can also encourage students to use home languages and English in creating dual-language identity texts, as illustrated by the *Dual Language Showcase* created collaboratively by Thornwood Public School (Peel District School Board), York University, and the Ontario Institute for Studies of Education of Toronto University beginning in 2001. Teachers can Google *dual language showcase* to see examples of students' dual language books in many languages.

Teach Cross-Language Features. Students can benefit from explicit instruction comparing and contrasting their home language and English. Cognate languages are languages that descend from the same language, like English, Spanish, and French that all descend from Latin language. Similarities across cognate languages are found at the word, sentence, and discourse levels. Cognates are words that are nearly the same in two languages, such as *decidir* in Spanish and *decide* in English. Comparisons of the grammar of the student's home language with English can also be helpful, such as pointing out differences between the order of nouns and adjectives in English and Spanish. In Spanish, adjectives generally come after the noun, as in *sombrero rojo* (hat red); in English, adjectives come before the noun, as in *red hat*.

Students may not automatically recognize these similarities, so teachers are urged to assist students in making these connections. Teachers are also reminded that the instruction in prefixes, suffixes, and root words that builds the vocabulary skills of non-ELLs is also beneficial for ELLs. Cognate languages are likely to have cognate prefixes, root words, and suffixes, and teaching students how to transform these word parts from one language to another (e.g., *-tion* in *transportation*; *-ción* in *transportación*) can greatly build students' vocabulary. Non-cognate languages, including Chinese and Japanese, may not make words from prefixes, root words, and suffixes as Indo-European languages do. Teachers can help students who use non-cognate languages build their English vocabulary by explicitly teaching about word formation in English.

Involve ELLs' Families in School Activities, Communicating with Them in the Language They Best Understand. Although cultural understanding of the role of parents in the schooling process varies, ELLs' parents can and should be encouraged to participate in school activities, just as the participation of non-ELLs' parents is encouraged. Clear explanations regarding how activities work (e.g., What is game night at an elementary school?) may be useful. Further, invitations and these explanations may need to be shared in the parents' home languages. Communication can be facilitated through the use of bilingual paraeducators, translation services, community volunteers, and other means. One more thought: In some cultures, a personal (verbal) invitation is needed to ensure attendance at an event. Bear this in mind when preparing for parent–teacher conferences; well-attended parent–teacher conferences represent an excellent opportunity to make connections with parents that can facilitate other types of school involvement.

Support Home Language Literacy Development to Enhance ELD. Although this volume focuses on learning content through English, we certainly advocate for the continuation and expansion of home language practices. Research supports the notion that home language skills can transfer to the new language (Wang, 2015). Further, support of students' home languages instills in them a sense of pride in their heritage, an important part of identity development. Teachers do not have to be fluent in a student's home language to emphasize its value. For instance, they can encourage parents to continue to use the home language at home with their children for speaking, reading, and writing activities. They can also encourage students who share the same home language to leverage that language for learning (García, Ibarra Johnson, & Seltzer, 2016).

Provide Multicultural and Home Language Books and Resources. Family literacy activities have been increasingly emphasized in recent years. It is empowering for families to see their own traditions and practices in the wide range of multicultural books that are now available. Non-ELLs and their families can also benefit from learning about other cultures through these texts. For ELLS and their parents, family literacy activities can also be fostered through the availability of such books in various languages. Readers can readily find home language resources online.

Use High-Quality Materials That Are Age Appropriate, Visually Supported, and Differentiated across ELP and Reading Levels. Teaching ELLs who do not read at grade level requires differentiation of materials. These materials must address standards-based curricular topics, but must also be accessible to students at lower levels of reading and language development. Age-appropriate, high-interest texts are encouraged. Readers can find high-quality, age-appropriate, lower-reading-level materials online.

Facilitate Interaction between ELLs and non-ELLs through Heterogeneous Grouping. Many ELLs do not speak English in their home environments and wholly depend on school-based language interactions to develop their English skills. Given that the continued use of the home language is to be encouraged, students must also be provided with plenty of time to practice and manipulate their newly developing language skills during the school day. ELLs need to interact with peers who have a strong command of the language during this time. It is necessary for these students to work not only with other ELLs but also with grade-level peers who can demonstrate appropriate use of both social and academic language. Heterogeneous grouping requires that ELLs not be grouped exclusively with one another or only with students receiving special education services. ELLs require opportunities to work with a range of more advanced speakers whose command of English assists in scaffolding ELLs' ELD. For example, ELLs and non-ELLs might be grouped together on a research project focused on a current events topic pertinent to the home countries of the ELLs in the class. In this way, all students bring expertise to be shared in the completion of the project, and the ELLs will benefit from the modeling of language by their more capable peers.

Develop Higher-Order Thinking across ELP Levels. Some teachers mistakenly assume that students at lower ELP levels are incapable of the higher-order thinking required for tasks that involve application, analysis, synthesis, creation, and evaluation. However, language level is not indicative of cognitive development. Though teacher creativity is required in designing appropriate and accessible activities, even students at level 1 are fully capable of engaging in higher-order thinking. For example, the placement of pictures in a simple Venn diagram exemplifies a student's ability to compare, contrast, and evaluate. Graphic organizers like this are an excellent way to foster higher-order thinking among ELLs with lower levels of ELP. Teachers can then provide students with the key vocabulary and sentence frames necessary to express their higher-order thinking according to their ELP levels.

Move from Concrete Activities to Abstract Concepts. Students new to English as the language of instruction need plenty of support to make sense of classroom lessons. This need is particularly significant when students are learning abstract concepts. In these situations, teachers must capitalize on more tangible examples (such as manipulatives and experiential activities) to facilitate understanding of the abstract concept, especially those involving multisensory experiences. For example, in a lesson about gravity, teachers might involve students in an activity where they ride an amusement park ride, providing a sensory experience at the outset.

Focus Error Correction on Specific Aspects of Language. Error correction during instruction should target only certain level-appropriate aspects of language. For instance, when teaching students at level 4, a brief contextualized lesson on the correct use of dependent clauses would be more appropriate than emphasis on a decontextualized list of grammatical constructions that might be overwhelming.

Make Use of Peer Tutors and Volunteers. There are countless benefits to be gained through peer tutoring and creating a team of volunteers to assist with classroom learning. Peer tutors learn about others and hone teamwork skills, while volunteers can expand their understanding of "the cultural other." Best of all, learning is fostered and relationships are built. Both authors have enjoyed the benefits of engaging the assistance of student and community-based volunteers in our classrooms. These individuals can be invaluable in supporting the learning of ELLs of all ages and extending overstretched budgets. Remember to provide these tutors with guidance in what topics to address with ELLs and with strategies to use during their tutoring sessions.

Create a Print-Rich Environment. While word, language, and concept walls and posters may initially be considered as elementary teaching strategies, these all-important aids should be implemented in the secondary context as well. Many students prefer and even rely on visual learning, so the benefit of pictorially supported word, language, and concept walls and posters cannot be underestimated for the entire class, ELLs and non-ELLs. While word walls may be familiar to readers, language walls are designated areas of the classroom that focus on larger chunks of language necessary in the student work. For instance, a teacher may post suggested phraseology for giving opinions such as, "I believe that _____" or "It seems to me that ____." Concept walls are areas that introduce entire concepts, like magnetism, using visuals and relevant words and language. In such cases, pictures, photos, and icons are all appropriate supports.

Teach Students to Participate in Their New Culture. In many schools, the ratio of ELLs to ELD teachers is very high. This discrepancy means that all teachers must not only teach language but also serve as cultural brokers for newcomers. Anyone who has ever traveled to another country understands the tremendous value of a kind soul willing to share insights about the "rules of the game" in the new context (e.g., how to hail a taxi, how to greet individuals of different status). As educators of students new to U.S. culture, we must embrace this role and assist newcomers in making sense of the norms and conventions of U.S. culture. This assistance may include such simple things as how to get a turn on the playground swings or how to negotiate the cafeteria lunch line. Additional examples include norms of body language, eye contact, and personal space; how to politely apologize or make requests; and other facets of the culture.

Support Paraeducators with Clear Guidance about Working Effectively with Students and Families. Paraeducators are invaluable resources to teachers who serve ELLs and to the students themselves, and they often have bilingual abilities. However, many paraeducators may not have a teaching background. Further, these all important staff members are not always afforded the professional development that teachers receive. Therefore, teachers must provide clear guidance to these instructional partners about the characteristics of ELLs at different ELP levels, instructional strategies appropriate for individual students, and ways to meaningfully and accurately assess these students. For example, rather than handing over a textbook and saying "Teach her Chapter 5," teachers must give paraeducators specific teaching and assessment guidelines and expectations that are appropriate for individual students. In addition, teachers must support paraeducators, whether they are bilingual or not, in serving students from diverse language backgrounds. By sharing cultural and linguistic insights, including those gained in collaboration with others, teachers can empower paraeducators to effectively assist students from a range of cultural and linguistic backgrounds in the learning process.

Serve Appropriately Identified ELLs in Talented and Gifted Programming. A lower ELP level does not preclude an ELL from participating in talented and gifted programming. Specialists can utilize the information presented in this book to tailor their services to the unique needs of talented and gifted ELLs.

Maintain English Language Instruction for ELLs Receiving Special Education Services across ELP Levels. Special education teachers do not always possess expertise in how to assist students in the language development process. Further, there seems to be a common, though mistaken, belief that students cannot "double dip," or receive services from two programs (e.g., ELD and special education programs) simultaneously. In fact, correctly identified students should receive all programming to which they are entitled. Providing these services calls for collaboration across programs, with both the ELD teacher and the special education teacher sharing their expertise about the best outcomes for the student.

Ensure Equitable ELL Participation in All Curricular and Extracurricular Programming. When analyzing membership in each curricular or extracurricular group, it must be noted whether there is balanced and proportional representation of all students, as articulated in the 2015 Dear Colleague Letter issued jointly by the United States Office of Civil Rights and the Department of Justice. In terms of extracurricular activities such as music lessons, band, chorus, school newspaper, after-school clubs, and drama and sports teams, teachers should not overlook the benefits of participation for ELLs. Such activities can provide ready-made social networks based on common interests, simultaneously promoting interaction and accelerating language development. For example, one high-school band teacher agreed to provide summer trumpet lessons for a newly arrived level 1 9th grader. As a result, the student, who had never had music lessons previously, was able to participate in the marching band during all four years of his high school career, making friends, attending school events, traveling with the band, and enhancing his language development. Subsequently, a program to collect donated musical instruments from graduating seniors was implemented so that elementary ELLs whose families might be unable to afford the monthly rental cost for an instrument, could begin to study music at an early age with their non-ELL peers. Fueled by the success of this effort, teachers began to investigate the equity of other school programs.

Conclusion

This chapter began with five guidelines for getting started with effective teaching and assessment of ELLs, focusing on grade-level placement, setting students at ease, taking a student-centered approach, using appropriate scaffolding, and drawing on students' home languages and cultures. The chapter then delved into the topic of academic language, describing what is meant by that term and offering recommendations for teaching this language to ELLs. Next, various classroom strategies for use with ELLs at all ELP levels were described in detail, with each strategy listed and explained and a classroom-based example provided.

Professional Learning Activities

1. **Identifying Language Demands in Standards, Assessment, and Instruction**

   Select one unit of instruction that you have implemented in your classroom, or one that you are preparing to implement soon. Identify the language demands, or how students will need to use oral and written language, throughout that unit of instruction.

   a. What content-area standards does this unit target? (Write out the standard).

   b. What are the primary ways that students need to use oral (listening and speaking) and written (reading and writing) language for academic purposes in this unit of instruction?

   c. How will the students' performance be assessed throughout this unit? How will students need to use oral and written language to complete these assessments?

   d. Make a list of the sequence of activities in this unit of instruction. Identify how students will need to use oral and written language to engage in each of these activities.

2. **Planning for Strategy Implementation**

    a. Make a list of the three assignment/assessment strategies discussed in this chapter that you consider to be most important:

    b. Why is each of these strategies important?

    c. When will you begin to employ these strategies? List specific assignments/assessments.

    d. Make a list of the three instructional strategies discussed in this chapter that you consider most important:

    e. Why is each of these strategies important?

    f. When will you begin to employ these strategies? List specific assignments/assessments.

Chapter 4

Differentiating for Students at Level 1

There needs to be a lot more emphasis on what a child can do instead of what he cannot do.

—DR. TEMPLE GRANDIN

The ability to recognize and meaningfully address the range of student capabilities at each level of English language proficiency (ELP) is an important factor in successful differentiation for English language learners (ELLs). To illustrate, we begin with scenarios based on two different 7th-grade level 1 ELLs: Corina, a student with limited or interrupted formal education (SLIFE) and Fajar, who is at grade level in his home language. Next we examine the student descriptors for level 1 ELLs to understand what these students know and can do with listening, speaking, reading, and writing in English. Then we use an example assignment to demonstrate how teachers can differentiate assessment and instruction for level 1 students like Corina and Fajar who have very different instructional needs and learning trajectories. The chapter concludes with assignment/assessment and instructional strategies that teachers can use to meet level 1 ELLs "where they are" so that these students can comprehend and engage with grade-level content-area instruction and progress along the English language development (ELD) continuum.

While the strategies suggested here are designed to elicit and support language production for level 1 students in listening, speaking, reading, and writing, teachers are reminded to push students to reach ever higher targets, providing scaffolding in instruction and assignment/assessment designed to support students' advancement to the next level of content and language proficiency. Teachers can support students' language development by eliciting level 1 language and, where possible and appropriate, providing and eliciting examples of level 2 language production.

Variation in Students' Backgrounds

Student Scenarios

Corina is a 7th-grade student who has just arrived from Guatemala and enrolled in an urban middle school. In the classroom, her teachers note that she often keeps to herself with downcast eyes. She does not communicate verbally with classmates or the teacher, though she sometimes responds to some commonly used classroom verbal cues that are visually supported. Teachers are concerned that when presented with a textbook, Corina is unsure of how to hold or open the book. She is unable to write her name or even hold a pencil.

Fajar is a 7th grader from Indonesia who has just begun to attend the same urban middle school. He, too, is silent in class but teachers immediately notice that he seems ready to try to engage with print materials. Though he can only respond to basic verbal commands at this point, Fajar can write his name and can copy writing from the textbook and other print materials.

While both students are in the 7th grade, they exemplify differences between students in the SLIFE category (Corina), who have not had opportunities to develop literacy in their home language, and students who can demonstrate grade-level achievement in their home languages (Fajar). Though both Corina and Fajar fall within the same ELP level, they are very different in terms of their preparedness to participate in middle school learning activities. Each requires distinctly different and specific approaches to assessment and instruction that take into consideration the variation in their academic preparation.

As a student who has not learned to read or write in any language, Corina must receive early literacy instruction as soon as she enrolls in a U.S. school, despite the fact that this kind of literacy instruction is not typically part of the middle school curriculum. As students in the SLIFE group arrive in the upper grades, the urgency for immediate and effective literacy instruction dramatically intensifies. Remedial literacy instruction that is designed to shore up earlier instruction may be available in some middle school contexts, but this approach is inappropriate for students in the SLIFE category. Rather, students like Corina need separate instruction that is grounded in best practice for initial literacy development and, at the same time, sensitive to the needs of culturally and linguistically diverse learners.

Classroom teachers at the upper grade levels cannot be expected to provide this intensive developmental literacy instruction in their content classrooms. Instead, school districts must create programs to meet the literacy development needs of older SLIFE. They likely need early reading instruction such as that provided with intensity and frequency for most ELLs during their first five years of school on a regular and ongoing basis. Students in the SLIFE group have missed years of stories read aloud in English, rhymes, songs, and playground chants to tune their ears to a different phonological system and provides a foundation for phonics and fluency. They lack these years of repetition and vocabulary building in English in contextualized settings at home that build their oral language development and fluency. Early literacy instruction must have an explicit focus as part of the core ELD program. Statistically, Corina is considered at risk and will likely drop out if she does not receive this type of literacy instruction.

In contrast, Fajar comes to the classroom having already developed grade-level literacy in his home language. This fact makes him fundamentally different from Corina in terms of his assessment and instructional needs. The research literature clearly demonstrates that literacy skills acquired in one's home language transfer to the new language (Dressler & Kamil, 2006; Wang, 2015), thereby accelerating and supporting the process of learning to read in the new language. While Corina has little to no experience with print to draw on in becoming an English reader and writer, Fajar is prepared to transfer and apply his previously developed skills to learning English reading and writing.

Student Descriptors

Level 1 ELLs come to English-medium classrooms at very early levels of ELP. Some of these students may be in a state of shock, having come from situations vastly different from U.S. classrooms. As a result, newcomer students are often unclear about what to expect and how to behave in their new environment. Many times, such students attempt to integrate into their new schools by copying the conduct of non-ELLs. Further, these newcomers display predictable characteristics of the typical language learning and cultural adjustment processes. However, these behaviors may be interpreted by some educators as indicative of inappropriate attitudes, learning difficulties, or cognitive challenges. This potential confusion requires an informed advocate who understands both the language learning process and the cultural factors that affect each student's integration into the classroom. Every teacher who works with an ELL must be that advocate.

Teachers also need to remember that not all level 1 ELLs are the same. For example, a student may not be at level 1 in all four domains of listening, speaking, reading, and writing. It is common for students to perform at level 1 in writing and reading while performing at higher levels in listening and speaking. Teachers are urged to look beyond students' composite ELP test scores to ascertain the ELP levels of their students in each domain. Furthermore, the student descriptors within level 1 show a range of capabilities. This range means that, while Corina and Fajar are both level 1 students, what they can be expected to do with language is different. Furthermore, because Corina comes to

Table 4-1   Student Descriptors, Level 1

Listening	Speaking	Reading	Writing
■ Begins to recognize often-heard words and phrases when supported contextually ■ Requires frequent restatement or paraphrasing ■ Begins to develop awareness of the sound system of English	■ Possibly silent ■ Produces often-heard words, memorized phrases, or self-generated language to express meaning or ask questions ■ Supports communication with nonverbal cues ■ Begins to produce the range of sounds of English	■ Gains meaning primarily from visual support ■ May start to transfer home language literacy skills to English ■ Develops reading skills in English when provided with high-quality, visually supported reading instruction	■ May draw or copy written text ■ May write or dictate individual letters, words, or phrases to convey meaning.

school with limited former education, her content learning and academic language and literacy development are likely to be much slower than Fajar's. In all cases, teachers should have high expectations for what their ELLs can do with content and language and use their understanding of these students' ELP levels and other background factors to push them to realistic and attainable levels of achievement. Table 4-1 summarizes the student descriptors for level 1 in listening, speaking, reading, and writing.

Listening

In terms of listening, level 1 ELLs may be hearing sounds not generally articulated or heard in their home languages. This initial stage of language learning is important because being able to hear and recognize new sounds is a precursor to articulating sounds verbally. Given their current ELP level, these students cannot be expected to make sense of a lecture or grade-level text independently. Instead, they must rely on context clues in the environment to construct meaning from classroom-based communication. Teachers also need to remember that level 1 students can engage in content learning that requires critical thinking, taking into consideration what these students can do with listening in English.

ELLs at level 1 listening begin to recognize often-heard words and phrases, especially when they are supported contextually. For example, teachers can make the instruction "sit down" comprehensible to level 1 listeners by gesturing toward the student's chair or by modeling the act of sitting down. These students also may need frequent restatement or paraphrasing to comprehend teacher talk and classroom activities. During this early stage of listening development, ELLs start becoming aware of the sound system of English.

Speaking

Teachers should not make the mistake of thinking that level 1 students who are silent are not learning. In terms of speech production, these students are often experiencing a "silent period" (Krashen, 1982), absorbing and processing new input in preparation for future language production. The length of this silent period is variable; some students may not produce spoken language for days, weeks, or months. At level 1, oral communication is generally brief, sometimes memorized, and often characterized by individual words or memorized phrases like "How are you?" At the earlier stages these students may be able to respond by pointing to pictures or using other nonverbal cues. In contrast, students at the higher end of level 1 may also generate original chunks of language. Level 1 speakers also begin to produce a range of sounds in English.

During this time, students' language development is largely focused on "survival English," an important aspect of social language. We encourage every teacher to take responsibility for assisting students to learn the formulaic language related to successful daily activities and tasks (e.g., "Good morning" or "How are you?") by promoting interaction with peers. These informal interactions assist ELLs in becoming comfortable and in developing a repertoire of meaningful words or phrases to successfully take care of "social business," whether on the playground, in the lunchroom, in the hallway, or in other contexts. Opportunities for sustained peer interaction should also be embedded in daily instruction. Engaging with peers allows ELLs to develop successful communication skills by manipulating language and modeling non-ELLs. Such linguistically developmental opportunities might be the only times the ELL engages with non-ELLs, particularly if English is not spoken in the home.

In terms of academic language, students at level 1 are, of course, only starting the journey toward proficiency in English. They are just starting to become familiar with general vocabulary and language structures, though they may begin to be aware of some of commonly used academic language practices in classroom routines, such as requests to take out or put away classroom materials.

Reading

All level 1 readers gain meaning primarily from visual support, and they develop reading skills in English when provided with high-quality, visually supported reading instruction. However, before new English sounds and letters can be matched, ELLs must have a strong foundation and familiarity with a growing vocabulary of concrete terms in English and a foothold on oral language development. With these foundations providing firm support rooted in comprehension, ELLs are best prepared to increase familiarity with the range of English sounds, or phonemic awareness, and to match letters to those sounds.

The difference between level 1 ELLs who can read in their home languages and those who cannot quickly emerges. Students like Corina who have not had the opportunity to develop literacy skills in any language cannot yet be expected to garner meaning from print. Instead, such students must rely on context clues like pictures and other supports to make sense of print-based materials. In contrast, students who have reading skills in their home languages, such as Fajar, may begin to transfer these skills to reading in English.

Writing

As with reading, the writing skills of level 1 ELLs are just beginning to emerge. With appropriate instruction, these students can begin to produce some written language. At the lower end of the level 1 continuum, their written work may take the form of drawing or copying letters, words, or longer stretches of text. As writing ability develops these students may, depending on their level in speaking, also dictate letters, words, and phrases to convey meaning. Again, the differences between students who have not yet learned to read and write in their home languages and those who can transfer writing ability from their home language must be recognized and acknowledged. Students with limited home language literacy skills naturally take longer to progress in the area of writing than their counterparts who can read and write in the home language. Even copying letters may be a laborious process for students like Corina. Graham (2010) offers some important words about handwriting:

> If students cannot form letters, or cannot form them with reasonable legibility and speed, they cannot translate the language in their minds into written text … that can lead to a self-fulfilling prophecy in which students avoid handwriting, come to think of themselves as not being able to write, and fall further and further behind their peers (p. 20).

This realization about students who are learning to write in English is a call to action for all teachers who work with ELLs. All teachers need to know the characteristics, script, concepts of print, and so forth of the home languages of all their students. Many school districts are dropping handwriting classes because non-ELLs rely on technology from early ages. We maintain, however, that the teaching of handwriting is non-negotiable for ELLs, especially those whose home languages do not use the Latin script, thus making handwriting essential for writing fluency.

All teachers who work with level 1 ELLs need to know what these students can do with listening, speaking, reading, and writing. Equipped with this understanding, teachers can look at their units of instruction and lesson plans to determine whether their level 1 students can comprehend and engage with grade-level activities. It is more than likely that level 1 students cannot participate in classroom activities without scaffolding and support. These student descriptors help teachers set realistic language-based expectations for level 1 ELLs and guide teachers' efforts to differentiate assignments/assessments and instruction.

A Word about Language Objectives

After teachers determine the essential learning of an assignment, they identify content objectives, which should be more or less the same for all students. Language objectives should explicitly indicate how students need to use oral and written language to reach the content objectives for a lesson, both those required for effective communication during each activity throughout the lesson and those required to demonstrate essential learning. Language objectives can be written for the lessons that are aligned with what ELLs can do with listening, speaking, reading, and writing in English. Teachers are advised to use the level 1 student descriptors when crafting appropriate language objectives for level 1 students.

For example, the content objectives might ask students to explain the steps they used to solve a math word problem, compare and contrast a historical and contemporary event, or summarize the key findings from a science experiment they conducted. Teachers then look at the content objectives of the lesson and ask themselves what the oral and written language demands of the lesson are. Next teachers specify how students need to use oral and written language to participate in each activity in the assignment and to demonstrate what they know and can do relative to the content objectives and essential learning of that assignment. With a clear understanding of the language demands of the assignment in mind, teachers are prepared to write and differentiate language objectives. Specifically, the language objectives ask students to use oral and written language to explain (the steps they used to solve a math problem), compare and contrast (a historical and contemporary event), or summarize (the key findings of a science experiment). Teachers need to remember that all students can use academic language to explain, compare and contrast, and summarize in ways that allow them to demonstrate their learning relative to the essential learning and content objectives. However, a level 1 student cannot be expected to use language in the same way as a level 3 student or a non-ELL. Teachers therefore turn to the student descriptors for listening, speaking, reading, and writing to identify appropriate language objectives for level 1 students (see Table 4-1).

Example Differentiated Assignment

· ·

Recall that the assignment we use to exemplify differentiation for ELLs across ELP levels is for students to write a set of instructions using an introduction; sequential organization; detailed description using appropriate grade-level vocabulary, sentence structures, and transition words; and a conclusion for a self-selected content-based process. The essential learning for this assignment is clarity in communicating steps in a content-based process, use of transition words, and logical sequencing, and is the same for all students, regardless of their ELP level.

All students in the class, including Corina and Fajar, are encouraged to choose the task for which they write instructions, which allows them to draw on a content-based process that they know something about or that they are interested in learning. The teacher has encouraged Corina and Fajar to work together to write a set of directions for making a peanut butter and jelly sandwich. Corina and Fajar have recently been introduced to these sandwiches and they like them a lot.

Corina and Fajar are in the 7th grade in a state that uses the Common Core State Standards (CCSS), and this assignment is aligned with the Grade 6–8 CCSS in English Language Arts–Literacy in History/Social Studies, Science, and Technical Subjects (www.corestandards.org./ELA-Literacy/WHST/6-8/). Teachers of other grades can choose the appropriate grade groups of their state-mandated college- and career-ready standards. The relevant parts of the standards for this example assignment are boldfaced:

- CCSS.ELA-Literacy.WHST.6–8.2
  Write informative/**explanatory texts, including** the narration of historical events, scientific procedures/experiments, or **technical processes**.
- CCSS.ELA-Literacy.WHST.6–8.2.a
  Introduce a topic clearly, previewing what is to follow; organize ideas, concepts, and information into broader categories as appropriate to achieving purpose; include formatting (e.g., headings), graphics (e.g., charts, tables), and multimedia when useful to aiding comprehension.
- CCSS.ELA-Literacy.WHST.6–8.2.b
  Develop the topic with relevant, well-chosen facts, definitions, **concrete details,** quotations, or other information and examples.
- CCSS.ELA-Literacy.WHST.6–8.2.c
  Use appropriate and varied transitions to create cohesion and clarify the relationships among ideas and concepts.
- CCSS.ELA-Literacy.WHST.6–8.2.d
  Use precise language and domain-specific vocabulary to inform about or explain the topic.
- CCSS.ELA-Literacy.WHST.6–8.2.f
  Provide a concluding statement or section that follows from and supports the information or **explanation presented.**

Teachers are encouraged to look closely at their assignments, and at the standards reflected in those assignments, to identify the language demands of each classroom activity. This assignment focuses on the domain of writing, and all students will need to use writing to explain (the steps in a content-based process), describe (each step of the process), and sequence (those steps). Of course, it is unreasonable to expect a level 1 ELL like Corina or Fajar to use the same kind of oral and written language to perform this task as we would expect from non-ELLs in a general education classroom. That said, it is reasonable for level 1 students to demonstrate their performance relative to the essential learning, taking into consideration what they can do with language at this level in their ELP. Teachers then draw on the student descriptors for level 1 writers and differentiate the language-based expectations for these writers. Teachers' quick analysis of how students are expected to use oral and written language in each assignment also benefits the non-ELLs in the class because of its explicit focus on academic language, which includes, but is not limited to, academic vocabulary.

Table 4-2 presents our example assignment differentiated for three levels of students: non-ELLs, level 1 writers, and level 2 writers. This portion of the template starts with the assignment for non-ELLs in the first column, reflecting backward design, which starts with the outcomes for the entire class. Including the expectations for non-ELLs on the differentiation template also reflects the expectation that differentiating instruction and assessment for ELLs is an integral part of the work of the general education teacher, not something additional or isolated. The second column includes the assignment for level 1 writers, with the language-based expectations and scaffolding and support differentiated to meet students like Corina and Fajar at their independent ELP level. The third column includes the language-based expectations and scaffolding and support for level 2 writers. Teachers need to keep in mind the next higher ELP level when working with individual students, to push them toward the kinds of language production needed at that level.

As we can see, the assignment has been adjusted to make it accessible for level 1 writers, with reduced language-based expectations and greater scaffolding and support. When considering students like Fajar and Corina, teachers should remember that, although the level 1 language-based expectations are reasonable for both students based on the student descriptors for level 1 writers, Corina may need much more time to complete the task than Fajar. Corina also needs the additional scaffolding and support denoted with the SLIFE acronym in the table.

To summarize, teachers can differentiate any assignment for level 1 writers by

- Maintaining the standards-based content or topic and essential learning for all students
- Clearly articulating the oral and written language demands for each activity of the assignment
- Adjusting the language-based expectations based on the level 1 student descriptors and assignment/assessment strategies for writing, while keeping the essential learning in mind

- Providing the necessary scaffolding and support for level 1 writers based on the instructional strategies discussed later in this chapter.

Of course, this example is just one way to differentiate this particular assignment. Curricular goals can be achieved in many ways, as long as teachers ensure that language-based expectations are appropriate to students' ELP levels and that necessary scaffolding and support are in place. Teachers also need to organize their assignments/assessments and instruction in ways that push students along the ELD continuum reflected in the student descriptors.

There are different ways that general education and ELD teachers can collaborate to create the necessary assignments/assessments and instruction for level 1 ELLs in the general education classroom. For instance, ELD and classroom teachers might work together to plan a differentiated assignment, and the ELD teacher might pull level 1 ELLs out of the general education classroom for supplementary language instruction and support. Another possibility is that the ELD and general education teachers co-teach the lesson, with both teachers in the classroom, using collaboratively planned activities designed to meet the needs of all students, regardless of ELP level. After reflecting upon the lesson, the general education and ELD teachers identify next steps in content and language instruction based on what they learned through their reflections. This approach illustrates the method used by teachers who engage in a student-centered continuous cycle of learning. Teachers who share responsibility for educating ELLs are encouraged to think creatively for effective ways to ensure that these students can learn content and language at school.

Assignment/Assessment Strategies

This section moves beyond our example assignment for 7th-grade ELLs and presents assignment/assessment strategies that teachers can use with level 1 students at any grade level in any content area. Focusing on assignment/assessment strategies before instruction strategies helps teachers clarify what they can expect their level 1 students to know and be able to do with content and language at the end of an activity, lesson, unit of instruction, or report period. When teachers teach with the end in mind, learning outcomes tend to improve.

We assume that assignments are a type of assessment, and that assessment strategies should mirror assignments. We also emphasize that level 1 students should not be subjected to an unfamiliar testing format when asked to demonstrate their content knowledge.

Recognizing that large-scale standardized assessment tools and classroom-based assessment tools designed for monolingual English speakers are inappropriate for level 1 ELLs, teachers must develop sensitive and useful assessment

Table 4-2 Example Assignment Differentiated for Level 1

Assignment: *Write a set of instructions using an introduction; sequential organization; detailed description using appropriate grade-level vocabulary; sentence structures; and transition words; and a conclusion for a self-selected content-based process.*

Standards-Based Content or Topic (from the curriculum)

For a content-based process

Non-ELL	Level 1	Level 2
Language-Based Expectations		
Write a set of instructions using	*Copy words and phrases for a set of instructions using*	*Write a set of instructions using*

■ *Introduction*
■ *Sequential organization*
■ *Detailed description with*
  ○ *appropriate grade-level vocabulary*
  ○ *grade-level sentence structures*
  ○ *appropriate and varied transition words*
■ *Conclusion*
		■ *Simple sentences*
		■ *Introductory sentence*
		■ *Sequential organization*
		■ *Ordinal transition words (first, second, third)*
		■ *Simple description using pretaught vocabulary*
		■ *Concluding sentence*

Non-ELL	Scaffolding and Support	Level 1	Level 2

Non-ELL

Using

- Model assignment
- Teacher demonstration of the task using a "think-aloud"
- Sequential graphic organizer for planning writing
- Language wall with sequencing words and key sentence structures
- Feedback designed to push students to produce accurate grade-level writing

Level 1

Using

- Level 1 model assignment
- Teacher demonstration of the task using a "think-aloud"
- Sequential graphic organizer for planning writing
- Photographs of relevant content-based processes
- Language wall with sequencing words (focus on ordinal numbers)
- Word and picture cards featuring needed content vocabulary (to be used when labeling the poster)
- Supplementary "think-aloud" demonstration of labeling
- Pictorially supported procedure texts
- Realia related to processes
- Additional work on introductory literacy skills (for SLIFE)
- Additional work on handwriting skills (for SLIFE)
- Additional time to complete the assignment (for SLIFE)
- Level-appropriate feedback designed to push students to the next level of writing development

Level 2

Using

- Level 2 model assignment
- Teacher demonstration of the task using a "think-aloud"
- Sequential graphic organizer with sentence starters for planning writing
- Photographs of relevant content-based processes
- Language wall with sequencing words (focus on ordinal numbers, then, next)
- Poster of needed simple sentence structures
- Word and picture cards featuring needed content vocabulary
- Supplementary "think-aloud" demonstration of simple sentence or paragraph writing
- Pictorially supported procedure texts
- Realia related to processes (to use in teaching and writing)
- Additional work on early literacy skills (for SLIFE)
- Additional work on handwriting skills (for SLIFE)
- Additional time to complete the assignment (for SLIFE)
- Level-appropriate feedback designed to push students to the next level of writing development

---

Essential Learning: *Clarity in communicating steps in a content-based process, effective use of transition words, and logical sequencing.*

Language Demands: *Use writing to describe each step in a process, sequence those steps, and explain how following these steps leads to the completion of the process.*

procedures that take into account the cultural and linguistic strengths and needs of these students. Teachers are wholeheartedly encouraged to "think outside the box" in creating new ways to gather information about what ELLs know and can do with content in English and in their home languages. Knowing what level 1 students can do with listening, speaking, reading, and writing, and understanding relevant student factors such as prior education, home language literacy, cultural orientation, and other relevant experiences, should inform the development of more appropriate and meaningful assessment procedures. In particular, knowledge of level 1 students' linguistic abilities prepares teachers to craft tasks appropriate for these students that are still aligned with essential learning in the content standards and curriculum. The resulting assessment procedures should yield authentic evidence of the content knowledge and skills of students whose ELP levels preclude their meaningful participation in assessments designed for non-ELLs. Teachers and administrators are reminded that appropriate assessment procedures can only occur at the intersection of student ELP level, relevant student background factors, and essential learning.

Including level 1 ELLs in daily instruction and assessment based on the content standards and curriculum designed for all students is crucial. Such inclusion represents best practice and is essential for maximizing ELL access to the curriculum; it is also critical for achieving academic parity. Remember that ELLs do not have the luxury of waiting until they are fluent in English to engage in essential learning of content material. From the first day in a U.S. school, each ELL plays "catch-up" with non-ELL peers, having to backfill language and content, tasks further complicated by cultural factors. As a result, the achievements of ELLs and non-ELLs are disparate from the beginning. Teachers must, through competent instruction and assessment, empower their students to take charge of their own learning, join their non-ELL peers in achievement, and reach their full potential.

All Domains

Teachers are reminded when assessing ELLs (and non-ELLs!) that assignments/assessments and instruction must be aligned in terms of both content and format. While it is obvious that students should only be assessed on what was taught, teachers must also remember that level 1 ELLs cannot be expected to linguistically demonstrate learning that has not been explicitly taught because of their emerging levels of English. That is, ELLs must be assessed using a format similar to the format of instruction. For example, if students are taught a concept using a graphic organizer and other visual supports, they should also be given the benefit of those scaffolds when they are assessed.

The following strategies can be used when developing assignments/assessments for level 1 students in all domains.

Create and Use Assignments/Assessments That Allow Students to Demonstrate Content Learning without Language Mastery. As level 1 ELLs begin to understand and produce English, they are likely to understand much more than they are able to demonstrate using only language. Empowering these students through teacher-created assessments that capitalize on what level 1 students can do with language is essential to their academic development and motivation. For example, rather than expecting a level 1 student to complete a multiple-choice test focused on story comprehension, a teacher might ask the student to sequence pictures to demonstrate understanding of the plot of the story.

Focus on Correct Answers Instead of Errors and Omissions. To encourage newcomers, teachers can increase student engagement by focusing on successes rather than shortcomings. Making a special effort to recognize and validate level 1 students' attempts to communicate pays dividends as students increase language production in a comfortable environment. For example, if a level 1 ELL recounts the steps in a process like washing one's hands, teachers should focus on the student's communication of the process and the intended meaning without correcting grammar or pronunciation.

Allow Students to Complete Assessments with the Support of a Bilingual Teacher or Paraeductor. Students at level 1 may understand far more than they are able to express in English. For this reason, bilingual teachers and paraeducators can be invaluable in assessing what students know and can do in the content areas. This support can be provided to students individually or in a small-group setting. One example of bilingual support would be explaining test questions in the student's home language. A second example would be translating parts of test questions, if language is not part of what is being assessed and graded. These supports both lead to a more accurate picture of what students know and can do in the short term and to increased student independence in the long term.

A third type of support that falls in a somewhat separate category would be allowing students to process content in their home languages. This approach can pay large dividends in terms of content learning. Working with a bilingual paraeducator can transform the assessment experience into one that facilitates both learning and assessment. While some teachers may be concerned that turning the test into a teaching and learning situation seems to constitute "giving students the answers," we must remember the purpose of our entire enterprise: student learning. If the ELL gains understanding of a given concept only at the time of the assessment, so be it! This result is better than no learning at all. Such situations may call for repeated, or cyclical, assessments later to ensure that learning has stuck. This cyclical assessment is appropriate and necessary, particularly if the assessment was the student's first opportunity to learn the material. Affording students the "opportunity to learn," even during an assessment, is an inherent part of fairness, as articulated in the Standards for Educational and Psychological Testing (AERA, APA, & NCME, 2014). If test procedures are unfair, then the whole assessment process loses utility. The usefulness of the assessment is lost because, without fairness, validity becomes questionable. If test scores do not truly reflect what students know and can do, the interpretations of the student's test score are invalid and the entire assessment procedure is meaningless.

Under no circumstances should a test be translated in its entirety. Doing so tends not to result in equivalent tests (Solano-Flores & Trumbull, 2003) and is an unreasonable demand to place on bilingual paraeducators.

Differentiate Grading by ELP Level. Realizing that listening and speaking are skills typically acquired before reading and writing skills, teachers should consider weighting oral demonstrations of learning more heavily for students at lower ELP levels. If, however, the student has learned English in isolation, or in contexts that focus on reading and writing without the benefit of authentic verbal interactions as is the case in some programs abroad, teachers could consider weighting written demonstrations of learning more heavily. Such linguistically responsive assessment practices recognize the continuum of language development while seeking to ascertain student learning in the content areas.

Since ELL teachers already have access to ELP assessment data, they know the reading and writing abilities of their level 1 students. Because teachers know that listening and speaking usually develop before reading and writing, it makes sense at level 1 to weight the domains of listening and speaking more heavily for grading purposes than those of reading and writing. There is no reason to punish a language learner for a predictable language development phenomenon. The oral demonstration of the desired content knowledge and skills should be given the greatest weight in determining an ELL's grade. Grammar should probably not be graded at level 1.

Explain Directions for Assignments/Assessments Orally and Provide Visual Support. To accurately determine what level 1 ELLs know and can do, it is imperative that students understand the assignment/assessment tasks at hand. Although some students at level 1 in reading and writing may exhibit higher levels of listening and speaking, the majority of these students likely have emerging listening and speaking skills. It is therefore recommended that special attention be given to the directions. While oral explanation certainly facilitates the understanding of written directions, teachers are also advised to provide visual clarification in the form of realia, icons, manipulatives, modeling, and demonstrations. Only when students understand the task can their performances be considered true indications of what they know and can do in the content areas.

Equipped with this understanding of assignment/assessment strategies that teachers can use across all domains, we turn now to strategies to assess listen-

Table 4-3   Assignment/Assessment Strategies for Level 1 Students

Listening	Speaking	Reading	Writing
▪ Evaluate student comprehension through student nonverbal communication ▪ Ask for a physical demonstration of understanding	▪ Use verbal cues to prompt repetition or short responses ▪ Assess orally to elicit words and phrases ▪ Allow home language oral responses	▪ Use high-quality, visually supported, age-appropriate reading materials matched to students' English language development and reading levels ▪ Elicit physical responses ▪ Ask for demonstration of understanding ▪ Prompt repetition of a teacher cue ▪ Ask students to retell stories using visual supports ▪ Assess orally to elicit words and phrases ▪ Support home-language reading	▪ Elicit beginning writing ▪ Ask students to complete visually supported graphic organizers ▪ Have students supplement early writing with visual support to enhance meaning ▪ Welcome home language writing

ing, speaking, reading, and writing. Table 4-3 provides a list of the strategies teachers can use to assess content understanding in the domains of listening, speaking, reading, and writing.

Listening

Because level 1 listeners are at the very early stages of language development, they may have difficulties demonstrating their listening comprehension of content-area concepts without considerable scaffolding and support. Nevertheless, these students can demonstrate their cognitively advanced understanding in a variety of ways, assuming that hearing is not an issue. Teachers must remember that students at lower levels of language proficiency are capable of higher-order thinking. Teachers need to keep an eye on essential learning and find creative ways to communicate the big ideas of the assignment without relying on oral communication. These assignment/assessment strategies provide the necessary scaffolding and support for level 1 students.

Evaluate Student Comprehension through Nonverbal Communication. At the very heart of learning and communicating in a new language is a student–teacher relationship that encourages and invites a student to participate, one in which a welcoming and supportive teacher works with a comfortable newcomer to facilitate both language and content learning. One way to achieve this goal with level 1 listeners is to use physical response to indicate understanding, as in locating or selecting by pointing, mimicking, and using gestures. For example, students can point to answer questions like "Where is your locker?" or "Which lunch do you want?" to demonstrate their comprehension. Another way that students can use physical response to demonstrate cognitive engagement is to mimic or repeat steps in a modeled activity like planting a seed. Students can also use physical response is to display judgment or evaluation by showing a "thumbs up" or "thumbs down" signal. Other kinds of gestures would include nodding or shaking of the head and raising a hand.

Note that intercultural awareness is essential when working with gestures. For example, the "thumbs up" signal has different meanings in different cultures, and students may use different techniques to get a teacher's attention (e.g., snapping in Germany). Teachers can explicitly teach what gestures used in the classroom mean, and help students become aware of cross-cultural differences.

Ask for a Physical Demonstration of Understanding. Level 1 students can demonstrate understanding by drawing, matching, and copying and using pictures or realia to sequence, categorize, prioritize, or evaluate, which are all important academic language functions. Demonstration is another way that students can show understanding of concepts without language mastery. For example, students can simply place objects in order to demonstrate sequencing or draw to demonstrate learning. Though it must be understood that not all ELLs are artists, students can create simple sketches to depict content knowledge and skills by drawing, for instance, habitats for different types of animals. Matching can also be used to ascertain student learning. For example, students can match various picture cards to nonverbally explain relationships between types of rock and how they are formed. Copying is another method that students can employ to demonstrate understanding, as in labeling layers of the rain forest. Students can also use realia and pictures to sequence concepts like the phases of the water cycle, categorize items like food groups, prioritize the levels of the food chain, and evaluate effective means of controlling erosion. Teachers simply need to identify a nonverbal means of communicating important classroom language functions—such as explain, argue, compare and contrast and sequence—and then teach students how to use these nonverbal cues to demonstrate content learning.

Speaking

When assessing level 1 students' content knowledge and skills using speaking, teachers must remember that these students may be at a preproduction stage of second language development. In other words, level 1 speakers may not yet speak in English. This level of language proficiency limits the activities in which these students can engage or participate. Nevertheless, level 1 speakers can demonstrate their cognitively advanced understanding in a variety of ways, that take into consideration what they can do with oral language. Furthermore, assessment opportunities using the following strategies lend themselves to incremental and graduated scaffolding, the ideal means for facilitating the simultaneous acquisition of language and content knowledge and skills.

Use Verbal Cues to Prompt Repetition or Short Responses. Repetition is another technique that teachers can use in ascertaining student learning. For example, teachers can ask students to repeat key "survival" words, like yes or no, in response to questions. Alternatively, students can be expected to produce short responses, whether individual words or memorized phrases in response to a teacher prompt. For example, in a categorizing task contrasting mammals, reptiles, and fish, a teacher might prompt, "What is this?" and the student responds, "mammal."

Assess Orally to Elicit Words and Phrases. Through authentic engagement with classroom learning and social activities, level 1 speakers can be expected to begin producing words and phrases in context. Teachers can consider their anecdotal observations of student interactions an appropriate indicator of students' learning or they can interview students to ascertain their content understanding. At this level, teachers can use and elicit everyday language that includes common, nontechnical language used in general communication.

Recall that most academic language does not typically appear in a social conversation and includes vocabulary and structures exclusive to classroom instruction, academic texts, and standardized (and often classroom) tests. Level 1 speakers may not be able to engage with this type of language. So, when assessing students in social studies, a teacher might ask these students to offer a one-word description about "what the *land* in states is like" rather than "what the *terrain* of states is like." The exception to this rule is when students have been explicitly taught key vocabulary; if a level 1 speaker has learned the word *terrain* in context, then the teacher can expect this student to comprehend and use this term.

Allow Home-Language Oral Responses. Level 1 speakers should also be allowed to respond in their home languages to demonstrate listening comprehension. To ascertain their understanding, teachers would need a working knowledge of the students' home languages or would need to rely on the assistance of a bilingual professional. This strategy could be used to determine if students understand the meaning of a given word in English. For example, the teacher might say the word in English and the student responds with the word or definition in the home language.

Reading

It is important to keep in mind that an ELL's age is an inadequate predictor of literacy development in the home language. Further, a focus on early literacy is essential for older level 1 readers whose literacy is just beginning to emerge. Teachers must ensure that the explicit development of literacy skills assumes a high priority. It should be noted that this is not remedial reading instruction; rather, this may be a student's first exposure to literacy instruction of any kind.

Since the student is acquiring English while working to catch up with non-ELL peers, special attention must be given to integrating meaningful content and literacy instruction. For high school students, this instruction must facilitate literacy development to empower students to earn graduation credit in a timely manner. This urgency may require that new classes or programs be developed and put in place to offer level 1 readers the opportunity to engage with the curriculum, achieve academically, and graduate from high school.

Recall that level 1 readers should not be expected to gain meaning from print alone. However, level 1 readers can draw on their emerging listening skills to engage with information that is read aloud, as long as it is visually supported. Students who have not yet had the opportunity to develop literacy skills should also be have opportunities to learn the alphabet, print directionality, book-handling skills, phonemic awareness of the sounds of English, letter–sound relationships (phonics), and vocabulary. Students can demonstrate their learning using early reading skills through the following assignment/assessment strategies.

Use High-Quality, Visually Supported, Age-Appropriate, Reading Materials Matched to Students' Reading Levels. If reading is required for assignment/assessment tasks, teachers should employ extensive visual support to facilitate students' understanding of the task. For example, a teacher might use a diagram of the water cycle on a test and ask students to match key words to the various parts of the diagram, rather than expect students to match words to printed definitions. Level 1 readers must not be expected to read tests to demonstrate their learning.

Elicit Physical Responses. Teachers can ask level 1 readers for physical responses to assess reading skills and content understanding. For example, students can point to specific letters of the alphabet or to a picture of a word that represents a category of an animal, vegetable, or mineral. Level 1 readers can also be asked to raise their hands to indicate their recognition or understanding of, for example, a specific sound or word.

Ask for a Demonstration of Understanding. Students can demonstrate and use early reading skills in a variety of ways. They can sequence pictures to show understanding, such as scenes from a story that they have seen acted out with puppets. Drawing can also be used to indicate comprehension. For instance, students could be asked to sketch an example of a cell after a visually supported science lesson. Matching could be used in a variety of academic ways, as in having students match a letter to a picture of a word that starts with the sound of that letter. Finally, mimicking is a viable assessment method for early reading skills. Level 1 readers can demonstrate book-handling skills by turning pages appropriately. These students can also role-play the actions of a character or act out their interpretations of layers found in the rain forest.

Prompt Repetition of a Teacher Cue. Repetition can be used to assess level 1 readers' early reading skills development and content understanding. For instance, these students can simply repeat after the teacher who utters a letter name or sound accompanied by visual support, like a picture or object, to ensure accurate pronunciation. This repetition also extends to word practice. Level 1 readers can also recite sentences that are read aloud, as long as they are visually supported, to ensure comprehension of the content. Finally, repetition of visually contextualized poems, rhymes, chants, and songs can be used to demonstrate content learning, if the words are made comprehensible through some type of sensory support.

Ask Students to Retell Stories Using Visuals. Level 1 readers can understand contextualized oral presentations of written material, including read-alouds of stories and other texts. However, visual supports, such as props and acting, are crucial to this understanding. Only when teaching has been made comprehensible can these students be expected to internalize information and demonstrate understanding. Level 1 readers can, depending on their level of spoken language proficiency, retell stories and texts to demonstrate learning. Keep in mind, however, that these students may need to make use of visual supports in their retelling to bridge gaps in their communication. For example, to retell a story a level 1 reader could use props, storyboards, timelines, acting, or other realia like puppets to reenact the story.

Assess Orally to Elicit Words and Phrases. Oral testing is a far better means to assess student learning than expecting level 1 readers to produce writing on traditional paper-and-pencil tests. Most students at this level can produce words and phrases in response to oral questions. Teachers are advised to "count" their observations of student responses to oral questions as test data. According to many in the field, oral language development is a critical aspect of early literacy for all students, including level 1 readers. Early literacy should therefore be an integral component of assessment of both reading skills and content, particularly at the early ELD stages.

Support Home Language Reading. The ability to read in the home language should not be underestimated in terms of its value and support in learning to read in English. If students can already read in their home language, they are likely to benefit from the support of content materials in those languages, particularly if they can read in their home language about the topic they are reading about in English at school. It is not difficult for teachers to find readings about school topics in Spanish and some other languages. Although test translation is not recommended, something as simple as a glossary of terms that students know in the home language might assist a level 1 reader in completing an assignment/assessment task.

Even if students have not yet learned to read in their home language, they can benefit from early reading instruction in that language. This, of course, requires having a teacher who is fluent in the student's home language and skilled in the teaching of reading in that language. The results of such early literacy instruction can and should be assessed using home language materials, bearing in mind that the language of a test should be the same as the language of instruction.

Writing

Level 1 writers arriving at U.S. schools require explicit and differentiated class-room attention to acquire the needed writing skills in English. While learning to write in a new language is a significant challenge for all students, students who have learned to write in their home language can transfer important writing skills to English. Given planned, focused, and differentiated attention in writing, these level 1 writers can immediately start the process of catching up to their non-ELL peers.

An ELL who has not yet developed writing skills in any language, regardless of age, urgently needs explicit instruction in the form of a comprehensive, well-planned program exclusively for students who do not have experience with the written word. The development of writing skills in English generally takes students who have not had the opportunity to develop home language literacy much longer than students who already have home language literacy in place. In fact, some informed and proactive schools identify ELLs who are not yet able to read and write in their home languages for placement in intensive programs that focus on emergent reading and writing skills.

The need for such specific and explicit development of foundational reading and writing cannot be overstated. This instruction must be highly contextualized and focused on meaning, rather than consisting of isolated drills and decontextualized exercises. It is incumbent on schools that serve students who are just beginning to develop literacy skills in any language to "meet them where they are" and ensure academic parity with their non-ELL peers. The first non-negotiable step to academic achievement in the United States is making certain that every student can read and write in English. Schools should be prepared with a concrete, research-based response plan for any student who arrives without developed home language reading and writing skills, regardless of the student's age. This type of targeted literacy instruction is the gateway for these students to reach academic success.

Students who come to U.S. schools with developed literacy skills in their home language have a far simpler task, especially if they can read and write at or above grade level. However, these students still require explicit attention to reading and writing development in English. Moreover, if these students come from language backgrounds that do not share the English alphabet (e.g., Chinese, Japanese, Arabic, Hindi), they require support similar to that for their counterparts who have not yet developed literacy skills in the home language. While students literate in home languages that use writing systems unlike the English alphabet understand the concepts of reading and writing, they require specific early literacy instruction related to phonemic awareness, letter formation, concepts of print, letter–sound relationships, and so on.

By definition, level 1 writers are at the beginning of the continuum of English writing development and can be expected to produce only limited amounts of print. In fact, it is appropriate for teachers to credit drawing and copying as legitimate writing skills at this early stage. Clearly, students cannot be expected to complete writing assessments that are appropriate for their non-ELL peers. A possible exception would be for students in kindergarten or 1st grade, where early writing development is the focus of instruction for all students. Further, for any level 1 writer, absolute accuracy, neatness, and clarity are unreasonable expectations. Teachers should think in terms of appropriate levels of production for a non-ELL beginning writer. With visual support in instruction, level 1 writers can represent their learning on paper through drawing, copying, dictating, labeling, and writing short phrases. Following are some appropriate writing assessment strategies for level 1 writers.

Elicit Beginning Writing. Level 1 writers can demonstrate understanding of content-area information through various early writing activities. For example, drawing is an early approximation of written communication. Students can create sketches of the types of animals studied to demonstrate content learning. Producing individual letters and numbers and combinations thereof, as in a dictation assignment, is a reasonable expectation for level 1 writers. These learners can also be credited with writing when copying the written word, as in labeling the stages of the butterfly's life cycle on a diagram or poster. They may also generate writing of words and phrases on their own, though many errors are likely to be present.

Ask Students to Complete Visually Supported Graphic Organizers. The beauty of graphic organizers is that they add a deeper dimension to content that allows students to apply knowledge, make connections, and understand interrelationships. Graphic organizers serve as an excellent springboard for teachers to employ in supporting level 1 writers because they help these students articulate ideas and relationships that they intuitively know but need scaffolding and modeling to express. For example, a student could complete a Venn diagram using pictures and, possibly, words or phrases to compare and contrast the United States and his or her country of birth. Such graphic organizers provide teachers with information on what students have learned and what they can do.

Require Students to Supplement Early Writing with Visual Support to Enhance Meaning. Level 1 writers begin to communicate meaning through pictures and then add the written word. When writing ability starts to develop, these pictorial representations should not be eliminated; rather, the use of pictures should continue to support of students' attempts to communicate meaning. Teachers can keep a supply of old magazines in the classroom for this purpose, as well as allow students to draw or use digital images to make their early writing more comprehensible.

One particularly powerful writing assignment for level 1 writers takes the form of journaling. In one version of this assignment, students complete a weekly journal describing what they did on the weekend. This assignment is an excellent entrée into the world of writing for students at the beginning of the language learning process because it is explicitly linked to student experience and can build on home and community funds of knowledge. Further, it helps students to internalize the fact that writing is "thought on paper," which is especially important for students who are writing for the first time. As an additional benefit, teachers get to know about their students' interests and activities. To enrich the journal, students can supplement their writing with pictures or drawings to support the clarity of their communication.

Welcome Home Language Writing. Teachers can support level 1 writers (like Fajar) who are literate in the home language by encouraging writing in their home languages, as appropriate. Even if the teacher is not fluent in the student's home language, this beginning practice can be useful in promoting student engagement, appropriate classroom behavior, and self-esteem. Collecting home language writing samples can be a meaningful assessment practice in terms of understanding the extent to which the student is literate in the home language. Even though teachers may not understand students' home language writing, they can recognize that extended writing likely represents more advanced writing than the painstaking creation of isolated words or letters. Further, allowing the use of the home language can demonstrate an acceptance of and respect for the student's heritage. Allowing writing in the home language will, in the long run, encourage increased student production and can be a scaffold to writing in English.

Teachers who want to gauge student understanding by allowing responses in the student's home language must understand the language or rely on the assistance of another school professional who does. Examples of this sort of writing assessment would include a description of the student's family or neighborhood or a daily journal about the student's activities at home.

Having considered appropriate assignment/assessment strategies for level 1 students across the four domains of listening, speaking, reading, and writing, teachers can better create assignment and assessment tasks and procedures well suited to students who are early in the process of acquiring English. Assessing the content knowledge and skills at the lower ELP levels is necessarily limited to activities that do not depend heavily on high levels of language use.

Instructional Strategies

The next step in the differentiation process is for teachers to identify ways that prepare level 1 students to demonstrate their learning on teacher-created differentiated assignments/assessments. This targeted and differentiated instruction, which prepares level 1 students to engage with level 1 assignments/assessments, is the topic of this section.

To prepare level 1 students to demonstrate content knowledge and skills, teachers should take the following four action steps:

1. Carefully examine any assumptions they might have about an individual student's background knowledge and language development.
2. Become familiar with the student's background, including issues of language, literacy, culture, and previous schooling.
3. Identify the independent level of each student, and then provide appropriate and strategic instruction to advance the students' language development and content learning.
4. Use timely and appropriate differentiated instruction to open the door to the essential learning in the curriculum and that requires students to use oral and written English for academic purposes according to their ELP levels. Simultaneous instruction of content and its associated academic language contributes to content learning and language development and is the responsibility of all teachers.

Because of the widely varying abilities of ELLs and non-ELLs in any given classroom, meaningful instruction will, by necessity, look different as teachers work to meet the instructional needs of individual students rather than aiming for the middle. As you think about your own teaching, ask yourself if you see a wide range of student abilities. Then consider if it makes sense to teach a child content well beyond her or his level of readiness, or if it is preferable to teach to the student's instructional level.

When teaching ELLs, teachers must remember the importance of matching instruction to student needs, particularly in relation to the student's ELP level, home language literacy, prior schooling, and cultural background. Educators who teach according to students' needs know that differentiating the instruction of content is not watering down the curriculum; it is facilitating access to it. Because each student, ELL or non-ELL, is advancing on a personal trajectory toward grade-level achievement, the content standards must remain the same for all students, and the essential learning within each standard must be the focus of teaching. In the current standards-based environment, teachers are charged with making grade-level curriculum accessible to all students, regardless of their backgrounds or ELP levels. Unless teachers embrace this task, students can never be expected to achieve at grade level. For example, if the grade-level curriculum calls for the writing of five-paragraph essays, a level 1 student cannot be expected to perform this task. Instead, based on the standard, the teacher should use instructional strategies that help the student build on what he or she can currently do with writing, such as drawing pictures or copying letters or words, to begin the journey toward grade-level writing. Developmentally, such differentiation affords ELLs the foundation they need to reach grade level.

All Domains

This section presents a general instructional strategy that supports the simultaneous learning of content and language across the four domains of listening, speaking, reading, and writing. Teachers can use this strategy to make grade-level content-area instruction accessible to all students, particularly ELLs at level 1.

Provide Sensory Support for Every Lesson. Teachers should, as much as possible, incorporate objects, pictures, hands-on materials and experiences, nonverbal communication, demonstrations, modeling, and simulations in every lesson for students at level 1. This kind of sensory support can be used to enhance instruction in all four language domains. Sensory support includes involving each of the five senses to the extent possible. Teachers can use this kind of support to scaffold new learning by allowing students to relate new information to existing knowledge.

By providing a sensory anchor, students have a meaningful basis on which to understand new vocabulary, concepts, and facts. For example, one of our favorite teacher cartoons depicts a teacher and students in a roller coaster car poised at the top of a steep hill. Just before plummeting, the teacher announces, "Today, class, we are going to learn about gravity!" Imagine how the students felt during the experience—for students unfamiliar with the feeling of a roller coaster descent, the precipitous experience built background; others were able to connect new terminology to a familiar feeling. The result of this sensory experience is that all students could attach the new vocabulary word (*gravity*) to the event with accompanying sights and sensations and expand learning from there.

Table 4-4 presents instructional strategies that teachers can use to make grade-level content comprehensible and engaging to ELLs at level 1 in the domains of listening, speaking, reading, and writing.

Table 4-4 Instructional Strategies for Level 1 Students

Listening	Speaking	Reading	Writing
▪ Teach basic commands by modeling actions ▪ Use simplified, correct language, repeating or paraphrasing as needed ▪ Allow sufficient wait time ▪ Model the completion of graphic organizers to build higher-order thinking ▪ Employ think-alouds to model processes and language	▪ Encourage involvement in discussions by eliciting nonverbal or brief communication ▪ Scaffold the use of academic language by providing simple sentence frames ▪ Concentrate on student's meaning rather than on grammatical correctness ▪ Reward all attempts to communicate	▪ Implement a high-quality, research-based, culturally and linguistically appropriate reading development program ▪ Use extensive visual supports so that students can derive meaning from print ▪ Support grade-level content using comprehensible reading materials with extensive visual support ▪ Teach early reading skills ▪ Build background and help students to make connections to prior learning and experiences ▪ Read or sing visually supported stories or texts to students, using props and acting to increase comprehension and develop the oral language skills necessary for reading ▪ Use shared, shared-to-guided, and guided reading ▪ Implement language experience stories ▪ Model the use of graphic organizers	▪ Ask students to communicate through cutting and pasting images or drawing ▪ Scaffold content and academic language production by providing simple sentence frames and models ▪ Use modeled, shared, and guided writing activities ▪ Accept drawing, copying and labeling, and self- generated approximations of words and phrases in lieu of grade-level writing ▪ Focus on correct answers instead of errors and omissions ▪ Create and use identity texts ▪ Model the use of graphic organizers to build higher-order thinking

Listening

The following instructional strategies focused on listening are effective for students with limited formal education, like Corina, and those with stronger educational backgrounds, like Fajar.

Teach Basic Commands by Modeling Actions. An important way to ensure that students at level 1 listening engage in classroom activities, thus paving the way to language production, is to teach basic commands such as, "Please close the door" or "Open your book," by modeling those actions. Often referred to as total physical response (TPR), this technique allows students to participate in classroom activities during the earliest stage of language acquisition. For example, teachers might state and demonstrate basic classroom instructions such as "Please sit down" or "Take out your pencil" a few times and have newcomers mirror their actions. After several repetitions, students should be able to respond to teacher commands without teacher modeling. Having learned basic classroom phrases in English, students are on their way to building a larger repertoire of vocabulary and phrases that allow them to participate in classroom activities.

Use Simplified, Correct Language, Repeating or Paraphrasing as Needed. Simplifying communication with students is another strategy that can facilitate listening comprehension. However, this strategy does not need to extend to oversimplification or ungrammatical use of language. For instance, well-meaning teachers may be tempted to speak to students at level 1 listening only in the present tense, thinking that doing so improves student understanding. However, while this practice may be somewhat helpful in the short term, it is unlikely to be helpful in the long term. Such oversimplification only delays the inevitable need for ELLs to attend to the sounds of various affixes that affect word meaning. Only when students develop sensitized listening skills can they become prepared for language production and classroom participation.

Further, educators should remember that while simple repetition for students can be helpful, sometimes complete rephrasing is necessary to access terminology that the student can recognize. For example, a teacher might paraphrase "Would you like to get a drink?" to "Do you want some water?" to use language that might be more familiar to a student new to English. Finally, remember that loud repetition can be offensive and is unlikely to foster understanding.

Allow Sufficient Wait Time. Many teachers recognize that increasing wait time leads to improved classroom performance for all students because it allows necessary cognitive processing to take place. Wait time is particularly useful for students at level 1 listening who, even when they might have understood instruction in

English, benefit from an extra moment to process language and content to demonstrate understanding. Remember that these students are working in a language that is new to them while they learn new content, so sometimes as much as ten additional seconds are needed.

Model the Completion of Graphic Organizers to Build Higher-Order Thinking. Students of all ages at level 1 listening can engage in higher-order thinking, including application, analysis, synthesis, evaluation, and creation. However, these students must be supported, particularly in the early stages of language development. Higher-order thinking can be facilitated when teachers point out important ideas and their relationships during instruction by modeling the completion of visual aids such as concept maps and Venn diagrams, to name a few types of graphic organizers. This modeling can be done in different ways, including the use of an LCD projector, Elmo, Smart Board, or other advanced technology during the presentation of information.

Employ Think-Alouds to Model Both Processes and Language. Another way in which educators can make learning new content processes and language accessible to students at level 1 listening is through think-alouds. In this strategy, teachers model a thought process using a whiteboard, an LCD projector, or other technology to show students how the process works. Thinking aloud provides students with generalizable language templates with which to articulate thoughts in English. For example, a teacher might model how to scan a text for important dates in a reading passage by "thinking aloud" throughout the demonstration. ELLs and non-ELLs can certainly benefit when teachers model cognition in this way.

Speaking

The following strategies are effective for SLIFE learners like Corina and students with stronger educational backgrounds like Fajar.

Encourage Involvement in Discussions by Eliciting Nonverbal or Brief Communication. Students at level 1 speaking are often at the preproduction stage of language development, which means that teachers can expect very little speech production. However, these students can comprehend input and make sense of classroom events as they develop familiarity with the phonemic (sound) system of English and with the meanings of various words and phrases. To encourage beginning oral production, teachers can pose questions in a way that allows for nonverbal responses, like nodding and pointing.

In addition, individual words like *yes, no, pencil, friend,* and memorized chunks of language like "How are you?" represent language development at level 1. These verbalizations must be recognized and encouraged as communication, regardless of the student's grade level. Teachers should introduce level 1 speakers to new vocabulary according to the level 1 student descriptors for speaking. It is unrealistic for teachers to expect students to use new terminology in full sentence form. Note that general, formulaic, and memorized language, rather than academic language, typifies level 1 comprehension and production. Finally, remember that students should not be forced to speak; rather, they need opportunities and encouragement.

Scaffold the Use of Academic Language by Providing Simple Sentence Frames. Teachers should model the use of accessible academic language to facilitate level 1 speakers' use of both social and academic language necessary for academic contexts. For example, teachers can use a simple sentence frame like "The rabbit has fur. The _____ has scales." Students are not expected to know the word *scales*, but they can engage in learning and in language production by identifying the animal that has scales using everyday terminology. This kind of simultaneous language and content teaching can be artfully employed as a part of regular classroom instruction rather than as a separate language lesson. That is, teachers can model and frame language and interactions with students that support students at level 1 speaking, while still teaching the content for all students, ELLs and non-ELLs alike.

Concentrate on Students' Meaning Rather Than on Correct Grammar. Another consideration for teachers of students at level 1 speaking is that the vocabulary of these students is so limited that it may hamper their attempts to communicate. At this stage, teachers should focus on the intent of the student's message rather than on the correctness of pronunciation, vocabulary, or grammar. A receptive and encouraging attitude can elicit even greater effort on the part of a beginning language learner. One teacher showed that she understood the message when her student said, "I go shopping yesterday." This teacher also modeled correct language by responding, "Oh, you went shopping?"

Reward All Attempts to Communicate. Teachers can help students build confidence by rewarding their attempts to communicate. As with language acquisition by toddlers, students of all ages at level 1 speaking respond positively to sustained encouragement of their attempts to communicate. This encouragement, however, needs to be culturally responsive and not make students uncomfortable. For example, teachers could respond to a student's attempt at communication without singling out the individual for correction, thereby allowing the student to preserve "face." The development of a culturally sensitive, respectful, and encouraging classroom environment, fostered by all members of the classroom learning community, will facilitate language and content learning by allowing ELLs to focus on learning instead of issues of safety and belonging.

Reading

Students at level 1 reading build on their emerging listening and speaking skills to support their reading development in English. Thus, reading instruction should be accompanied by a strong oral language component, especially for students who are just learning to read in any language. When teachers know what their students can do with reading in the home language, they are better prepared to select appropriate reading strategies for level 1 readers in English. Teachers are encouraged to draw on the following instructional strategies.

Implement a High-Quality, Research-Based, Culturally and Linguistically Appropriate Reading Development Program. The needs of students who have yet to develop literacy skills in any language are different from the needs of those who can read in their home languages. Even at level 1 reading, these students' differential needs must be considered and addressed. Practically, this means that even at emergent reading levels, students who have little or no prior literacy experience must be afforded extra time and appropriate instruction to develop the necessary skills to enter the world of literacy. In contrast, their ELL peers who are literate in their home languages can transfer some of their literacy skills to the learning of English. The need is particularly acute for an increasing number of older students arriving in U.S. classrooms without previous schooling or reading skills in any language. The students with little to no prior literacy experience represent a crisis in today's classrooms that can be averted by explicit, age-appropriate, needs-based, and meaningful literacy instruction. Schools must assume this important responsibility, particularly at the middle and high school grades, or these students have little chance to learn how to read, let alone be afforded parity of access to the curriculum.

In one example, a responsive high school enlisted the help of a retired kindergarten reading teacher as a volunteer who taught early reading skills to a high school–age student from South Sudan. Her sustained support assured that this student was able to develop the requisite skills to participate in the high school curriculum and graduate in a timely manner.

Use Extensive Visual Supports So That Students Can Derive Meaning from Print. Remember that level 1 readers are typically unable to derive meaning from print alone. Teachers can make use of visual supports beyond those found in reading materials to support these students' textual comprehension. Visual support can include content-related posters and pictures to serve as springboards for discussion and vocabulary development. Teachers can explicitly connect the content in these visuals to printed words in the text. Teachers or other students can also transfer this language to the pictures themselves in the form of labels that students can continually access when posted in the classroom. These thematic pictorial supports provide students with ready references that they can draw on throughout a unit of instruction, enabling improved vocabulary and content understanding.

Support Grade-Level Content Using Comprehensible Reading Materials with Extensive Visual Support. Teaching all students according to the same content standards requires that students at level 1 reading receive instruction that is relevant to curricular essential learning, yet adapted to their linguistic needs and abilities. Grade-level reading materials are not appropriate for these students except in kindergarten and, possibly, 1st grade. As a result, alternative or supplementary content materials must generally be relied on to address the needs of level 1 students above 1st grade. These materials must reflect the content area addressed in the lesson or unit and serve as a foundation on which students can build content-area understanding, despite their beginning reading skills in English.

When addressing the needs of older level 1 readers, it is not generally recommended to use elementary school materials, as these are unlikely to be age appropriate. Older students may feel insulted by materials that they consider babyish, and this feeling can detract from motivation. Instead, teachers should look for engaging, high-quality materials that are tied to the curriculum, written at a lower reading level, and include colorful and realistic visual supports. Funds for these kinds of supplementary materials can sometimes be obtained from parent–teacher groups, civic and church organizations, and the school board. Fundraisers are another option for creative teachers to stretch their materials budgets to meet a wide range of student needs.

Teach Early Reading Skills. Students at level 1 reading should not be expected to read independently; they first need to gain basic listening and speaking skills (Franco, 2005). Franco asserts that this need is based on the importance of phonemic awareness—the understanding of the sound system of English. She further emphasizes that students need to be able to aurally identify and reproduce sounds in English that they may not have heard or articulated previously in their home languages before being expected to orally produce those sounds while reading. During this time, typical developmental and engaging activities might include rhyming, chants, segmentation, and syllabification. For older students, these activities may take place outside the content classroom supported by an ELD teacher, paraeducator, or trained volunteer.

Although Franco (2005) suggests that independent reading should begin when students can speak in sentence form, we remind teachers of the difference between students who have not learned to read in their home language and students with a foundation in home language literacy. Some students at level 1 reading may be able to read at an earlier stage, particularly if they can read in their home language, which provides a strong support for reading development in English.

Two other important early reading skills are the alphabetic principle and concepts of print (Kauffman, 2007a). The alphabetic principle involves recognizing the names of letters and their shapes. Concepts of print encompass a variety of skills including book-holding, understanding print directionality, one-to-one matching of spoken and written words, making connections between illustrations and graphics and print, and recognizing punctuation marks. The alphabetic principle and the concepts of print can be developed simultaneously with phonemic awareness. However, only when a foundation of phonemic awareness is firmly in place should instruction move to letter–sound relationships (phonics) and identification of the written word.

Note that phonics can present challenges for students who read in other languages because, in the Roman alphabet, individual letters may produce different sounds in English than they do in the students' home languages. For example, in Vietnamese the sound for the letter v is sometimes pronounced as /y/ is pronounced in English. A firm base of these early reading skills (phonemic awareness, alphabetic principle, concepts of print, phonics) is necessary for English reading development.

Build Background and Help Students Make Connections to Prior Learning and Experiences. Teachers must ensure that all students in the classroom share the background knowledge and skills needed to successfully engage in learning. If students come from a range of backgrounds, this knowledge and these skills may need to be built within the context of classroom learning. For instance, if the topic is tornadoes, students from countries where tornadoes do not occur must be given some background knowledge about this type of storm. This background knowledge may be developed using simple pictures or a video clip, if the instruction focuses on basic aspects of tornadoes.

Teachers must also remember that students do not automatically connect new learning to prior learning and experiences, so they need to assist students in making these connections. For example, if the topic is the Civil Rights movement, connections can be made for students in other countries by quickly presenting examples of similar issues in their countries of origin.

Read or Sing Visually Supported Stories or Texts with Students Using Props and Acting to Increase Comprehension and Develop Oral Language Skills Necessary for Reading. When presenting readers at ELP level 1 with text materials, teachers should make every effort to ensure that these students understand the information represented by the printed word. Such efforts are likely to include going out of one's comfort zone by performing planned charades or using acting to facilitate student comprehension. Any prop that can foster understanding is a useful addition when using this strategy. For example, we know of a teacher who dressed up like a bee for the science lesson on bees. This attention-getting strategy could also extend to content learning when parts of the costume could be capitalized on for teaching about the insect's anatomy. This is the sort of thoughtful presentation that will support early readers' understanding of materials that are read aloud to the class.

Use Shared Reading, Shared-to-Guided, and Guided Reading. Knox and Amador-Watson (2002) provide excellent guidance regarding how to structure balanced literacy instruction for students at ELP level 1 reading. They illustrate the fact that a balanced approach to teaching reading to these students includes read-alouds, shared reading, shared-to-guided reading, guided reading, and, of course, independent reading, accompanied with spelling and phonics instruction.

In shared reading, as described by Knox and Amador-Watson, the teacher reads a (big) book to students while classroom discussion is focused on strategy use and topics related to the text. In shared-to-guided reading, the teacher offers the support of a shared reading lesson during guided reading. In guided reading, the teacher plays the role of a coach, assisting students with strategy use, questioning, and discussing the reading by looking at parts of the text together, before students read on their own. The goal is to create independent readers. Finally, in independent reading, the student reads on his or her own. The same text may be used throughout this cycle of instruction; through the teacher's gradual release of responsibility, the recycling and repetition of language, and extended practice, students can develop confidence and facility in reading. Fountas and Pinnell (2017) provide further advice on guided reading for all students, including ELLs.

Implement Language Experience Stories. The language experience approach allows teachers to use students' own words as texts for teaching reading. Following a shared experience, like baking a cake, students collaboratively dictate stories while the teacher or another student acts as the scribe. Then these nonfiction stories are used as material for teaching reading. For instance, teachers can cut apart the story, giving each student a sentence. Students then work collaboratively to sequence these sentence strips. Taken a step further, these sentences could be cut apart; then students can reconstruct the sentences. This approach, which allows for recycling and repetition of students' language, is ideal for situations when literacy resource materials are scarce. It supports students in developing skills such as comprehension, word recognition, and fluency. In this case it is appropriate for teachers to adjust ungrammatical language to accurate prose when transcribing for students. The goal is to create model texts for classroom use.

Model the Use of Graphic Organizers. Graphic organizers are an excellent scaffold for student construction of meaning from print materials as they move toward higher ELP levels in reading. Students at ELP level 1 are known to have sophisticated thoughts and ideas despite their early levels of reading in English. Graphic organizers provide a way to represent these ideas and serve as a scaffold for ELLs to articulate facts and make connections to print materials. Teachers should explore a variety of organizers, being sure to incorporate visual and pictorial support into this type of student work. For instance, after reading a story, the teacher could use a Venn diagram or T-chart to model how to compare and contrast two characters in the story.

Writing

As is the case with reading development, students like Fajar who can write in their home languages progress more readily toward higher levels of writing development in English than their peers like Corina who have yet to learn to write in any language. Students who are not yet able to write in their home languages require more focused and explicit early writing instruction and increased time for practice to develop their writing abilities. Such practice is essential. Like learning to read, learning to write is a requirement for school success and does not occur incidentally. Rather, students who are new to writing, particularly those in middle and high school, need instruction that is at the most basic level. Further, this writing instruction must be tailored to the needs of students just learning to write in a language that they barely know. This type of instruction can be supported by paraeducators and skilled, trained volunteers who can work with students individually or in groups at their specific instructional levels.

Students who cannot read or write in their home languages, and who constitute an increasing proportion of ELLs in U.S. schools, are greatly at risk. They continue to drop out at higher rates than their non-ELL peers, are underrepresented in colleges and universities, and are unable to fully participate in their communities unless they receive the instruction that they need. Following is a list of strategies designed to assist students at ELP level 1 writing, whatever their level of home language literacy development, in developing writing skills in English.

Ask Students to Communicate by Cutting and Pasting Images or Drawing. In teaching early writing, use students' background knowledge and experiences to validate and value what each student brings to the classroom. Invite students to depict familiar ideas and concepts by drawing or by cutting, pasting, and gluing images to become comfortable with the representation of information in print. This kind of activity serves as a concrete step toward more abstract, or letter-based, representations in print as students increase their writing proficiency.

For students who have not had the opportunity to develop writing skills, manual dexterity and eye-hand coordination must also be developed. Time spent learning basic drawing, cutting, pasting, and gluing techniques increases facility with a writing instrument when learning to form letters.

Because they live in an age of computers, cell phones, and text messaging, all students need dexterity for daily activities. Further, legible handwriting is essential for success in many school-based and job-related tasks. Purposeful teaching of sometimes overlooked manual skills traditionally learned in U.S. schools at the elementary level helps give all students, particularly ELLs, the requisite manual dexterity for writing, keyboarding, and the like. Teachers can embed such developmental activities when creating posters or cutting pictures or labels for other projects.

Scaffold Content and Academic Language by Providing Simple Sentence Frames and Models. For students to begin writing in English, they must be provided with clear guidance and solid examples. Often, formulaic sentences such as, "The rabbit has fur. The _____ has scales" are good starting points for written production. Teachers should post sentence frames as models for student reference in their print-rich classroom environments. Students can begin by completing sentence models with a single word (like *fish* in the preceding example), then with phrases, and ultimately write sentences on their own as their writing skills develop. With this sort of scaffolding, students more readily begin the process of learning to write in English.

Use Modeled, Shared, and Guided Writing Activities. As with reading, we recommend the balanced literacy approach presented by Knox and Amador-Watson (2002) and others for use with ELLs at early stages of writing development. According to this approach, writing instruction should include modeled, shared, and guided writing prior to expectations of independent writing. In this type of balanced literacy instruction, modeled writing includes the presentation of the writing process with overt attention to letter–sound relationships and writing conventions. In shared writing, the teacher acts as a scribe for the language that the teacher and students collaboratively compose. In guided writing, the student writes with teacher support. For example, as part of an elementary unit on basic weather patterns, a teacher could write a sentence about the weather with student input. Then students could write their own sentences with teacher guidance and eventually, as their writing skills increase, write sentences independently.

Accept Drawing, Copying and Labeling, and Approximations of Words and Phrases in Lieu of Grade-Level Writing. Since teachers in any grade are likely to have students at level 1 writing in their classes, it is helpful to remember that the progress of these students toward achieving a content standard can only be shown through level 1 writing capabilities. By definition, these ELLs are unlikely to be able to write on grade level, with the exception of kindergarten and, possibly, 1st grade students. For that reason, teachers must accept forms of communication that are commensurate with level 1 ELP as defined by the level 1 student descriptors for writing. Written communication produced by level 1 writers needs to target the content standard and take the form of drawing, copying and labeling, or original brief or formulaic writing, often with significant errors, in accordance with the student's ELP level.

Focus on Correct Answers Instead of Errors and Omissions. Teachers must focus their attention on the intent of the message presented through level 1 student writing. Errors are to be expected, given that these writers are just beginning to learn English. For example, a student might write, "Go mall Friday. Shoes," when she or he means, "I went to the mall on Friday and bought some shoes." Teachers who focus on the essence of student communication rather than on incidental errors encourage students to continue their efforts toward higher levels of writing development. For example, if a student laboriously copies a word but reverses a letter, overlook the error while focusing on the effort and the result at this early stage.

Ask Students to Create and Use Identity Texts.

> Identity texts are the product of students' creative work or performance.... Students invest their identities in the creation of these texts, which can be spoken, signed, visual, musical, dramatic, or combinations in multimodal form. The identity text then holds a mirror up to students in which their identities are reflected in a positive light. (Cummins & Early, 2011, p. 3)

Often an extremely motivating approach, honoring students' personal stories and histories supports students in preserving, maintaining, and developing their personal identities while they acquire English. Students' experiences provide the perfect vehicle for authentic writing, vocabulary building, and self-expression. Drawing on students' funds of knowledge (Gonzalez, Moll, & Amanti, 2005) allows ELLs to engage meaningfully as contributing members of the classroom community. In one such example, Jones-Vo's K–12 ELLs each contributed her or his immigration story to a bound volume entitled, *Kaleidoscope of True Stories.* This inspirational collection of stories spanned all ELP levels with contributions ranging from 1st-grade drawings that included falling bombs to high-school multipage essays recounting details of refugee camps. Housed in each district building's media center, the book became a sought-after resource for teachers, administrators, and others.

Model the Use of Graphic Organizers to Build Higher-Order Thinking. Having received instruction using visual supports and allowing for drawing; cutting, pasting, and gluing images; copying and labeling; and approximating words and phrases, students can enrich their expression by applying these strategies to graphic organizers. While grade-level expectations may stipulate that students write sentences on the organizer, students at level 1 writing must be allowed to demonstrate content understanding according to their ELP level. This means that students may fill in the graphic organizer with images, drawn or cut and pasted, and shorter bits of language.

Instruction That Integrates Language Domains

Beginning at level 1 and throughout the language development process, teachers are advised to integrate all four language domains (listening, speaking, reading, and writing) into daily curricular activities. After school many ELLs return to homes where English is not spoken. Teachers should therefore purposefully embed language-rich activities that integrate all four domains into the school day, when students can manipulate, practice, and improve their English. Recall that SLIFE learners like Corina need even more support as they work to develop literacy skills in English. As such, tying reading and writing activities to speaking and listening activities is especially helpful for students with backgrounds such as hers.

Conclusion

The assessment and instructional strategies discussed in this chapter can be applied either across multiple domains or within a single language domain. While some newcomers arrive exhibiting level 1 skills in listening, speaking, reading, and writing, other students can exhibit different levels across language domains. For example, many South Sudanese students have arrived in U.S. classrooms at level 1 in reading and writing, but at level 2 or 3 in listening and speaking. When teachers notice that a student's ELP level varies by language domain, they should adjust the assignment/assessment and instructional strategies to target the student's level of language development for each domain.

Another important consideration is that students can possess level 1 skills at any age. For example, many high schools currently struggle with an increased enrollment of older students at level 1. Educators are encouraged to carefully consider the urgent needs of these students regarding literacy development and to take steps to provide the essential instruction that can mean the difference between academic engagement and success instead of academic failure and likely dropping out of school.

Professional Learning Activities

Working individually or with others in professional learning communities, differentiate the first four assignments for Corina and Fajar. For assignment 5, choose the assignment and differentiate it for at least one of the ELP level 1 students in your class. When differentiating for ELP level 1 students, remember that they may be at different ELP levels in listening, speaking, reading, and writing.

Differentiating for Corina and Fajar

For assignments 1–4, differentiate the language-based expectations and the scaffolding and support needed for level 1 students, Corina and Fajar. Recall that Corina and Fajar are both 7th-grade students at level 1 in all domains. However, Corina is described as a SLIFE, and Fajar is more or less at grade level in his home language.

1. Read the assignment above the template.
2. Read the essential learning and language demands below the template.
3. Review the standards-based topic, language-based expectations for non-ELLs.
4. Complete the template to show the differentiated assignment for Corina and Fajar by adding appropriate language-based expectations and scaffolding and support for these students.

After you complete the template, read on for additional insight on how to differentiate the assignment.

Assignment 1: *Write a five-page report about a country using internet sources*

Standards-Based Content or Topic (from the curriculum)	
About an assigned country	

Non-ELL	Level 1
Language-Based Expectations	
Write a five-page report	■ ■ ■ ■
Scaffolding and Support	
Using ■ *Internet resources*	*Using* ■ *Internet resources* ■ ■ ■

Essential Learning: *Research and summarize an assigned country.*
Language Demands: *Use writing to describe, explain, and summarize.*

Show both Corina and Fajar a sample of a completed poster that shows the key points about a country. Choose appropriate buddies from the class who know how to support Corina's and Fajar's learning. Demonstrate how to copy letters, words, and sentences, emphasizing how to know what information to copy. For example, the teacher could highlight portions of a document to be copied onto a poster and clarify (by modeling) that those are the only segments to be copied.

Allow Corina to focus on her country of origin. Pair her with a strong student who is interested in helping others and who has patience with Corina's unique needs. Allow this partner to take the lead by demonstrating online research and writing up the report. Corina's report should consist of a poster showing the main ideas of her research using pictorial representation, such as pictures, maps, and flags found on the internet. Given that Corina is still learning basic letter formation, she could cut labels for the poster from a list typed by her buddy and affix them to the poster. In this way, Corina can demonstrate her learning by using pictures and labels. The cutting and gluing give Corina practice with school-related materials and activities that may be new to her. Demonstrate how to use scissors and glue and allow her to practice before working on the final poster. Corina will also need extra time to complete her poster and would benefit from the assistance of a paraeducator or the teacher in accomplishing the task.

Fajar should also make a poster while working with a buddy. Because he is familiar with the English alphabet, he is more likely to be able to neatly write labels and short descriptions on the poster by hand. In this way, Fajar can demonstrate his understanding of the topic according to his ELP level.

Assignment 2: *Give a 3-5 minute presentation about a current event*

Standards-Based Content or Topic (from the curriculum)	
About a current event	
Non-ELL	**Level 1**
Language-Based Expectations	
Give a 3-5 minute presentation	• • • • • •
Scaffolding and Support	
Using ■ *Information found online, in newspapers, and in magazines*	*Using* ■ *Information found online, in newspapers, and in magazines* • • • •

Essential Learning: *Summarize a current event and present information.*
Language Demands: *Use writing and speaking to describe, explain, and summarize.*

Keep in mind that level 1 students are likely in the silent period, so giving even a simplified speech in front of a classroom of students is inappropriate. Some students may be willing to do so in their home languages, but their willingness would depend on the individual student and the audience. If Corina is willing to give a short speech in her home language (worthwhile in terms of self-esteem alone), recall that she will be unable to read about the current event. She has to learn about the event from a bilingual individual or perhaps on a Spanish language news site. She may be able to summarize information about a current event through the creation of a poster with pictures or clip art. She could share key words with the content or ELD teacher, a paraeducator, or a trained volunteer to demonstrate her learning. It may be necessary for the paraeducator to repeat prompts for Carina to demonstrate what she knows.

Fajar needs similar supports. His home language literacy does not necessarily bear on the giving of the presentation. However, if Fajar is willing to give the presentation in his home language, he can read about the current event in his home language. Home language materials are a must for Fajar if this is the expectation. A news website and print materials in his home language could help with this assignment.[1]

Corina's and Fajar's teachers are encouraged to select current event topics based on the availability of high-quality information pertaining to issues in each student's country of origin. Find home-language news sites for both students. It is important to ensure that material for Corina is presented orally because she is unable to garner meaning from print independently, even in her home language. Model the creation of a poster for both students, model the presentation for Fajar, and provide both students with opportunities to practice sharing information in a comfortable setting.

Assignment 3: *Read a textbook chapter and answer the chapter questions*

Standards-Based Content or Topic (from the curriculum)	
For a textbook chapter	

Non-ELL	Level 1
Language-Based Expectations	
■ *Read and answer questions*	■ ■ ■ ■
Scaffolding and Support	
Using	*Using*
■ *The textbook itself and environmental print (e.g., labeled posters in the classroom)* ■	■ *The textbook itself and environmental print (e.g., labeled posters in the classroom)* ■ ■ ■ ■

Essential Learning: *Summarize, synthesize, and explain general information about the chapter topic.*

Language Demands: *Use oral and written language to summarize, synthesize, and explain general information.*

This assignment is inappropriate for Corina or Fajar. Recall that neither student is ready to gain meaning from print in English. Instead, they need to be able to learn the information through demonstrations, pictures, graphs, charts,

---

[1] Teachers should avoid using instant translation websites to translate documents for students or parents. These websites may not produce accurate translations and may result in more confusion than clarification.

videos, and so forth. Only then can they be expected to demonstrate content knowledge and skills. If the textbook is visually supported, it can help students to learn information about the assigned topic.

During instruction, as noted, ensure that material addressed in the textbook chapter is presented to level 1 students through demonstrations, pictures, graphs, charts, video, and so forth so they have access to the same curricular information as the other students. The textbook can certainly be used to achieve this end; teachers can model how to use the supporting features like headings, bold print, and pictures found in the textbook to learn about and understand the topic. Information pertaining to the print features is more meaningful to Fajar than Corina, but both students can benefit from this type of instruction. Individual support from a paraeducator or other individual would also be helpful. Recall that Corina, as a SLIFE learner, needs intensive reading and writing instruction that is age appropriate and designed for ELLs with limited formal schooling.

Assignment 4: *Complete a multiple-choice and short answer assessment from the textbook*

Standards-Based Content or Topic (from the curriculum)	
For a curricular topic	
Non-ELL	**Level 1**
Language-Based Expectations	
Complete a textbook-based multiple-choice and short-answer assessment	■ ■ ■ ■ ■ ■ ■ ■ ■
Scaffolding and Support	
Using	*Using*
■ *Only the information on the test and committed to memory*	■ *The information on the test and committed to memory* ■ ■ ■ ■ ■ ■

Essential Learning: *Display information learned about a given topic.*
Language Demands: *Use reading and writing to summarize and explain.*

This assignment is entirely inappropriate for either Corina or Fajar. Instead, teachers must create an assignment that is appropriate for level 1 students, and that incorporates the essential learning of the unit. Teaching must be made accessible through the use of demonstrations, pictures, graphs, charts, videos, and so forth. Students must also become familiar with the methods they are expected to use to demonstrate their learning. This familiarization is especially critical for Corina who has little to no experience with school-based learning tests.

Given her limited formal education, Corina is likely to need extra time to complete any assessment that requires literacy skills. That is, she needs more time than Fajar because he is able to transfer some reading and writing skills from his home language. Prior to completing a written assessment, however, Corina needs intensive literacy instruction to prepare her.

Differentiating for Your Students

For assignment 5, choose an assignment from your curriculum. Differentiate the assignment for a student in your class at ELP level 1. Consider how student background factors like prior schooling, home language literacy, cultural orientation, and challenging experiences are likely to influence this student's content and language learning in your classroom.

1. Write the assignment above the template.
2. Identify the essential learning and language demands, and write this below the template.
3. Fill in the standards-based topic, language-based expectations for non-ELLs and for your student at ELP level 1.
4. Plan and implement the assignment in your classroom. If possible, videotape the lesson, or invite an ELL coordinator or coach to observe it. Focus on the teacher's use of appropriate differentiation strategies for students at level 1 in any domain.

Assignment 5: _____

Standards-Based Content or Topic (from the curriculum)	

_____

Non-ELLs	Level 1
Language-Based Expectations	
▪	▪ ▪ ▪ ▪
Scaffolding and Support	
Using ▪	*Using* ▪ ▪ ▪ ▪

Essential Learning: _____

Language Demands: _____

Share your template with your colleagues, and explain why you made the choices you did. When you implement the lesson in your class, reflect on how your focal student uses oral and written language in each of the activities you planned. If you videotape the interaction, work with your colleagues to explore the scaffolding and support you provided. In any case, collect evidence of your student's content and language performances, identify your student's strengths, and list possible next steps for instruction.

Chapter 5

Differentiating for Students at Level 2

Their goal wasn't to stand out because of their differences; it was to fit in because of their talents.

—MARGOT LEE SHETTERLY

Teachers must remember the role that they play in moving students along the continuum of language development, scaffolding English language learners' (ELLs') production in listening, speaking, reading, and writing to the next higher English language proficiency (ELP) level. This chapter focuses on the needs of students at ELP level 2 by describing student characteristics and assignment/assessment and instructional strategies. However, teachers should keep in mind that the range of level 2 production is broad. They should think in terms of what students can currently do and what they need to learn to do next. Such purposeful vigilance supports students in advancing along the continuum of language development to the next level, level 3, by providing (or eliciting, where possible and appropriate) examples of level 3 language production.

Variation in Students' Backgrounds

Student Scenarios

Bayan is a 10th-grade student from Iraq. She is a recent Kurdish refugee and has observed violence toward her family. She did not attend formal school in Iraq. She seems sad and withdrawn; some of her teachers suspect she has post-traumatic stress disorder (PTSD). Her family arrived without basic belongings and lives well below the poverty level. In terms of language, Bayan answers formulaic questions with memorized statements and can participate in academic conversations only minimally. She often uses incomplete sentences and phrases orally to convey complete thoughts but is only able to write with considerable effort because she is not literate in Kurdish.

Estefania is a 10th-grade immigrant student from Costa Rica who has arrived with her parents, who are professionals in a large international company, and her younger brother. She is from the capital city and enjoyed the benefits of private schooling there, where she performed on grade level. She is an outgoing, fashion-conscious student who is happy to be attending her new high school. Estefania seeks opportunities to interact with classmates in social and academic contexts. Though her English is just beginning to emerge, she has begun to use some general academic words and phrases, even in her writing.

Bayan and Estefania are at opposite ends of the level 2 spectrum of abilities because of their experiences with previous instruction. As a student with no prior schooling, Bayan's task in building literacy skills in English is far more daunting than that of Estefania, who can readily transfer skills learned in Spanish to English. Bayan will need more time to develop her foundational abilities in literacy than Estefania. With these divergent needs in mind, teachers must recognize that all students at level 2 do not have the same instructional needs.

Similar to Corina, one of the students at level 1 discussed in Chapter 4, Bayan urgently needs basic, initial literacy instruction designed to be culturally and linguistically sensitive to her needs. As such, remedial reading classes created for non-ELLs cannot work for Bayan. Educators must embrace the responsibility to teach foundational reading and writing skills in a meaningful, contextualized approach (as opposed to decontextualized drill-based approaches) so that students like Bayan can access content curricula. Particularly for older students with limited or interrupted formal education (SLIFE) who arrive having missed basic, developmental reading instruction at the elementary level, providing such meaning-based beginning instruction in reading and writing is the critical difference between student success and failure in U.S. schools. As with students at level 1, classroom teachers cannot be expected to provide this extensive instruction solely within the context of their content teaching; instead, it is incumbent upon school districts to create programs to meet the particular needs of students in the SLIFE group. These students must learn to read and write.

In contrast, Estefania's academic readiness is supported by her previous schooling experience and her positive attitude toward her new school. She enjoys being a teenager in the United States and has made several friends already. Because of these combined factors, Estefania is ready to continue and expand her learning and is much less in need of separate, basic literacy instruction than her classmate Bayan.

Student Descriptors

Students at level 2 start to use language in generative ways rather than rely on basic, typically memorized, language. These students are beginning to develop

Table 5-1   Student Descriptors, Level 2

Listening	Speaking	Reading	Writing
■ Begins to respond to frequently heard language with continued dependence on context, paraphrasing, and repetition ■ Begins to build content and academic vocabulary	■ Uses phrases and simple sentences to communicate about common experiences and situations ■ Begins to produce content and academic vocabulary ■ Errors often inhibit communication	■ May recognize and read frequently encountered words and phrases ■ Gains meaning from simple and familiar text with visual support	■ Dictates phrases and simple sentences ■ Writes phrases and simple sentences with occasional content and academic vocabulary when supported ■ Errors often obstruct meaning

academic language. Although their errors often hinder understanding, students at level 2 are far more communicative than their counterparts at level 1. However, when considering what students at level 2 can do with English, teachers are reminded to check students' ELP levels in listening, speaking, reading, and writing separately, rather than assuming that a composite score of 2 means that the student scored at level 2 in each language domain. Table 5-1 summarizes the student descriptors for level 2. We turn now to a description of each language domain within level 2.

Listening

The listening ability of students at level 2 is characterized by comprehension of simple, contextualized sentences related to social and academic content. These students are likely still becoming familiar with new sounds in English, relying on commonly heard words, chunks of words, and expressions to construct meaning. Because students at level 2 can generally comprehend words and phrases before producing them orally in English, teachers can ask students to sort pictures into categories to demonstrate their understanding of academic language functions such as identify, summarize, and explain.

Students at level 2 listening begin to respond to frequently heard language with continued dependence on context, which means that teachers need to provide the necessary context to support students' ongoing language development. For example, science teachers might show students at level 2 pictures of plants and animals from different climate zones (polar, temperate, and tropical), say the names of the plants and animals, and ask students to sort the pictures into categories representing the three climate zones. These students build content and academic vocabulary when given opportunities to learn that vocabulary in context. They would be expected to comprehend the vocabulary terms represented in the pictures that are associated with plants and animals in polar, temperate, and tropical climates.

Speaking

In terms of speaking, students at level 2 can use phrases and simple sentences, though they may rely on telegraphic speech (incomplete sentences that communicate complete thoughts), to talk in social and highly contextualized academic situations. Though these students' vocabularies are expanding to include general academic language, they often make mistakes that may prevent understanding. Pronunciation may be inaccurate because students at level 2 in speaking are likely still developing phonemic (sound) awareness and the ability to produce new sounds in English. These students are also expanding their ability to use language for academic purposes. For example, students at level 2 in speaking can ask simple questions and provide brief answers to questions, for example, to agree or disagree. These students can also produce simple definitions for academic terms.

Reading

The reading abilities of students at level 2 include a growing receptive understanding of the sounds of the English alphabet. These skills must be firmly in place before students are expected to match the sounds with letters. In other words, students must develop general phonemic awareness before incorporating phonics, which focuses on the visual representations of sounds in the written word. Students like Estefania who can read and write in their home languages start to recognize written language more readily than their classmates who have yet to develop literacy skills in their home languages. Further, students who are able to read and write in their home language may even appear to be reading full passages, relying on home-language phonetic learning to read aloud without comprehension (also known as *word calling*). This ability to apply sounds to letters does not mean that the student comprehends what she or he is reading. Teachers may be deceived, thinking that oral fluency in reading or speed in word calling indicates reading comprehension. However, only after the student learns vocabulary, preferably thematically and contextually, is she or he able to comprehend text and actually read.

With respect to reading comprehension, students at level 2 in reading may recognize and read frequently encountered words and phrases. These students gain meaning from familiar and simple text with visual support. For example, after a concrete demonstration of the stages in the water cycle, students at level 2 can be expected to read a simple text on that topic. After the demonstration and reading of the text, students can be expected to identify the stages of the water cycle process, perhaps using pictures.

Writing

Students at level 2 in writing range from those who can write in phrases using everyday and academic language to those who can create simple sentences. Errors are common and are likely to impede meaning. The student who cannot write in her or his home language is likely to continue writing with level 2 characteristics for a longer period of time than a student who can write in his or her home language. That student can transfer writing skills from the home language to English and is likely to move to level 3 (expanded sentences) with relative ease in comparison with his or her classmate who cannot write in the home language, like Bayan. Students at level 2 in writing can complete sentence frames with key phrases, for example, to identify, recount, explain, and persuade.

A Word about Language Objectives

The student descriptors presented in Table 5-1 provide a snapshot of what students at level 2 can do independently with listening, speaking, reading, and writing in English. Teachers can use these student descriptors to identify appropriate language-based expectations and develop language objectives for students at level 2 in any domain. Equipped with this understanding, teachers are ready to differentiate assignments/assessments and instructional strategies for the students at level 2 in their classes. This approach helps teachers meet ELLs at their level and move them along the ELD continuum within the context of their content-area instruction.

Example Differentiated Assignment

The example assignment used for all of the level-specific chapters in the book is differentiated in Table 5-2 for students at levels 2 and 3. Recall that for this assignment, students are to write a set of instructions using an introduction; sequential organization; detailed description using appropriate grade-level vocabulary, sentence structures, and transition words; and a conclusion for a self-selected process. Here we focus on a 10th-grade math class that includes Bayan and Estefania. The teacher aligns the assignment with the 10th-grade math standards, and prepares the lesson for all students, with attention to what Bayan and Estefania can do with listening, speaking, reading, and writing in English. The essential learning for this assignment is clarity in communicating steps in a content-based process, use of transition words, and logical sequencing, and it is the same for all students, regardless of ELP level. The teacher looks at this assignment, which focuses on writing, and identifies the following language objective for the class: All students will use writing to explain the steps in a concrete process, describe each step of the process, and sequence those steps.

All students in the class, including Bayan and Estafania, are to choose the math task for which they write instructions, which allows them to choose to write about a process that they know something about or that they are interested in learning.

While level 2 is the focus of this chapter, teachers must always be aware of the expectations for students at subsequent levels to push students toward those levels of language development. For this reason, level 3 expectations are also provided in this example. Additional considerations for students in the SLIFE group, like Bayan, are included in the scaffolding and support section in Table 5-2. Readers are reminded that, as with all of the example assignments in this book, this is just one way to differentiate language-based expectations and provide scaffolding and support.

Teachers can collaborate in many ways to facilitate the simultaneous learning of content and language for students at level 2, with the general education and ELD teacher both working to support students as they learn language and content simultaneously. For example, the ELD and content teachers might work in a collaborative arrangement, where they co-plan, co-teach, and co-assess. There are different ways that teachers can structure their co-teaching partnership, based on local resources and constraints (Honigsfeld & Dove, 2017).

Assignment/Assessment Strategies

As with students at level 1, large-scale standardized assessment tools and classroom-based assessment tools designed for non-ELLs are inappropriate for students at level 2. With this in mind, educators must apply their understanding of what students at level 2 can do with English and their home language in the domains of listening, speaking, reading, and writing, as well as these students' prior schooling, cultural orientation, and experiential backgrounds to create appropriate avenues for them to demonstrate content knowledge as they are developing English. Only in this creative and resourceful way can teachers gain an accurate understanding of what these students know and can do in the content areas.

All Domains

Teachers can use the following strategies with students at level 2 in the domains of listening, speaking, reading, and writing. The strategies help teachers assess what these students can do with content, taking into consideration their ELP level. Teachers can use evidence of students' performance to make decisions about instruction.

Table 5-2   Example Assignment Differentiated for Level 2

Assignment: *Write a set of instructions using an introduction; sequential organization; detailed description using appropriate grade-level vocabulary, sentence structures, and transition words; and a conclusion for a self-selected content-based process.*

Standards-Based Content or Topic *(from the curriculum)*		
For a content-based process		

Non-ELL	Level 2	Level 3
	Language-Based Expectations	
Write a set of instructions using	Write a set of instructions using	Write a set of instructions using
■ Introduction	■ Simple sentences	■ Simple, compound, and a few complex sentences
■ Sequential organization	■ Introductory sentence	■ Introduction (two sentences)
■ Detailed description including	■ Sequential organization	■ Sequential organization
○ appropriate grade-level vocabulary	■ Ordinal/transition words (first, second, third)	■ Ordinal/transition words (first, second, then, next)
○ grade-level sentence structures	■ Simple description using pretaught vocabulary	■ Increasingly precise description using increasingly academic pretaught vocabulary
○ appropriate and varied transition words	■ Concluding sentence	■ Conclusion (two sentences)
■ Conclusion		

Non-ELL	Level 2	Level 3
	Scaffolding and Support	

Using

Non-ELL

- Model assignment
- Teacher demonstration of the task using a "think-aloud"
- Sequential graphic organizer to plan writing
- Language wall with sequencing words and key sentence structures
- Feedback designed to push students to produce accurate grade-level writing

Using

Level 2

- Level 2 model assignment
- Teacher demonstration of the task using a "think-aloud"
- Sequential graphic organizer with sentence starters to plan writing
- Photographs of relevant content-based processes
- Language wall with sequencing/ordinal transition words (then, next, first, second)
- Poster of necessary simple sentence structures
- Word and picture cards featuring needed content vocabulary
- Supplementary "think-aloud" demonstration of simple sentence or paragraph writing
- Pictorially supported procedure texts
- Realia related to processes (to use in teaching and writing)
- Additional work on early literacy skills (for SLIFE)
- Additional work on handwriting skills (for SLIFE)
- Additional time to complete the assignment (for SLIFE)
- Level-appropriate feedback designed to push students to the next level of writing development

Using

Level 3

- Level 3 model assignment
- Teacher demonstration of the task using a "think-aloud"
- Sequential graphic organizer with an increasing use of complex sentence starters to plan writing
- Photographs of relevant content-based processes
- Language wall with sequencing/ordinal transition words (then, next, first, second)
- Word and picture cards featuring increasingly academic vocabulary
- Supplementary "think-aloud" demonstration of paragraph writing
- Simple, compound, and complex academic sentence frames posted in the classroom
- Pictorially supported procedure texts
- Realia related to processes (to use in teaching and writing)
- Additional work on basic literacy skills (for SLIFE)
- Additional time to complete the assignment (for SLIFE)
- Level-appropriate feedback designed to push students to the next level of writing

Essential Leaning: *Clarity in communicating steps in a content-based process, effective use of transition words, and logical sequencing.*

Language Demands: *Use writing to describe each step in a process, sequence those steps, and explain how following these steps leads to the completion of the process.*

Create and Use Assignments/Assessments That Allow Students to Demonstrate Content Learning without Language Mastery. As students at level 2 acquire language and content simultaneously, it is likely that content understanding will supersede their linguistic ability to express that understanding. As a result, to understand what these students know and can do in a given content area, teachers must create assessments that tap into students' knowledge and skills without depending on proficiency in oral or written English. Such flexibility in assessment allows students to demonstrate, in a variety of ways, complex concepts and ideas that they are not yet able to articulate in English. When teachers develop assignment/assessments that separate content knowledge from language production, they gain more accurate insight into the content learning of ELLs at level 2. Examples of flexible assessments include posters rather than essays, short answer oral tests instead of paper-and-pencil multiple-choice tests, and demonstrations rather than reports.

Focus on Correct Answers Instead of Errors and Omissions. In the same way that students at level 1 respond positively to sustained encouragement, students at level 2 derive support from continued emphasis on their successes rather than their shortcomings. Maintaining a positive and receptive classroom environment allows students to focus their concentration and energy on learning language and content. This positive focus also reduces anxiety in the classroom and builds the confidence of students at level 2, as it does for those at level 1. For example, when a student at level 2 says, "I go store last night," teachers demonstrate understanding of the statement and simply rephrase ("Oh, you went to the store?").

Allow Students to Complete Assignments/Assessments with the Support of a Bilingual Teacher or Paraeducator. Like their level 1 counterparts, students at level 2 are likely to understand far more than they are able to express in English. The linguistic abilities of bilingual teachers and paraeducators can provide a much-needed bridge for students at level 2 in completing assignment/assessment procedures. This support can be provided individually or possibly in a small-group setting that includes students from the same language background. This support may come through an explanation of directions in the student's home language or the translation of parts of test questions—if language is not part of what is being assessed and graded. Students at level 2 may also process content with bilingual educators as a means of learning and demonstrating what they know and can do in the content areas. These home language supports provide an important scaffold that helps students demonstrate what they know and can do with content.

Teachers should remember, however, that tests should not be translated in their entirety. This process typically results in nonparallel tests, rendering the results very difficult to interpret. Therefore, teachers should not ask that tests be translated fully by school personnel or others.

Table 5-3   Assignment/Assessment Strategies for Students at Level 2

Listening	Speaking	Reading	Writing
■ Explain directions for assignments and assessments orally, and provide visual support ■ Ask for a physical demonstration of comprehension	■ Allow occasional home language oral responses ■ Assess orally to elicit phrases and simple sentences	■ Use high-quality, visually supported, age-appropriate reading materials matched to students' English language development and reading levels ■ Prompt student repetition of a teacher cue ■ Assess orally to elicit phrases and simple sentences ■ Support home language reading by providing appropriate materials	■ Elicit writing of phrases and simple sentences ■ Have students complete visually supported graphic organizers with phrases and simple sentences ■ Have students supplement writing with visual support that enhances meaning ■ Welcome home language writing, as appropriate

Differentiate Grading by ELP Level. As is the case with students at level 1, students at level 2 typically develop listening and speaking skills before reading and writing. For this reason, these students' oral demonstrations of content understanding should be weighted more heavily than their written demonstrations.

Next we describe assignment/assessment strategies that teachers are encouraged to use with students at level 2 in listening, speaking, reading, and writing. Table 5-3 presents these strategies for easy reference.

Listening

Teachers can use the following strategies to support students at level 2 in listening.

Explain Directions for Assignments/Assessments Orally, and Provide Visual Supports. Teachers must ensure that students understand the expectations of each assignment and assessment task if the results of that work are to be accurate indicators of what students know and can do. Because students at level 2 in listening are still at early stages of English listening development, teachers are urged to use visual supports, such as realia, icons, manipulatives, and models to enhance student understanding of the task at hand. For example, teachers could show students a model of a completed diorama when giving instructions. This strategy is essential because if students do not fully comprehend what they are expected to do, the resulting scores are meaningless.

Ask for Physical Demonstration of Understanding. It is common for language learners' listening comprehension to develop more quickly than their speaking production. Teachers should therefore encourage students to use nonverbal communication to demonstrate what they can understand. For example, in math class teachers might ask students at level 2 to explain their understanding of a word problem involving multiplication by manipulating shapes to demonstrate what they understand. In language arts class, teachers might ask groups of students to act out a story that had been read aloud.

Speaking

Because students at level 2 in speaking are still at the early stages of language development, they need considerable scaffolding and support to produce oral language for academic purposes. Teachers can support their speaking efforts by using the following strategies.

Assess Orally to Elicit Phrases and Simple Sentences. At level 2, as students continue to develop their language skills, teachers can continue to test orally because speaking is likely the student's major productive domain. Such oral testing should be considered instead of testing designed for non-ELLs. For example, if an essay test item were to state "Synthesize your learning about volcanoes," an oral assessment could be based on discussion of a picture of a volcano. The teacher could point to the volcano, eliciting what the student knows by asking, "What is it? What is happening?"

Allow Occasional Home-Language Oral Responses. As students at level 2 acquire English skills, they often draw on their existing home language vocabulary while developing a vocabulary in English. Such linguistic versatility should be perceived as an advantage for bilinguals and students who know more than two languages. Interchanging words of two languages and substituting words when the term in one language is inaccessible are useful and common developmental linguistic tools that should not be perceived as a hindrance. One student was overheard saying, "I dropped my *zapato* (Spanish for *shoe*) on the *suelo* (Spanish for *floor*)." Such an expression is cause for celebration because the student is obviously acquiring vocabulary and syntax, as well as generating a complete sentence. In this case, the student is using both languages communicatively and correctly. This example clearly shows how students can apply home language skills to the new language, setting the stage for increasingly advanced student-generated oral language production.

Further, full responses to assignment/assessment tasks in a student's home language may be accepted at times for different reasons. On occasion, a teacher may simply want to allow the student an opportunity to showcase her or his home language skills to the rest of the class. In another situation, the teacher may want to build a student's communicative confidence. Other times, the teacher may grade the student's content understanding based on a home language response—for example, if the teacher is proficient in the student's home language, if there is a bilingual school staff member available to assist, or if a bilingual volunteer can lend a hand.

Reading

The following strategies can be applied when assessing the reading skills of students at level 2 and when reading is involved in the content assessment process.

Use High-Quality, Visually Supported, Age-Appropriate Reading Materials Matched to Students' Reading Levels. Students at level 2 in reading have not yet developed the reading skills to read tests designed for non-ELLs. If reading is a required part of a testing procedure, then suitable texts must be used, and visual support to aid comprehension must be provided. If reading is not being tested, however, the language load of the test must be reduced to the extent possible. One means to this end is the use of simplified texts and plenty of visual support.

Prompt Student Repetition of a Teacher Cue. When students at level 2 in reading repeat what the teacher has said, either in words or song, teachers can ascertain their reading skills and content understanding. For instance, a teacher might ask a student to repeat a short sentence read aloud to check for accurate pronunciation. In the content areas, teachers might use songs or raps to teach content. If a student is able to perform the song or rap with visual support, for example, by pointing to pictures at appropriate times during the performance, this ability could be taken as evidence of content learning.

Assess Orally to Elicit Phrases and Simple Sentences. This technique is the same as that for speaking, as described earlier. For example, the student could engage in a short question-and-answer session focused on reading a linguistically appropriate passage, such as an informational passage focused on different types of trees, which includes visual supports. In another example, the student could sequence story cards with simple captions.

Support Home-Language Reading by Providing Appropriate Materials. Students who can read in their home languages can capitalize on those skills during test taking. For example, a glossary in the student's home language can help him or her negotiate written material on a content test. For students who are given the benefit of literacy instruction in the home language, progress in this endeavor can and should be tested using that language. In other words, students learning to read in Spanish should be tested in Spanish.

Writing

As with reading, students who have not yet learned to write in their home languages are likely to take longer to develop sufficient writing skills to move from level 2 to level 3 than their counterparts who have learned to read and write in their home languages. The arduous nature of developing literacy skills in an entirely new language must be considered when testing these students using writing. It may take students like Bayan who have limited home language writing skills longer to produce written answers or products than students like Estefania who can read and write in her home language.

Elicit Writing of Phrases and Simple Sentences. Regardless of age or grade level, students at level 2 in writing can only be expected to produce writing as delineated in the student descriptors, that is, using phrases and simple sentences. For example, a middle school assignment to write a five-paragraph essay would need to be adapted to include only phrases and simple sentences. This product would need to be graded according to the student's ability to meet the adapted expectations, rather than rating the assignment according to the non-ELL expectations for a full five paragraphs.

Teachers can elicit phrases and simple sentences by providing sentence frames, giving students pictures or other visual prompts tailored to content needs, and modeling the writing process. For instance, an academic sentence frame to describe a food chain might be "[picture of birds] eats [picture of worms]." The student supplies pretaught words like *bird* and *worms* from memory, likely using invented spelling. Students might also access a visually supported word or language wall.

Have Students Complete Visually Supported Graphic Organizers with Phrases and Simple Sentences. Graphic organizers continue to be an excellent tool to gauge student learning at level 2 in writing, just as they were at level 1, because they have also been used for the instruction of that learning. It is critical for teachers to remember that assessment formats must be familiar to students; the assessment phase is not the time to introduce new formats for students to use in showing what they know and can do. Teachers must not make assumptions about students' ability to demonstrate learning through means not explicitly taught, particularly students at early ELP levels.

Allowing students at level 2 in writing to use scaffolding during assessment enables them to better demonstrate what they know and can do in the content areas. Though the teacher may expect non-ELL students to write answers in complete sentences without the aid of a graphic organizer, she or he can view the graphic organizer and the differentiated linguistic expectations as a data-driven practice that allows students to demonstrate their knowledge and skills as fully as possible. One example of this type of support is a graphic organizer with a word bank for students to use in comparing the desert and the tundra.

Have Students Supplement Writing with Visual Support to Enhance Meaning. Because the writing of students at level 2 likely includes many errors and omissions that hinder understanding, requiring these students to use visual supports such as drawings, magazine pictures, and clip art in their writing is necessary to reinforce their communication in a meaningful way. For example, students can be required to write a weekly journal entry about their weekend activities. The expectations, varying with student abilities, are that students use pretaught vocabulary to describe at least five activities using phrases and simple sentences. This written journal entry must include a relevant picture, either drawn or snipped from a magazine, and glued onto the journal page. Another example is having students write a description of a picture provided by the teacher.

Welcome Home Language Writing, as Appropriate. This technique parallels that used for speaking, in that students can be allowed to insert words from their home language into their writing in English. As with speaking, students can gain confidence in their ability to communicate, which fuels motivation and effort. This ability to use both languages in the same phrase is a valuable developmental device that should be appreciated rather than discouraged. Teachers may also allow students to write in their home languages to honor those skills and build student confidence. Such writing can even be used for grading purposes if someone is available to translate the answer, which might be, for example, a narrative about a family tradition. In addition, students who are learning to write in their home languages can also make use of those languages in testing of their progress in those programs.

Instructional Strategies

Having reviewed a range of strategies that can be used to elicit evidence of level 2 students' learning, we turn to instructional strategies that facilitate student success on differentiated assignments/assessments. This approach follows the backward-lesson-design model (Wiggins & McTighe, 2006), wherein teachers determine what outcomes students must achieve and then design instruction to support that achievement.

Before teachers select instructional strategies for students at level 2, they are encouraged to begin with four important steps:

1. Examine your own assumptions about what your students can do.
2. Learn about students' backgrounds.
3. Determine students' instructional levels based on content knowledge and skills, as well as levels of language proficiency in English and in the home language to the greatest degree possible.
4. Teach essential learning from the curriculum and its associated language in a differentiated manner.

Students at level 2 have begun the ELD process and, with the support of knowledgeable teachers and appropriate instruction, steadily progress toward English language levels on par with non-ELLs and grade-level academic performance.

All Domains

Teachers who work with students at level 2 should use the following strategy across the language domains of listening, speaking, reading, and writing.

Provide Sensory Support for Every Lesson. As with students at level 1, teachers are reminded to capitalize on the five senses of their students at level 2 in order to make instruction meaningful and memorable by using, for example real objects, pictures, hands-on materials and experiences, nonverbal communication, demonstrations, modeling, and simulations. For example, if a family and consumer science teacher is discussing the five different tastes (sweet, salty, sour, bitter, and umami), students at level 2 should be afforded the opportunity to sample foods of each category. Experiential and sensory learning contributes to long-term learning, providing "mental Velcro" to which students can attach new vocabulary and conceptual learning.

Table 5-4 presents instructional strategies for students at level 2 in the domains of listening, speaking, reading, and writing.

Listening

The following strategies support students at level 2 in listening as they work to aurally comprehend content and language.

Use Simplified, Correct Language, Repeating or Paraphrasing as Needed. Teachers are reminded that using language understandable to the student at level 2 is essential. Taking care to speak simply but correctly, teachers can engage these students in basic exchanges about social topics such as family and personal interests, as well as general academic topics related to the curriculum. Students are also be well served by teachers who repeat and paraphrase. Such conscious reinforcement supports development of a receptive repertoire of English words and phrases.

Allow Sufficient Wait Time. Because students at level 2 in listening continue to require extra processing time, this strategy gives them a cognitive window for constructing meaning from speech before the opportunity is lost. This strategy is also helpful for non-ELLs, who can deepen their cognitive processing of teacher input when given additional time to think (even up to 10 seconds).

Model the Completion of Graphic Organizers to Build Higher-Order Thinking. Graphic organizers help students at level 2 in listening to make connections and can assist them in developing metacognitive skills, "thinking about their thinking." Such explicit support of content processing makes thinking visible. Teachers can model appropriate ways to express ideas in English by helping students to

Table 5-4   Instructional Strategies for Students at Level 2

Listening	Speaking	Reading	Writing
■ Use simplified, correct language, repeating or paraphrasing as needed ■ Allow sufficient wait time ■ Model the completion of graphic organizers to build higher-order thinking ■ Employ think-alouds to model both process and language	■ Encourage involvement in discussions by eliciting phrases or simple sentences ■ Scaffold content and academic language by providing appropriate sentence frames ■ Concentrate on students' meaning rather than on grammatical correctness ■ Reward all attempts to communicate	■ Implement a high-quality, research-based, culturally and linguistically appropriate reading development program ■ Use extensive visual supports so that students can derive meaning from print ■ Support grade-level content using comprehensible reading materials with extensive visual support ■ Teach early reading skills ■ Build background and help students make connections to prior learning and experiences ■ Read or sing visually supported stories or texts to students, using props and acting to increase comprehension and develop oral language skills necessary for reading ■ Incorporate shared, shared-to-guided, and guided reading. ■ Implement language experience stories ■ Model the use of graphic organizers	■ Scaffold content and academic language by providing sentence frames ■ Incorporate modeled, shared, and guided writing activities ■ Accept phrases or simple sentences in lieu of grade-level writing expectations ■ Focus on correct answers instead of errors and omissions ■ Correct and use identity texts ■ Model the use of graphic organizers

fill out their organizers. Graphic organizers can serve as a way to make sense of content and as a note-taking device. For example, a teacher could model the completion of an outline about the solar system.

Employ Think-Alouds to Model Process and Language. Teachers can use this valuable strategy to help students at level 2 in listening understand how to do certain tasks and to model appropriate language use. For instance, in a lesson on paragraph writing, the teacher could demonstrate the process of writing a good topic sentence by thinking aloud during the process of writing such a sentence in front of the class. In this way, teachers can exemplify both the cognitive process and the necessary language to complete the process.

Speaking

The following strategies are designed to facilitate the language and content learning of students at level 2 in speaking.

Encourage Involvement in Discussions by Eliciting Phrases or Simple Sentences. Students at level 2 in speaking typically understand far more than they are able to articulate. As a result, they benefit greatly from encouragement and patience as they begin to produce spoken English. While students at level 2 in speaking are often able to cognitively process at high levels, they frequently report feeling "babyish" because of their diminished ability (in comparison to that in their home languages) to communicate verbally. This level of language production is a predictable product of normal linguistic development, rather than an indicator of limited cognitive ability. Nevertheless, it can be demoralizing for these students.

As a result, teachers should approach students at level 2 in speaking with positive assumptions about their cognitive abilities and their desire to expand their speaking abilities. Teachers should also maintain high expectations for student performance, working to elicit appropriate levels of language production. This process can be facilitated by using visual supports for student responses. For instance, when asking a student at level 2 for an example of an amphibian, the teacher might provide a variety of pictures of examples and nonexamples that have been previously discussed. Another key technique for eliciting student speech at this level is to allow students to discuss possible answers with a "shoulder partner" (a student at a higher ELP level) or a small group. Such heterogeneous grouping assures that ELLs are exposed to more developed examples of language use, thus facilitating their learning of how to articulate content knowledge appropriately.

Scaffold Content and Academic Language by Providing Appropriate Sentence Frames. As students at level 2 in speaking expand their vocabularies and speech production, they need opportunities to practice and manipulate academic language to the greatest extent possible. Teachers can, based on essential learning, accelerate the process of language development by modeling academic language and embedding opportunities to use such language. Specifically, teachers can use sentence frames as examples of academic language structures and vocabulary that students can draw on. This strategy benefits ELLs and non-ELLs, who are also learning academic English. For instance, students at level 2 in speaking can complete simple sentence frames such as "The rabbit has ____" and "The fish has ____" with the words *fur* and *scales*. This content-based language focus ensures that English language learning and content learning occur simultaneously. Teachers are also urged to provide students at lower levels of language proficiency with guidance in how to ask for assistance and clarification in polite

ways by providing sentence frames such as, "Could you please help me with
_____?" or "Could you tell me what _____ means?"

Concentrate on Students' Meaning Rather Than on Correct Grammar. Students at
level 2 in speaking expend much of their attention in accessing meaningful vocabulary in English to formulate phrases and simple sentences, checking against
what they already know and comparing their English production to their home
languages. When these students do produce some speech, teachers can support
and encourage increased oral production by continuing to focus on meaning
instead of providing detailed corrections. For example, when a student says,
"Teacher, water?" the teacher could simply give the student a pass to get a drink.
Corrections can overwhelm the student at level 2 in speaking and may result in
reticence, frustration, and delayed speech production. These students are better
served if teachers focus on providing meaningful input, expanding vocabulary
development, and embedding opportunities for peer interaction.

Reward All Attempts to Communicate. Like students at level 1, students at level 2
in speaking benefit from a positive and receptive environment and can be discouraged or embarrassed if they are singled out for correction. Consider your
own foreign language learning experiences; many teachers themselves report
giving up on learning a new language because of feelings of inadequacy when
their speech was picked apart by teachers who were overly focused on accuracy
at the beginning stages of language development. Instead, teachers can respond
to student communication in a welcoming and inclusive fashion that honors
these students' progression toward language development, accepting the recog-
nizable approximation while encouraging the student to expand and sustain
communication efforts. For instance, if a student at level 2 in speaking were to
say "health homework," a study hall teacher could simply begin to provide assistance rather than insisting on a perfectly articulated request. It should be
noted that this omission of minute correction is not intended to reinforce errors. Rather, teachers must recognize that speaking errors, particularly those
made systematically, are part of a learning process on the path to accuracy.

Reading

As with students at level 1, the distinct needs of students at level 2 who can read
and write in the home language and those who cannot continue to profoundly
affect students' progress toward grade-level English language production in different ways. Teachers are reminded that students, such as Bayan, who cannot
read in their home languages require more explicit reading instruction and support than their counterparts, like Estefania, who can read in the home language.
Students like Estefania can transfer previously learned reading skills to English,
making the process of learning to read in English much easier. Programming

focused on early reading development is essential for students at level 2 who cannot read in any other language so that they can gain the requisite skills to access the standards-based curriculum. Skilled, trained, reading teachers and volunteers can play a key role in providing this support.

Implement a High-Quality, Research-Based, Culturally and Linguistically Appropriate Reading Development Program. Students at level 2 in reading who have not learned to read in the home language need explicit focused instruction in how to read, regardless of age. This calls for the development of programming that is tailored to the needs of ELLs, rather than enrolling such students in remedial instruction designed for non-ELLs who have had early literacy instruction. This programming must be culturally and linguistically sensitive in terms of materials, ensuring that making meaning is the focus of the reading instruction rather than isolated drill approaches. In districts with small numbers of students who cannot read in any language, a well-trained and well-supported paraeducator or volunteer may play a key role in delivering this instruction. As an example of appropriate programming nonfiction reading materials focused on curricular topics could be the basis for oral language development and reading skills for students at level 2 in reading.

Use Extensive Visual Support So That Students Can Derive Meaning from Print. Visual supports like posters and pictures are essential for the reading development of students at level 2. Such comprehensible depictions provide contextualization that these students can draw on to increasingly make sense of the printed word. Various kinds of visual supports, including posters, pictures, diagrams, and models provide a much-needed bridge to higher levels of reading development. Texts without contextualizing visual support are likely to be incomprehensible to students at level 2 in reading, who should not be expected to gain understanding from what is likely to be perceived as uninteresting or meaningless.

Support Grade-Level Content Using Comprehensible Reading Materials with Extensive Visual Support. Engaging students at level 2 in the content-area reading curriculum can be accomplished with meaningful materials. At the higher grades, grade-level materials are unsuitable for students at level 2 in reading. Teachers therefore need to creatively assemble a body of accessible and comprehensible resources that is tied to the content curriculum, but better suited to the ELP levels of the ELLs in their classes. Teachers are encouraged to seek funds for such materials from parent–teacher groups, civic and church organizations, and the school board, if classroom budgets do not support the purchase of these necessary materials.

Teach Early Reading Skills. Students at level 2 in reading who are not yet speaking at sentence level should not be expected to gain meaning from print through independent reading (Franco, 2005). As part of the development of prerequisite oral skills, Kauffman (2007a) clarifies that students must have the opportunity to build phonemic awareness in English. By phonemic awareness, we mean the ability to hear, identify, and manipulate phonemes, which are the smallest units of sound that can differentiate meaning. Students at level 2 in reading must also (continue to) learn the alphabetic principle (the names of the letters and their shapes) and a range of skills falling under the label of *concepts of print*, including the following:

- Book-holding skills
- Understanding of print directionality
- Understanding of the one-to-one matching of spoken and written words
- Understanding of the connection between illustrations and graphics and print
- Understanding of punctuation marks (Kauffman, 2007a, p. 148)

These students must also be provided with meaning-based instruction in phonics to prepare them for independent reading, according to Kauffman (2007a). As an example, teachers can use environmental print, such as content and language objectives, as the source of this type of early reading skill instruction.

Build Background and Help Students Make Connections to Prior Learning and Experiences. To facilitate student success, teachers must ensure that all members of the classroom community have the prerequisite knowledge and skills needed to actively engage in the learning process. Given the diversity of today's classrooms, this requirement means that teachers must know their students' backgrounds, and account for likely variability in what students know by teaching needed background information. Teachers must also help students to make connections to their own backgrounds in terms of prior learning and experiences because many students do not do so on their own. For instance, students at level 2 in reading might think about celebrations in their countries of origin when learning about Thanksgiving in the United States because there are similar celebrations in other countries.

Read or Sing Visually Supported Stories or Texts to Students, Using Props and Acting to Increase Comprehension and Develop Oral Language Skills Necessary for Reading. Although students at level 2 in reading are gaining ground in terms of their listening skills, teachers who read or sing stories and other texts to students need to provide visual support to facilitate understanding. When the language presented is comprehensible, students can appropriate it for their own use. This kind of presentation of written material can assist with students' comprehension and their own language production. For example, a teacher might dress in character when reading the "Emancipation Proclamation" to students. Props might include pictures relating to slavery that could be referred to during the reading of the speech. Role-playing can also enhance comprehension.

Incorporate Shared, Shared-to-Guided, and Guided Reading. Although shared, shared-to-guided, and guided reading may be perceived as elementary classroom teaching strategies, students of all ages at level 2 in reading benefit from such specific and targeted instruction. In shared reading, the teacher and students read an enlarged text together, discussing various points throughout the reading. Then students read this same text on their own, repeatedly, developing increasing fluency. In guided reading, the teacher guides small groups of students in reading a common text that is at their instructional (rather than their frustration) level. The teacher can provide individualized instruction as students read individually and simultaneously "under their breath." Shared-to-guided reading (Knox & Amador-Watson, 2000) is designed to bridge shared and guided reading by providing extra scaffolding to students during the guided reading process. All of these strategies foster early reading development in students at level 2 in reading.

These three approaches are exemplified in a unit about arctic biomes in which the teacher starts with an appropriate passage that is read using shared reading. Students then focus their efforts on high-quality, age-appropriate, lower-reading-level books on the same topic that could be read using shared-to-guided and guided reading techniques.

Implement Language Experience Stories. This approach allows students at level 2 in reading to create texts with the assistance of the teacher to be used in reading instruction. After a shared experience, such as a field trip to the zoo, students work together to write a description of the outing, with the teacher acting as a scribe. Teachers must elicit the full range of abilities, pushing students at level 2 in reading toward level 3, and ensure that the written language is grammatically accurate. They then use these student-generated texts as reading material for instruction. Both early reading (e.g., phonics) and reading (e.g., fluency, comprehension) skills can be taught with such pieces of writing.

Model the Use of Graphic Organizers. Teachers can help students at level 3 in reading to make sense of texts and to make connections among ideas through the use of graphic organizers. These organizers can serve as a link to assessment activities that can make use of the same instrument, allowing these students to demonstrate what they know and can do. For example, when teaching a unit on the Civil War, students can categorize big ideas like military leaders, states involved, and key issues related to the North and the South by using a T-chart.

Writing

The developmental distinction between students at level 2 in writing who can and those who cannot write in their home languages continues to manifest in different ways as both groups advance in the area of writing. Students like Bayan who cannot write in their home languages require more intensive instruction and more time than students like Estefania who can transfer writing skills from the home language to become strong writers in English. This important need cannot be slighted, overlooked, or neglected. School districts must take purposeful steps to make certain that plans for instruction include the crucial needs of these newcomers, since their lack of writing ability positions them for failure in school.

Scaffold Content and Academic Language by Providing Sentence Frames. This strategy applies equally to speaking and writing. Students at level 2 in writing require explicit instruction in how to frame their thoughts in English and repeated opportunities to practice. While these students can only produce phrases and simple sentences, they can begin to incorporate academic language into their writing, if aided by visually supported examples such as word walls, concept walls, and teacher modeling. Teachers can also provide simple sentence frames for learners at level 2, such as "The rabbit ____ fur." or "The fish ____ scales." These can elicit the student's use of simple present tense sentences using new academic vocabulary. Non-ELLs can also benefit from explicit instruction in how to use academic language rather than social language in the content areas. For example, teachers might extend students' production of content vocabulary by posting "The roots _____ water." with a picture to guide students to use an academic word like *absorb* rather than an everyday word like *drink* in an academic sentence.

Incorporate Modeled, Shared, and Guided Writing Activities. Knox and Amador-Watson (2000) and others understand these kinds of instruction within a balanced literacy framework. When teachers employ modeled writing with students at level 2 in writing, they show these students the process of writing, writing conventions, features such as letter–sound relationships, and how to choose a genre that is appropriate for a task. In shared writing activities, teachers invite students to collaborate with them in producing written text that is displayed for all to see. Teachers and students can work together to create templates that students can use to generate their own future writing. Guided writing allows students to work on their own writing, but with teacher support. A workshop approach to writing enables teachers to meet students where they are and to individualize one-on-one instruction and feedback. For instance, as a precursor to asking students to create word problems in math class, the students could be taught to write sentences.

Accept Phrases or Simple Sentences in Lieu of Grade-Level Writing Expectations. While remembering the need to push students to the next ELP level, teachers are, nevertheless, encouraged to maintain a flexible attitude about the writing of students at level 2. These students must be afforded the time and opportunity to develop their writing, just like their non-ELL peers in the early elementary grades. All ELLs must be allowed to incrementally learn to write in English. Teachers are advised to accept phrases and simple sentences from students at level 2 in writing. Because ELP test data indicate that this level of production represents maximum capability at this stage of linguistic development, higher demands are unreasonable. For example, if non-ELLs are expected to write a two-page biography, students at level 2 in writing might write phrases or simple sentences to communicate meaning about their assigned person, supplemented with visual support. The length of the assignment is, by necessity, shortened.

Focus on Correct Answers Instead of Errors and Omissions. As with speaking, teachers must focus on the content conveyed by students at level 2 in writing, rather than on the errors that might be present in expression. When correcting writing for these students, select one or two areas for feedback, such as content concepts, verb tense, or use of articles, and disregard other errors. Overwhelming students with corrections of every inaccuracy is unlikely to facilitate learning. In fact, it can have the opposite effect by demoralizing a student who worked very diligently to produce the submitted product.

Ask Students to Create and Use Identity Texts. Identity texts tap into students' individual creativity and are based on their personal background and experience. Creating identity texts motivates students and helps them to assume a fully vested role in the classroom community. As such, they have equitable standing and are able to contribute to classroom discourse. For example, three of Jones-Vo's 7th-grade students presented about their countries of origin and refugee experiences as part of the school's Celebration of Diversity, alongside community leaders and other experts. These same students were later invited to present at a similar event in a nearby district, providing them the opportunity to strengthen their identities as capable ambassadors and experts.

Model the Use of Graphic Organizers. As with other language domains, graphic organizers can serve as an excellent support for the writing development of students at level 2 in writing. Organizers like Venn diagrams or semantic webs completed during listening and reading activities can be used as springboards for writing. Alternatively, students at level 2 can produce writing by completing a graphic organizer. Visual supports throughout these organizers are essential and enhance concept development. For instance, a teacher could use a T-chart to allow students to categorize and label pictorial examples of living and non-living things.

Instruction That Integrates Language Domains

The more authentic a teaching and learning activity is, the more likely it is to integrate the language domains of listening, speaking, reading, and writing. Although strategies for these domains have been presented separately, teachers are urged to integrate the language domains and the appropriate strategies for each throughout their teaching. This natural approach to language use in the classroom lends itself to logical and real applications. For example, students might create presentations about their home countries in which they research, prepare a written slide presentation with visual support, and deliver a speech to the class, possibly with a partner or cooperative group where each student has an assigned, productive role.

Conclusion

Readers are reminded that students sometimes function at different levels of ELP in different domains. If a student exhibits level 2 writing and level 3 speaking, for example, the use of level-specific strategies for each language domain is necessary. Teachers can use a wide variety of assignment/assessment and instructional strategies to meet the range of needs in their classrooms.

In addition to demonstrating different levels of proficiency across domains, students can also demonstrate different levels of language proficiency at any age. That is, students at level 2 might appear in elementary, middle, or high school classrooms. Teachers must choose strategies that are in keeping with their students' ELP levels, regardless of student age.

Professional Learning Activities

Working individually or with others in professional learning communities, differentiate the first four assignments for Bayan and Estefania. For assignment 5, choose the assignment and differentiate it for at least one of the level 2 ELP students in your class.

Differentiating for Bayan and Estefania

For assignments 1–4, differentiate the language-based expectations and the scaffolding and support needed for level 2 students Bayan and Estefania. Recall that Bayan and Estefania are both 10th-grade students at level 2 in all domains. However, Bayan is a SLIFE learner and does not read in her home language, and Estefania is more or less at grade level in her home language.

1. Read the assignment above the template.
2. Read the essential learning and language demands below the template.
3. Review the standards-based topic, language-based expectations for non-ELLs.
4. Complete the template to show the differentiated assignment for Bayan and Estefania by adding appropriate language-based expectations and scaffolding and support for these students.

After you complete the template, read on for additional insight on how to differentiate this assignment.

Assignment 1: *Write a letter to a public official*

Standards-Based Content or Topic (from the curriculum)	
Voicing a concern about an issue _____	

Non-ELL	Level 2
Language-Based Expectations	
Write a letter to a public official	▪ ▪ ▪ ▪
Scaffolding and Support	
Using ▪ *Examples discussed in class*	*Using* ▪ *Examples discussed in class* ▪ ▪ ▪

Essential Learning: *Writing a letter in the correct format, formally voicing a concern.*
Language Demands: *Use writing to provide an account, evaluate that account, and argue for a position.*

For Bayan and Estefania, build sufficient background, support students in making connections to what they already know, preteach relevant vocabulary, and embed opportunities for interactions with non-ELL students. It is also necessary to provide students with models of what is expected, such as samples of successfully completed assignments, in this case a letter to a public official that voices a concern. Dissect this letter with the class, pointing out formatting issues, formulaic language, and appropriate formal business vocabulary. A letter template with sentence starters and a word bank that supports students in arguing their position can be used to guide their work. The letters Bayan and Estefania write should follow business letter format and should be graded in accordance with each student's level 2 language development capabilities. Such purposeful practices empower ELLs to be successful on adapted classroom assignments.

For Bayan, the assignment necessitates building background because it is unlikely that she has ever written a letter. Instead of having her write to a public official who she does not know, contextualize the assignment by asking her to write a very simple letter to the school principal about a concern at school. Remember it is likely that her listening and speaking levels will progress more quickly than her writing. Bayan is probably going to need additional support with the writing process because she has not had experience with writing in her home language and so has no skills to transfer to English. It takes Bayan longer than Estefania to demonstrate the English language skills needed to write her own letter.

Bayan may need to practice with a template that lays out the format of a business letter and includes some key words and structures. Bayan's SLIFE status may also necessitate the provision of extra time to complete the assignment. Bayan's teachers need to use appropriate differentiation strategies for her to access learning opportunities at school. When all teachers know how to provide appropriate scaffolding and support for students like Bayan, they can engage with classroom activities, learn content, acquire English for academic purposes, and achieve.

It is more likely that Estefania has experience in writing letters and is familiar with the notion of lobbying for her interests. Taking time to activate this background knowledge prepares her to participate in this assignment. Because Estefania is familiar with the genre of business letters, has grown up surrounded by print in the home (e.g., books, newspapers, grocery lists), and can transfer her Spanish writing ability to English, this assignment is less daunting for her than for Bayan. She is accustomed to the notion of "taking care of business" through reading and writing. In addition, Estefania can readily apply her background knowledge about the importance of adhering to a prescribed format in producing her letter. Her teacher, recognizing Estefania's readiness to receive academic instruction, should consider providing various basic academic sentence examples and frames (e.g., "I am writing to express _____" or "Thank you for your time"). Estefania may not need the letter template for more than general guidance, while Bayan's task may be to simply complete the template.

Assignment 2: *Read and respond to a novel about social issues*

Standards-Based Content or Topic (from the curriculum)	
Give a 5-minute summary and plot analysis	

Non-ELL	Level 2
Language-Based Expectations	
▪ *Read and give a 5-minute summary and plot analysis*	▪ ▪ ▪ ▪
Scaffolding and Support	
Using ▪ *A graphic organizer for the development of the summary and analysis*	*Using* ▪ *A graphic organizer for the development of the summary and analysis* ▪ ▪ ▪

Essential Learning: *Broaden understanding of social issues; develop reading comprehension by analyzing and orally summarizing a novel.*
Language Demands: *Use oral and written language to recount, summarize, and analyze social issues.*

The placement of Bayan and Estefania in a general education class that requires the reading of entire novels is questionable for students at ELP level 2. These students cannot be expected to participate in such assignments and should be provided with alternative programming that is aligned with their instructional level.

Rather than having these students read complex fiction, thematic nonfiction or simple fiction texts are recommended. These books should match the reading demands appropriate for students at level 2 in reading, include plenty of visual support, and represent familiar topics of interest. Students can then create a summary in the form of a poster that includes visuals labeled with phrases and simple sentences based on sentence frames provided by the teacher. The poster can serve as a scaffold for the oral presentation of the book. Students might organize their summary according to the organizational text features found in the book. Oral presentations would be done in small groups or for the teacher, paraeducator, or trained volunteer, one on one. Show Bayan and Estefania an example poster and demonstrate a simple narration to familiarize these students with the expectations for the assignment. They then read a visually supported text at their instructional level that addresses a social issue. They can collaborate with the teacher to create and discuss a visually supported word and concept wall, complete with representative photos, illustrations, and icons.

Part of Bayan's instruction must emphasize early reading development. Preteaching vocabulary is beneficial, especially for Bayan. Bayan needs this vocabulary because she has less facility than Estefania in decoding and other skills that make print more meaningful. Shared and guided reading is essential to assist Bayan in making meaning from the visually supported text and building fluency. The teacher could provide a graphic organizer to be filled out with assistance for Bayan to use as a model for her poster. Finally, the teacher, a paraeducator, or a trained volunteer must practice the narration with Bayan, modeling and having her repeat phrases and sentences.

The strategies described for Bayan will also be effective for Estefania, though Estefania is likely to progress more quickly because she has a richer academic background than Bayan.

Assignment 3: *Write a detailed lab report based on an experiment done in class*

Standards-Based Content or Topic (from the curriculum)	
Using the scientific method and our template for writing lab reports	
Non-ELL	**Level 2**
Language-Based Expectations	
▪ *Write a detailed lab report*	▪ ▪ ▪ ▪
Scaffolding and Support	
Using	*Using*
▪ *An experiment done in class*	▪ *An experiment done in class* ▪ ▪ ▪

Essential Learning: *Listing and describing the steps of the scientific method; writing a lab report with appropriate format and content.*

Language Demands: *Use oral and written language to list, describe, and write a lab report.*

Rather than writing the lab report from scratch, Bayan and Estefania can fill in a graphic organizer that includes visual support and lists the steps of the scientific method. They can describe what they did in the experiment at each step by completing sentence frames with provided language. Students can be provided with key words or sentence strips with accompanying pictures and icons that describe the steps of the experiment according to the scientific method. Students select and sequence these strips in the correct order as a prewriting activity. They then fill out a graphic organizer that includes a bank of words and phrases with accompanying pictures. Bayan and Estefania should each work with a partner whose English is stronger for guidance throughout the process. It is important that these partners be chosen wisely and given specific guidance in how to assist students like these. In this way, both Bayan and Estefania are able to recount what occurred during the science experiment.

Bayan needs additional assistance with the writing process and may also require extra time (more so than Estefania) to complete it because of her SLIFE background. Teachers need to remember that even forming the letters within the provided words may represent a challenge to this student who is learning to write for the first time. For this reason, the graphic organizer may be partially completed for Bayan.

Assignment 4: *Create a public service video*

Standards-Based Content or Topic (from the curriculum)	
Identifying the causes and solutions for global warming	

Non-ELL	Level 2
Language-Based Expectations	
▪ *Create a public service announcement*	▪ ▪ ▪ ▪
Scaffolding and Support	
Using ▪ *The support of a small group*	*Using* ▪ *The support of a small group* ▪ ▪

Essential Learning: *Identify causes of and solutions for global warming; use technical skills, such as running a video camera and using computer software to create a short video clip.*

Language Demands: *Use oral and written language to describe a public service message, state a position, agree, disagree, compare, contrast, and explain.*

This project represents an opportunity for the video group to mentor Bayan and Estefania, but the group needs explicit teacher guidance about how to do so. The group members must be explicitly taught how to welcome and effectively work with students at ELP level 2. Both Bayan and Estefania can benefit from the hands-on nature of the technology and the interaction with and mentoring of their group members. They can expand and practice their English by creating a poster, based on a model, and by narrating the poster on the public service announcement. The narration may take the form of speaking memorized lines, which may be supported by teacher cueing because the students might be nervous about the performance.

Bayan can participate in the video by using pretaught language and vocabulary about the causes of global warming while pointing to pictures on a poster showing sources of pollution. Her performance would be followed by a peer's explanation of each issue. In terms of the technological side of the assignment, Bayan needs explicit guidance on using the video technology and should shadow the other students, trying her hand at the technology once she has been taught how to use it. Bayan must not be left out of the technological work just because her English is at beginning skill level and she has little background experience with the technology. Bayan may need extra time with the writing portion of the assignment because she has not learned to read and write her home language.

While Estefania also needs the support of her group members, she may be more familiar with some of the technological requirements of the project because she attended school prior to coming to the United States and because her higher socioeconomic status has afforded her access to computers, video cameras, and so forth. Like Bayan, Estefania can be fully involved in production of the video, using pretaught language at the phrase and simple sentence level.

Differentiating for Your Students

For assignment 5, choose an assignment from your curriculum. Differentiate the assignment for a student in your class at ELP level 2. Consider how student background factors like prior schooling, home language literacy, cultural orientation, and challenging experiences are likely to influence this student's content and language learning in your classroom.

1. Write the assignment above the template.
2. Identify the essential learning and language demands and write this below the template.
3. Fill in the standards-based topic, language-based expectations for non-ELLs and for your student at ELP level 2.
4. Plan and implement the assignment in your classroom. If possible, videotape the lesson or invite an ELL coordinator or coach to observe the lesson and focus on the teacher's use of appropriate differentiation strategies for students at level 2 in any domain.

Assignment 5: _____

Standards-Based Content or Topic (from the curriculum)	

_____

Non-ELL	Level 2
Language-Based Expectations	
▪	▪
	▪
	▪
	▪
Scaffolding and Support	
Using	*Using*
▪	▪
	▪
	▪
	▪

Essential Learning: _____

Language Demands: _____

Share your template with your colleagues and explain why you made the choices you did. When you implement the lesson in your class, reflect on how your focal student uses oral and written language in each of the activities you planned. If you videotape the interaction, work with your colleagues to explore the scaffolding and support you provided. In any case, collect evidence of your students' content and language performances, identify your students' strengths, and list possible next steps for instruction.

Chapter 6

Differentiating for Students at Level 3

All educators must first share a sense of responsibility for providing an equitable education for ELs so that they will be willing to change the way in which they work with ELs to. . . .address ELs' specific linguistic and cultural needs through instruction.

—DIANE STAEHR FENNER

Incisive analysis of student abilities related to language proficiency levels leads teachers of English language learners (ELLs) to create useful and innovative assignments/assessments and instruction. This type of ELL-specific differentiation empowers students to express their understanding of content without having fully developed oral and written English for academic purposes. Communicating understanding of standards-based content using increasingly advanced language is the ideal vehicle to drive both enhanced content learning and language development. In this way, students receive instruction that offers the maximum benefit: simultaneous learning related to both grade-level content and English language development (ELD). In this chapter, we focus on the language development of students at level 3, describing these students in detail and outlining strategies that can help teachers keep students engaged, motivated, and on track.

While the suggested strategies are designed to elicit production for students at level 3 in listening, speaking, reading, and writing, teachers should maintain their efforts to push students to reach ever higher targets, while providing scaffolding in instruction and assessment. Such informed practice helps these students advance to the next level of language proficiency, level 4, by providing and eliciting (where possible and appropriate) increasingly refined examples of level 4 language production.

Variation in Students' Backgrounds

Student Scenarios

Toua, a Hmong 3rd grader born in a refugee camp in Thailand, is the son of parents from Laos. His family arrived in the United States two years ago and he initially struggled in school, partly because he had received no formal education prior to his arrival. As a result, he had no experience with reading and writing in his home language. In the past two years, Toua's parents have become gainfully employed and reestablished their network with the Hmong community. In terms of language, Toua quickly developed social language and his teachers wonder why he struggles academically because he appears to be fluent in English. His reading and writing are below grade level but his teachers suspect he might just be lazy.

Aung, a 3rd grader from Myanmar (formerly Burma), was also born in a refugee camp. Before arriving in the United States last year, Aung attended school in the camp and was taught in English by missionaries. His parents do not speak English at all and have had difficulty locating employment. Aung frequently misses school when he is excused to translate at the clinic for his parents. Aung's language skills allow him to communicate well in social situations and classroom instruction is meaningful to him, especially when contextualized and supported visually. Because his teachers in the camp paid particular attention to the conventions of writing, Aung perfectly forms the English alphabet and works very diligently to create accurate written products, though his work is below grade level. He also struggles to make sense of grade-level reading materials.

Toua and Aung, though both 3rd-grade refugees from Southeast Asia, are quite different in terms of their biographical profiles, which influence their instructional needs. The issue of home language literacy is a primary informant of differentiated lesson design in that Toua needs more explicit instruction in reading and writing than Aung, who can transfer some skills learned during his previous schooling experiences. Both Toua and Aung live in homes where English is never spoken.[1] As a result, both students require repeated and sustained efforts to embed interaction with the non-ELLs in their classroom in both social and academic situations. Such intentional opportunities for Toua and Aung to hear and practice English in authentic learning contexts are essential to their ELD.

Because Toua lives in an enclave community, he has many opportunities for cultural experiences and home language reinforcement. However, there are few occasions for him to use English outside of school, and he does not appreciate or recognize the need to learn academic English. His outgoing personality has helped him to engage with his classmates and develop a solid foundation of

---

[1] Teachers are reminded that maintaining the home language and culture is recommended and should not urge parents of ELLs to speak only English at home.

social English, but his academic language abilities lag behind. In this way, Toua typifies many students at level 3: They have developed the language they need for social interactions but still struggle with academic tasks because they are just beginning to develop academic vocabulary and a command of the more complex language commonly used in the content areas and testing. What may appear to some teachers as laziness on Toua's part is more likely his lack of understanding and background knowledge related to the academic tasks at hand. Toua may also not be as motivated to participate because he lacks a meaningful relationship with his teacher and perceives the teacher's possible frustration with him. This is a watershed moment for Toua; without explicit instruction in how to use language for academic purposes, he is likely to stagnate at level 3 indefinitely. He is in dire need of focused, specific, and sustained differentiated instruction to launch him toward higher English language proficiency (ELP) levels.

While Aung did receive instruction in English before coming to the United States, he does share two of the characteristics of Toua's biographical profile: he is also in the 3rd grade and lives in a home where English is not spoken. As a result, teachers should provide increased interaction opportunities within the school setting for language development to support both Aung and Toua. Toua's language has developed more slowly than Aung's because this is Toua's first experience with formal schooling. In addition, Toua has had fewer opportunities to develop his school-based socialization skills, a fact that might be evident in his classroom behavior. In contrast, Aung behaves quietly and cooperatively, seeming very content with the protocol of school behavior, working diligently and independently as needed. His painstaking handwriting is an example for other students. He is familiar with the format of a written page in terms of neatness, margins, headings, and the like. Because of his "jump start" on literacy in English, Aung is poised to advance on the ELD continuum. However, teachers worry that his increasing absences to translate for his parents have a negative impact on his progress.

Student Descriptors

Students like Toua and Aung at level 3 generally possess a strong foundation of social language and continue to broaden and deepen their academic language when supported with appropriate instruction. In terms of listening, students at level 3 still benefit from sensory support to construct meaning from more detailed and complex discourse. These students can speak and write using increasingly complex sentence structures, though errors sometimes inhibit communication.

Readers are reminded that they must check assessment scores in listening, speaking, reading, and writing individually when considering their students' ELP levels, rather than assuming that a composite score of 3 means that the

Table 6-1   Student Descriptors, Level 3

Listening	Speaking	Reading	Writing
■ Interprets meaning of sentence-level communication in social and general academic contexts ■ Understands main ideas of more complex oral discourse, particularly when supported visually ■ Continues to build repertoire of content and academic vocabulary and sentence structures	■ Generates simple sentences with minimal errors ■ Uses more precise and specific content and academic vocabulary and increasingly complex grammatical structures ■ More complex sentences contain errors that may inhibit communication ■ May appear fluent because of near mastery of social language ■ Content and academic language continues to develop related to concrete and abstract concepts	■ Derives meaning from increasingly complex sentence- and paragraph-level text with visual and teacher support ■ Draws on background knowledge and previous experiences to make sense of longer text	■ Writes increasingly complex sentences ■ Uses a wide range of social vocabulary and a developing range of content and academic vocabulary related to concrete and abstract concepts ■ Errors sometimes obstruct meaning

student scored at level 3 in each language domain. For example, it is relatively common to find students at composite level 3 who score higher in listening and speaking than in reading and writing. Because these students sound like they speak English, teachers may think that they can achieve in class without additional supports and scaffolds. However, these students still need considerable support with reading and writing in English. Teachers therefore need to know how to differentiate instruction and assessment in ways that use oral language to accelerate literacy development in English—and in the home language to the greatest degree possible. Table 6-1 summarizes the student descriptors for level 3 in the domains of listening, speaking, reading, and writing.

Listening

In the domain of listening, students at level 3 can grasp some main ideas of increasingly complex communication, though they still rely on sensory supports to better comprehend details. These students can interpret the meaning of sentence-level communication in social situations (e.g., on the playground or in the hallways) and academic situations (e.g., learning in the classroom). Students at level 3 in listening generally understand the main ideas of more complex oral discourse. For example, these students should be able to comprehend a mini-lesson in class that explains how to categorize animals and plants at different levels of the food chain, particularly when the explanation is visually supported. Students at level 3 in listening continue to build their repertoire of content and academic vocabulary and should polish and expand their listening ability by building vocabulary and knowledge of more complex grammatical constructions.

Speaking

In terms of speaking, students at level 3 can generate simple sentences with minimal errors. These students often attempt higher forms of complexity when they speak for academic purposes, and their errors sometimes inhibit understanding. Students at level 3 in speaking also continue to develop vocabulary and grammatical structures in speech related to both concrete and abstract topics. Because these students often have an extensive ability to communicate socially, teachers could be fooled into thinking that they have reached expectations for grade-level English language skills and therefore prematurely cease differentiation strategies.

Such premature and inappropriate cessation of the provision of ELL-specific teaching and assessment strategies can result in students who may get stuck at level 3 because of this lack of appropriate scaffolding and explicit and informed instruction. Teachers are therefore urged to base instructional decisions on meaningful data from academic state-approved ELP tests and classroom formative assessments designed to inform educators specifically about their students' ELP levels. Any other assessments that have been developed without the needs of ELLs in mind will yield far less useful or meaningful data on which to base instruction.

Reading

In level 3 reading, as in speaking, students continue to make sense of simple text and attempt to construe meaning from increasingly complex writing, still deriving benefit from sensory support to solidify understanding. Students at level 3 in reading can also make sense of more complex genres and texts when their reading comprehension is supported with an appropriate graphic organizer, such as a semantic web, T-chart, or matrix. Teachers can help students attach new academic language (vocabulary, sentence structures, and discourse markers) to the graphic organization of the content in texts that students are reading. Because at level 3 students use their background knowledge and experiences to make sense of increasingly complex and lengthy language and associated concepts, accessing and building student background related to experiences and knowledge is essential.

While the importance of background knowledge is consistent across all levels of language development, academic background knowledge takes center stage as linguistic and content complexity intensifies. It continues to be critical that teachers be fully knowledgeable about their students' social and academic backgrounds, drawing on students' biographical profiles, cumulative folders, and other evidence that can illuminate individual student characteristics, knowledge, and skills. Such an understanding of students' backgrounds provides educators with valuable insight about students' existing reading skills and helps to shape appropriate differentiated instruction.

Writing

At level 3 in writing, students can generate various types of social and academic language with increasing complexity because their writing development tends to mirror their speaking development. Though these students are prone to making errors that can obscure meaning, their vocabulary, sentence, and discourse structures are gaining sophistication. Students at level 3 in writing can produce narrative, expository, and persuasive texts about concrete and abstract topics, especially when their writing is supported with graphic organizers like those used in instruction. As when teaching reading, teachers are advised to incorporate what they know about their students' backgrounds into writing instruction, filling in appropriate background instruction where necessary.

A Word about Language Objectives

Recall that content objectives are derived from the essential learning of an assignment and that language objectives specify how students need to use oral and written language to participate in the range of classroom activities throughout that assignment. Teachers maintain content objectives as more or less the same for all students. In contrast, teachers have the freedom to creatively differentiate language objectives according to what students can be expected to do with listening, speaking, reading, and writing. The student descriptors for students at level 3 lay out what these students can be expected to do independently and with the kinds of instructional supports that encourage their development along the ELD continuum. Teachers can use these student descriptors to articulate the language-based expectations for students at level 3 and the language objectives for any content-area assignment.

Because all four language domains (listening, speaking, reading, and writing) have firmly taken root by level 3, students at this level are uniquely positioned to maximize the results of high-quality assignments/assessments and instruction that are linguistically differentiated.

Example Differentiated Assignment

Table 6-2 is excerpted from the example differentiated assignment we have been working with throughout this book, and here we focus on students who have

Table 6-2 Example Assignment Differentiated for Level 3

	Standards-Based Content or Topic *(from the curriculum)*	
	For a content-based process	
Non-ELL	**Level 3**	**Level 4**
	Language-Based Expectations	
Write a set of instructions using	*Write a set of instructions using*	*Write a set of instructions using*
▪ *Introduction*	▪ Simple, compound, and a few complex sentences	▪ Compound and complex sentences
▪ *Sequential organization*	▪ Introduction (two sentences)	▪ Introduction (two complex sentences)
▪ *Detailed description showing*	▪ Sequential organization	▪ Sequential organization
○ *appropriate grade-level vocabulary*	▪ Ordinal/transition words (first, second, then, next)	▪ Greater variety in transition words (e.g., after, as soon as; meanwhile)
○ *grade-level sentence structures*	▪ Use increasingly precise description, including pretaught academic vocabulary	▪ Increasingly precise description using increasingly grade-level content/academic vocabulary
○ *appropriate and varied transition words*	▪ Conclusion (two sentences)	▪ Conclusion (two complex sentences)
▪ *Conclusion*		

Non-ELL	Level 3	Level 4
	Scaffolding and Support	

Non-ELL

Using

- Model assignment
- Teacher demonstration of the task using a think-aloud
- Sequential graphic organizer to plan writing
- Language wall with sequencing words and key sentence structures
- Feedback designed to push students to produce accurate grade-level writing

Level 3

Using

- Level 3 model assignment
- Teacher demonstration of the task using a think-aloud
- Sequential graphic organizer with increasingly complex sentence starters to plan writing
- Photographs of relevant content-based processes
- Language wall with ordinal/sequencing words (first, second, then, next)
- Word and picture cards featuring an increasing use of academic vocabulary
- Supplementary think-aloud demonstration of paragraph writing
- Simple, compound, and complex academic sentence frames posted in the classroom
- Pictorially supported procedure texts
- Realia related to processes (to use in teaching and writing)
- Additional work on basic literacy skills (for SLIFE)
- Additional time to complete the assignment (for SLIFE)
- Level-appropriate feedback designed to push students to the next level of writing

Level 4

Using

- Level 4 model assignment
- Teacher demonstration of the task using a think-aloud
- Sequential graphic organizer with key complex phrases to plan for writing
- Photographs of relevant content-based processes;
- Language wall with a wide range of sequencing words (color-coded to push students to use more advanced transition words; such as after, as soon as; meanwhile) and complex sentence structures
- Word and picture cards featuring grade-level content/academic vocabulary
- A supplementary think-aloud demonstration of writing smooth transitions between ideas
- Compound and complex academic sentence frames posted in the classroom
- Pictorially supported procedure texts
- Realia related to processes (to use in teaching and writing)
- Additional work on more advanced literacy skills (for SLIFE)
- Additional time to complete the assignment if needed (for SLIFE)
- Level-appropriate feedback designed to push students to the next level of writing

Essential Learning: Clarity in communicating steps in a content-based process, effective use of transition words, and logical sequencing.

Language Demands: Use writing to describe each step in a process, sequence those steps, and explain how following these steps leads to the completion of the process.

reached independent level 3. Recall the example assignment: Students are to write a set of instructions using an introduction, sequential organization, detailed description, appropriate grade-level vocabulary, sentence structures, and transition words for a self-selected content-based process. The essential learning for this assignment is clarity in communicating steps in a content-based process, use of transition words, and logical sequencing and is the same for all students, regardless of ELP level. This assignment focuses on the domain of writing; students use writing to describe, sequence, and explain.

The assignment in this chapter focuses on a 3rd-grade science class that includes Toua and Aung. Recall that Toua's parents are from Laos. Toua was born in a refugee camp in Thailand and has never been to school. Aung was also born in a refugee camp, but he attended school at the camp and learned some English. The teacher needs to consider how these background factors influence the scaffolding and support that each student needs.

This portion of the template is differentiated for students at level 3 in writing, and the blank row at the top of the template includes language-based expectations. Column 1 is for non-ELLs and provides the grade-level language-based expectations for writing in this content-based assignment. Column 2 shows us what students at level 3 in writing can be expected to do independently with language, as well as the scaffolds and supports that help students move along the continuum of language development. Column 3 presents language-based expectations and scaffolding and support for level 4, which is the next ELD level. Students at level 4 in writing are included in this sample assignment so teachers remember to consider the next higher level of language proficiency in designing their expectations for students to push them to ever-higher levels of achievement.

To facilitate the learning and achievement of the ELLs in their classes, teachers can collaborate in a range of ways. For example, a teacher leader or leadership team may have expertise in teaching math and in educating linguistically and culturally diverse learners. The team might develop lesson plans for all math teachers who work with ELLs so that these students can reach a particular math goal or standard. Math teachers could then implement the lesson plans with their ELD colleagues in the math classroom. The teacher leader or coach could observe the math and ELD teachers implement the differentiated lesson and reflect on their practice with them. This approach is an effective way of using coaches, content teachers, and ELD teachers to build capacity in differentiating instruction.

Assignment/Assessment Strategies

Large-scale standardized assessment tools and classroom-based assessments designed for monolingual speakers of English are likely to be inappropriate for students at ELP level 3, yielding invalid information about what these students know and can do because the scores are clouded by language development that is still progressing. As a result, teachers must support ELLs by creating innovative assessments that are sensitive to the linguistic and cultural realities of their students at level 3 so the information gained about what these students know and can do in the content areas is accurate.

All Domains

The following assignment/assessment strategies are generalizable for students at level 3 across the domains of listening, speaking, reading, and writing.

Create and Use Assignments/Assessments That Allow Students to Demonstrate Content Learning without Language Mastery. Students at level 3 have developed the abilities to speak and write such that they can begin to participate more actively in assessments that require English language production. However, persistent errors may be present and may hinder the communication process. For this reason, assessment procedures for students at level 3 must not require language production beyond student capabilities. Instead, teachers are urged to allow students to demonstrate their learning in a variety of authentic ways to show their content knowledge taking into consideration what they can do with English. Teachers can ask students to generate sensory depictions of understanding, such as the creation of a slide presentation or a podcast, embedding the development of technology skills.

Allow Students to Complete Assignments/Assessments with the Support of a Bilingual Teacher or Paraeductor. Some students at level 3 continue to derive much-needed support from the assistance of a bilingual educator when completing assignments/assessments. However, at level 3, the type of bilingual support is likely to involve more clarification than extensive explanation. As with students at levels 1 and 2, this support can be provided individually or in a small-group setting of students with the same language background. For instance, an Arabic-speaking paraeducator could clarify the terms *potential energy* and *kinetic energy* to a small group of Arabic-speaking students who may not fully comprehend the academic English used to explain an assignment/assessment so that these students could demonstrate content understanding.

Differentiate Grading by ELP Level. Teachers should emphasize the positive and recognize that ELLs bring a wealth of background knowledge and contributions to the classroom. To ensure academic success for all students, teachers must advocate for parity of access, not only to the curriculum but also to educational opportunities including advanced courses, which are often determined by grade point averages. When grading students whose language abilities are not on grade level, teachers must distinguish what they are really grading. We advocate that *content* mastery, not *English language* mastery be the focus for grading students at level 3. Moreover, this emphasis should be based on test data that identify language development level. When a student is at level 3, he or she must be graded in a way that recognizes what the student can do with English, without penalizing him or her.

Explain Directions for Assignments/Assessments Orally and Provide Visual Support. To gain an accurate estimate of what students at level 3 know and can do in the content areas, teachers must ensure that students understand how to complete the assignment/assessment procedure. Hopefully, this has been clarified during instruction, but teachers are urged to use whatever means are appropriate, including realia, icons, manipulatives, and models, to ensure that all students comprehend what is being asked of them during assignments/assessments. For example, teachers could familiarize students with how to answer specific types of test items by modeling the process with a sample item, such as by drawing a line connecting a question and a response in a set of matching items.

Simultaneously Assess Content and Language Development. Since general education teachers usually teach language through their content, they are charged with assessing both language and content as appropriate, for example, by asking students to summarize, retell a story, question and respond, analyze, and evaluate. This approach of simultaneously assessing content and language is not new in U.S. classrooms; for instance, teachers routinely assess non-ELLs' vocabulary development in the content areas. At level 3, students are ready to participate in this kind of assessment, though only through differentiation. Teachers must carefully attend to the student descriptors for level 3 when creating assessments for students at this level, ensuring that the linguistic demands of these assessments are in accordance with students' current abilities. For example, when assessing the vocabulary knowledge in science (or any other content area) of students at level 3, teachers must remember that these students are not on grade level in terms of vocabulary development. However, these students have moved beyond general academic vocabulary and are capable of using more specific and precise vocabulary, as scaffolded during instruction. Such vocabulary may be assessed, though teachers could also consider using a word bank.

Table 6-3 provides a summary of assignment/assessment strategies that teachers can use with students at level 3 in listening, speaking, reading, and writing. Teachers are reminded to look individually at students' levels in each of the different domains to identify appropriate assignment/assessment and instruction strategies based on data about what their students can do with English in each domain.

Table 6-3   Assignment and Assessment Strategies for Students at Level 3

Listening	Speaking	Reading	Writing
■ Assess orally, using more precise and specific content vocabulary and increasingly complex grammatical structures ■ Provide visual supports to assess comprehension of more complex sentences and discourse	■ Expect students to produce more complex discourse and sentences using more precise and specific vocabulary ■ Expect language to reflect sentence-level frames and models used during instruction ■ Errors may inhibit communication	■ Use high-quality, age-appropriate, lower-reading-level materials that provide extensive visual support, expecting comprehension of increasingly complex sentence and paragraph-level text ■ Assess orally, using and expecting more precise and specific content vocabulary and increasingly complex grammatical structures ■ When traditional paper-and-pencil tests must be used, employ simplified English and visual support	■ Elicit writing of increasingly complex sentence structures using a developing range of general academic and content-specific vocabulary ■ When traditional paper-and-pencil tests must be used, employ simplified English and visual support

Listening

Teachers can use the following strategies when they assign/assess students at level 3 in listening.

Assess Orally Using More Precise and Specific Content Vocabulary and Increasingly Complex Grammatical Structures. Although students at level 3 in listening are still acquiring their English skills, they are capable of comprehending content-specific vocabulary that reflects increasing precision and specificity. Teachers are encouraged to use a wider range of general academic and specialized content-area vocabulary and more complex sentences about increasingly complex topics, providing concrete support.

Provide Visual Supports to Assess Comprehension of More Complex Discourse and Sentence Structures. Students at level 3 in listening can be expected to comprehend social and academic language about familiar or concrete topics. However, teachers do need to provide visual supports like graphic organizers, realia, manipulatives, and models when expecting students to comprehend complex sentences and discourse. Teachers are encouraged to use the same visual supports to assess listening that were used in instruction. For example, if the teacher used a graphic organizer to show the stages in the water cycle during instruction, he or she should use the same graphic organizer to support students' comprehension during assessment.

Speaking

Teachers can use the following strategies when creating assignments/assessments for students at level 3 in speaking.

Expect Students to Produce More Complex Discourse and Sentences Using More Precise and Specific Vocabulary during Assignments and throughout Assessment. Students at level 3 in speaking start to produce much more oral language about general academic and content-specific vocabulary they have studied, complex sentences that they have learned, and extended discourse that they have become familiar with. However, teachers need to target this more extensive vocabulary and complex oral language at the sentence and discourse level during instruction and use the same types of supports when assessing.

Expect Language to Reflect Sentence-Level Frames and Models Used during Instruction. To support students at level 3 in speaking, teachers are encouraged to use the same sentence-level frames and models for language that they used during instruction. Teachers must remember that there is no equation for determining what constitutes level 3 vocabulary; it extends beyond general academic language but it does not represent grade-level production. For instance, when discussing layers of the rain forest a student at level 2 in speaking might refer to its *top*. A student at level 3 might talk about the *ceiling*, whereas a student using grade-level vocabulary would use the term *canopy*.

Errors May Inhibit Communication. Because students at level 3 in speaking are producing longer and more complex oral language at the sentence, word, and discourse levels, their spoken language is likely to exhibit more errors. Teachers are encouraged to focus on content when using oral language to assess these students' content learning because that is the purpose of the assessment. Teachers can make note of the errors that students at level 3 make and focus instruction on the specific errors in sentence and discourse structure at another time, perhaps during designated ELD time. However, academic vocabulary that has been taught as part of content-area instruction is part of content learning, so it is fair game for assessment of students at level 3 in speaking.

Reading

Teachers can use the following strategies when creating assignments/assessments for students at level 3 in reading.

Use High-Quality, Visually Supported, Age-Appropriate Reading Materials Matched to Students' Reading Levels, Expecting Comprehension of Increasingly Complex Sentence and Paragraph-Level Text. Students at level 3 in reading are beginning to make sense of sentence and paragraph-level texts but are still below grade level in terms of English reading ability. To scaffold these students' reading ability, the use of visually supported lower-reading-level material is matched to student data. Whereas grade-level reading materials are unlikely to be at the instructional level of students at level 3, they should not be used to assess students at level 3 in reading either. The lower-reading-level materials used for scaffolding can contribute to increased comprehension and can be used as part of the assessment. In addition to finding lower-reading-level materials at public libraries, school libraries, area education agencies, and other venues, these materials can be obtained from a variety of publishers.

Assess Orally Using and Expecting More Precise and Specific Content Vocabulary and Increasingly Complex Grammatical Structures. Maintaining high expectations for students at level 3 in reading that are closely matched with the student descriptors helps these students continue their progress from level 3 to higher ELP levels. Only through the consistent teaching of precise general academic and content-specific vocabulary can teachers expect such vocabulary to be operational at the time of assessment. The same is true for the teaching and assessment of increasingly complex grammatical structures. Teachers must be explicit in their instruction and insistent on the production of general academic and content-specific vocabulary and increasingly complex grammatical structures during assessment. Further, teachers must recognize the purpose and responsibility of their assessment: to provide students at level 3 in reading the opportunity to perform to the best of their linguistic abilities, showcasing the highest extent of their content knowledge and skills. An example of increasing grammatical complexity would be moving from two simple sentences such as "Glass is hard. A diamond is harder." to a complex sentence using the comparative like "A diamond is harder than glass."

When Traditional Paper-and-Pencil Tests Must Be Used, Employ Simplified English and Visual Support. By definition, students at level 3 in reading cannot effectively demonstrate their content knowledge and skills on tests that require grade-level English reading skills. Further, the range of development at level 3 in reading is extremely broad, with students who are entering level 3 differing greatly from those at the upper reaches of level 3. Thus, the language of assessments must consider intralevel variations and provide supports for the beginning end of the level 3 spectrum. For instance, while students at the advanced end of level 3 in reading might not rely heavily on pictorial support like clip art, icons, or graphs, students just entering level 3 in reading would likely require such support to make sense of the assessment instrument. Simplified English may mean changing a passive construction such as "A [protractor] is needed to measure the size of an angle" to an active construction like "We use a [protractor] to measure the size of an angle." A picture of a protractor could also be included with this test item if vocabulary alone were being assessed (Fairbairn, 2007).

Writing

Teachers can use the following assignment/assessment strategies with students at level 3 in writing.

Elicit Writing of Increasingly Complex Sentence Structures Using a Developing Range of General Academic and Content-Specific Vocabulary. When prompting students to demonstrate their content knowledge and skills, teachers should call for level 3 production in writing. To do so, however, it is recommended that teachers frame their prompts using language that students are certain to comprehend.

Comprehension of the assessment prompt should not be part of what is assessed; rather, teachers should be assessing the written response to the prompt. If the prompt cannot be understood, then the teacher has no opportunity to evaluate a response. Once the student understands the task at hand, she or he can produce level 3 writing in response. Teachers may need to specify the kinds of vocabulary and grammar that are expected. For example, the teacher could explicitly say, "Use the words discussed in class and write in complete, detailed sentences," or the teacher could provide an academic sentence frame or two to model what is expected.

When Traditional Paper-and-Pencil Tests Must Be Used, Employ Simplified English and Visual Support. This strategy applies equally to tests of reading and tests of writing. Teachers must be sure to elicit responses using understandable language and visual supports, such as clip art and graphs, where needed. For instance, students could be asked to explain the plant growth process by sequencing and labeling pictures of a seed, a sprout, a seedling, and a plant.

Instructional Strategies

We begin this section with the guiding principles that teachers need to embrace when they are responsible for teaching content and language to students who are learning English as a new language. Effective ELL teachers need to do the following:

1. Examine their assumptions about working with students from the particular linguistic and cultural backgrounds in their classes
2. Learn about students' language, literacy, cultural, and educational backgrounds to identify what resources they can draw on

3. Determine students' instructional levels based on their content-area knowledge and skills and their ELD levels
4. Teach essential learning from the curriculum and its associated language in a differentiated manner

These critical action steps are keys to scaffolding student learning of language and content. The incorporation of all four critical action steps is never more important than at level 3, where students are often relegated to the status of "lifelong level 3s." In other words, without appropriate differentiated instruction, these students are at risk of failing to move beyond level 3.[2] Readers may be familiar with the term *long-term English language learner (LTELL)* that is sometimes used to refer to these students. We prefer not to use this term because it deflects responsibility for ongoing ELD from teachers and the school system.

Because students at level 3 have developed language abilities across all domains, the instruction and assessment strategies described in this section have distinctly powerful potential to scaffold student abilities—but only if they are appropriately applied. Without such appropriate instruction and assessment, students at level 3 may miss the opportunity to continue to develop higher levels of English and to achieve academically at school.

All Domains

Teachers can use the following strategies across all domains with students at level 3 in listening, speaking, reading, and writing.

Provide Sensory Support for Every Lesson. Sensory experiences—for example, using real objects, pictures, hands-on materials and experiences, nonverbal communication, demonstrations, modeling, and simulations—provide students with "mental Velcro" to which they can attach new learning of language and content. As grade-level content becomes more complex, this strategy continues to offer excellent support for students at level 3. For example, when starting a physics class focused on the topic of friction, the teacher could begin by asking students to rub their hands together to create heat. He or she could then build on this shared experience to introduce vocabulary and conceptual learning related to the topic of friction, making connections to what students already know through experience.

Explicitly Teach and Require Students to Use Increasingly Complex General Academic and Content-Specific Vocabulary and Sentence Structures. Because students have a

---

[2] Based on our own experience and on the input of teachers around the United States, non-ELLs may also use oral and written language according to the student descriptors for level 3, particularly in reading and writing. Such students need the same type of linguistically differentiated instruction as ELLs at level 3.

grasp of basic sentence structure and academic vocabulary at level 3, teachers must continue their informed developmental expectation that students must expand their abilities to generate more complex language. For example, science teachers can target language development by providing and eliciting more complex academic sentence frames such as, "*Despite the fact that* the polar ice cap is melting _____.*" Teachers can use academic sentence frames across content areas and should collaborate to ensure that such frames and general academic and content-specific vocabulary are implemented throughout the curriculum. Such intentional work to build academic language pays dividends when students participate in large-scale standardized testing, which often uses this type of formal language.

Table 6-4 presents instructional strategies in listening, speaking, reading, and writing for students at level 3. Teachers need to remember that students at level 3 overall may not be at level 3 in each of the four domains individually—students' listening and speaking skills often develop faster than their skills at reading and writing in English. Teachers therefore need to identify which students are at level 3 in which domains and use the strategies accordingly to push their students along the ELD continuum.

Table 6-4　Instructional Strategies for Students at Level 3

Listening	Speaking	Reading	Writing
■ Scaffold students' language development by using increasingly complex language, paraphrasing as needed ■ Allow sufficient wait time ■ Model the completion of graphic organizers to build higher-order thinking ■ Employ think-alouds to model both process and language	■ Provide opportunities for producing extended oral language through activities such as reporting and presentations ■ Scaffold extended oral language production by providing increasingly complex sentence frames ■ Concentrate on students' meaning rather than correct grammar	■ Implement a high-quality, research-based, culturally and linguistically appropriate reading development program ■ Use high-quality, visually supported, age-appropriate reading materials matched to students' reading levels ■ Build background and help students make connections to prior learning and experiences ■ Incorporate shared, shared-to-guided, and guided reading ■ Model the use of graphic organizers to build higher-order thinking	■ Provide opportunities for producing extended written discourse ■ Scaffold extended written language production by providing sentence-level frames ■ Incorporate modeled, shared, and guided writing activities ■ Accept increasingly complex sentences in lieu of grade-level writing expectations ■ Ask students to write expanded sentences using a range of complexity ■ Concentrate on students' meaning rather than grammatical correctness ■ Ask students to create and use identity texts ■ Model the use of graphic organizers

Listening

Teachers can use the following instructional strategies with students at level 3 in listening.

Scaffold Students' Language Development by Using Increasingly Complex Language, Paraphrasing as Needed. As students at level 3 develop their sophistication in terms of listening, teachers must concentrate on providing increasingly complex aural input. Students only enhance their recognition of more complex language if they receive such stimuli, contextualized through classroom activities. As teachers help students heighten their listening skills, they must be conscious of the incremental nature of language development and offer a range of paraphrases that clarify and restate meaning. For example, when asking a student about her or his science experiment, the teacher might ask, "What was the outcome of the procedure? That is, what happened?" In this way, students who did not understand the first question would still be able to participate through the support afforded by the second question. Through the sustained use of this strategy, teachers provide essential support that these students need to develop their listening skills.

Allow Sufficient Wait Time. As students at level 3 in listening attempt to process and generate increasingly complex language, they continue to benefit from (and require!) additional processing and wait time, even up to 10 seconds. When these students articulate academic sentence frames, especially for the first time, patience on the part of the teacher encourages sustained effort from the students and should lead to growth in language and content learning.

Model the Completion of Graphic Organizers to Build Higher-Order Thinking. Graphic organizers and concept maps continue to help students at level 3 in listening understand inter-relationships among concepts to facilitate higher-order thinking. These students can benefit greatly when teachers incorporate strategies that allow them to conceptualize more complex ideas while they are still learning English. Improving the comprehensibility and contextualization of content through graphic organizers facilitates the production of increasingly complex language in English. For instance, a social studies teacher could construct and complete a concept map when discussing the inter-relationships between political parties.

Employ Think-Alouds to Model Process and Language. This strategy can be used to teach specific processes for students at level 3 in listening, such as the writing of a summary. The teacher models steps for writing a summary, thinking aloud to describe both the cognitive processes and language that are part of the summary-writing process. These think-alouds can assist all students, ELLs and non-ELLs, in developing content skills and important general academic and content-specific language.

Speaking

The following instructional strategies can be used to scaffold and support students at level 3 in speaking.

Provide Opportunities for Producing Extended Oral Language through Activities Like Reporting and Presentations. Students at level 3 in speaking are uniquely prepared and motivated to participate in meaningful instruction through speaking, particularly when such activities are relevant, interesting, and authentic. The activities must be differentiated, and the student must receive appropriate support in carrying out the tasks. For example, one of the authors engaged students at level 3 in speaking through collaboration with a local university professor. Each student was to create a slide presentation based on personal experiences about how to teach English to speakers of other languages for future ELL teachers at the university. This authentic task was exceptionally motivating because the students drew on their own background knowledge as ELLs and presented their content to a real university audience. Supported by a template to develop the slide presentation, students grew in both writing and technology skills as they honed their speaking and presentation abilities. Such integrated development across domains offers an ideal avenue for language growth. In spite of the demanding task, these students succeeded with teacher and peer support (Vann & Fairbairn, 2003).

Scaffold Extended Oral Language Production by Providing Increasingly Complex Sentence Frames. When teachers are conscious of the necessity for language development, they are better prepared to insist on high-quality responses, including increasingly complex sentence structures and vocabulary. Rather than accepting one-word answers or social language as appropriate academic responses from students at level 3 in speaking, teachers can provide sentence frames like "As a result of the interaction of _____ and _____." Teachers must insist on high-quality responses from all students, avoiding the trap of responding to any utterance a student might produce. Insisting on high-quality responses supports all students as they prepare not only for more advanced education but also for viability in the future workplace. For example, avoid asking a question such as,

What is the name of the type of animal that can live on land and in water?

Such a question would likely elicit a one-word answer:

Amphibian

Instead, a teacher might ask a question that elicits the characteristics of the animal:

Who can tell me some characteristics of an amphibian?

Additionally, the teacher can provide an academic sentence frame, orally and in writing, for student reference. In this case, the academic sentence frame might be

Unlike reptiles, amphibians are characterized by the fact that they _____.

Concentrate on Students' Meaning Rather Than on Correct Grammar. Teachers must support the ELD of students at level 3 in speaking by embedding sustained teacher and peer interactions that scaffold speaking development. In this context, teachers should continue to concentrate on the meaning of student speech rather than on errors. Detailed corrections in speaking are not helpful to students at level 3. Rather, teachers should target limited, preidentified aspects of language for correction, such as the pronunciation of high-frequency academic words (e.g., *measure*). In this way, students learn to monitor their production incrementally rather than becoming overwhelmed by a variety of confusing error corrections. For example, teachers might insist on the use of dependent clauses in oral communication about content, having provided examples using academic sentence frames.

Reading

Implement a High-Quality, Research-Based, Culturally and Linguistically Appropriate Reading Development Program. The necessity of understanding a student's background in home language literacy cannot be overstated. The needs of students at level 3 in reading who are not yet able to read in the home language profoundly affect these students' progress toward grade-level reading ability. This progress is slowed, in part, because of their lack of reading skills relative to their peers who are able to transfer reading skill from the home language. These students require focused attention on reading and more time to develop and practice their reading skills. Skilled and trained reading teachers, paraeducators, and volunteers should (continue to) support students at level 3 in reading as they develop their reading skills because these students are ready to gain meaning from print independently.

While students who have had the opportunity to acquire literacy skills in their home languages are likely to progress at a faster rate, both groups require culturally and linguistically appropriate reading development programming that is effective for ELLs at this level. If these students do not receive targeted reading support, they continue to be at risk for school failure. To the extent possible, reading materials should reflect the full range of diverse learners in the classroom.

Use High-Quality, Visually Supported, Age-Appropriate Reading Materials Matched to Students' Reading Levels. Students at level 3 in reading cannot be expected to make sense of grade-level reading materials without significant support. The best way to support the mandate to teach all students to the same content standards is by using materials that match the developing reading level of students. To compensate for the inability to understand meaning presented in grade-level texts, materials that are written at a more accessible level and that incorporate a variety of visual supports must be provided for students at level 3.

Build Background and Help Students to Make Connections to Prior Learning and Experiences. Teachers must ensure that students at level 3 in reading begin learning experiences on a level playing field by building the background knowledge needed for success. Teachers can and should also guide students in making connections to their own background knowledge and experiences because many students do not automatically make such connections. For example, some students may have personal experience with the curricular topic of earthquakes. This type of background knowledge should be ascertained and brought to the fore in instruction.

Incorporate Shared, Shared-To-Guided, and Guided Reading. Because students at level 3 in reading continue to work toward grade level (with the possible exception of early elementary students), continuing or beginning to use shared, shared-to-guided, and guided reading is essential. Teachers are reminded that, regardless of the student's age, appropriate reading instruction is imperative. Shared, shared-to-guided, and guided reading provide irreplaceable and essential opportunities for students at level 3 in reading to practice and develop their reading abilities. Content-area books at appropriate reading levels can be used to teach reading while simultaneously supporting learning in the subject areas. Teachers might also consider sending accessible reading materials home with students, in the form of either level-appropriate curricular texts or reproducible books (Fountas & Pinnell, 2017; Knox & Amador-Watson, 2000).

Model the Use of Graphic Organizers to Build Higher-Order Thinking. Students at level 3 in reading can continue to capitalize on the integration of graphic organizers for their reading development, particularly as important scaffolding to the related domain of writing. By developing graphic-organizer literacy through a variety of visual representations for conceptualizing thoughts, relationships, and connections, students at level 3 can sharpen complex ways of understanding and articulating their thinking. These tools should be used routinely to ensure that these students have a ready schema to draw on for finetuning new learning—for example, a sequential graphic organizer, with visual support as needed, can be used to demonstrate understanding of how to complete a recipe.

Writing

Students at level 3 in writing in English who have yet to develop writing skills in their home languages likely require more time than their peers who can write in their home languages to progress in writing. As with the incremental development of grade-level reading skills, writing development of all learners is, in part, a function of practice over time. Thus, students at level 3 in writing must be afforded many opportunities to write, particularly in contextualized and meaningful situations, while receiving differentiated support.

Provide Opportunities to Produce Extended Written Discourse. Teachers can encourage students at level 3 in writing through activities such as journaling, report writing, and preparing presentations. This strategy applies equally to speaking and writing. With sufficient scaffolding, including templates and individual assistance, students at level 3 can create extended pieces of writing. Guided writing also may facilitate the creation of such pieces and reduce errors.

Scaffold Extended Written Language Production by Providing Sentence-Level Frames. Teachers can use sentence frames such as, "As a result of the interaction of _____ and _____," to support the writing development of students at level 3. This strategy applies equally to speaking and writing. As with word walls and concept walls, templates for broader discourse—language walls—should be accompanied by pictures, icons, charts, and other meaningful representations. Providing templates in the form of academic sentence frames and larger models for various forms of discourse builds a language repertoire for students at level 3 in writing to draw on across the curriculum. Such practical templates should be visibly posted in the classroom for ease of student reference. For example, teachers could post the format of a lab report, including the required components, supported visually. Again, the need for visual support is dependent on the student's level of language development, rather than on his or her age or grade level.

Incorporate Modeled, Shared, and Guided Writing Activities. As students at level 3 in writing learn that writing is an increasingly complex thought applied to paper, modeled, shared, and guided writing activities offer ways to enhance these students' writing abilities. When these students observe the teacher in modeled writing and interact with a peer or with the teacher, they can see what competent writing with increasing complexity looks like. Having experienced an appropriate writing model, level 3 writers can then apply that knowledge to their own practice in a guided writing setting (with teacher support) and, eventually, independently. These techniques could work well, for example, when these students are writing narrative or expository text in a workshop environment.

Accept Increasingly Complex Sentences in Lieu of Grade-Level Writing Expectations. Teachers must set their expectations for students at level 3 in writing in keeping with the student descriptors. While these students can write increasingly complex sentences with a developing range of academic vocabulary, they cannot produce grade-level writing because errors can obstruct meaning.[3] Students at level 3 in writing, like their counterparts at level 2, must be afforded sufficient time and opportunity to develop their writing, just as their non-ELL peers likely experienced in the early elementary grades. For example, if the assignment is for students to write a fairy tale, the writing of students at level 3 may be shorter and less complex in terms of structure and vocabulary than that of non-ELLs. Length would likely be diminished because of the increased time that it takes students at level 3 to produce writing.

Ask Students to Write Expanded Sentences Using a Range of Complexity. To ensure that students at level 3 in writing use a variety of increasingly complex sentence structures, teachers must provide, model, and post suggested academic sentence frames showing students how to combine simple sentences into compound sentences. This scaffolding allows students to write longer, more complex sentences commensurate with their capabilities at this level. Content teachers have an ideal forum to teach this meaningful augmentation of writing ability in the context of their subject areas. For instance, science teachers could ask students to combine simple sentences in science reports to create compound or complex sentences. Teachers should routinely hold students accountable for producing increasingly complex language, in writing and in speaking.

Concentrate on Student Meaning Rather Than Correcting Grammar. As with students on this same level in speaking, teachers should focus on students' meaning in writing rather than on errors included in the written message. Error correction should be limited to preidentified, level-appropriate aspects of language. For instance, if a student were to write, "When I finish graduating, I intend to visit Mexico," a teacher might ignore the grammatical inaccuracies in the first part of the sentence and simply continue the conversation.

Ask Students to Create and Use Identity Texts. Identity texts, in which students at level 3 in writing draw on their own backgrounds and experiences using English and their home languages, engage these students in meaningful language development. According to a student participant,

---

[3] The authors recognize that, in the lower elementary grades, increasingly complex sentences with significant errors may fall within the range of grade-level performance. Again, guidance must be interpreted in terms of grade-level norms for language.

I have my own inner skills to show the world … and I felt that those skills of mine are important also … I could actually show the world that I am something.… And that's how it helped me and it made me so proud of myself that I am actually capable of doing something.…I am something." (Cummins & Early, 2011, p. 50)

Because identity texts can often be adapted to meet requirements of grade-level content standards, they provide an important avenue for engaging and affirming students as intellectually capable and contributing members of the community. For example, inviting students to present on their own cultures and countries in a social studies unit positions them as classroom experts and affords them an often elusive status as knowledgeable and authoritative. Another benefit is that these identity texts provide all students with the opportunities to gain important perspectives on other countries and cultures.

Model the Use of Graphic Organizers. Graphic organizers can be used in conjunction with academic sentence frames as a springboard for complex language production. For instance, students at level 3 in writing might complete a Venn diagram comparing two countries and conclude by writing a summary based on the intersection of the two circles. The teacher could provide an academic sentence frame such as, "While India produces _____ and Thailand produces _____, both countries produce _____." Such explicit language instruction provides students with more complex ways to express content meaning that they intuitively understand but are unable to articulate, while providing a repertoire of templates for future use. All students, including non-ELLs, in the classroom benefit from this type of academic language instruction.

Instruction That Integrates Language Domains

As seen in the university–school partnership mentioned earlier, the more authentic a teaching and learning activity is, the more likely it is to integrate the four language domains of listening, speaking, reading, and writing. Teachers are urged to fully integrate instruction related to all four language domains to use all of them on a regular basis.

Conclusion

Teachers were encouraged to match strategies with student language proficiency levels for each individual language domain. That is, if a student is at level 3 in speaking but at level 1 in writing, strategies from level 3 should be applied to speaking and strategies from level 1 to writing. Teachers were also reminded that large-scale standardized assessment tools and classroom-based assessments designed for monolingual English speakers are likely to be inappropriate for students at level 3, yielding invalid information about what students know and can do because the scores are clouded by a student's ELP levels in listening, speaking, reading, and writing. As a result, teachers must support these students by creating innovative assessments that are sensitive to the linguistic and cultural realities of students at level 3 to gain accurate information about what these students know and can do in the content areas.

Professional Learning Activities

Working individually or with others in professional learning communities, differentiate the first four assignments for Toua and Aung. For assignment 5, choose the assignment and differentiate it for at least one of the level 3 ELD students in your class. When differentiating for students at ELD level 3, remember that they may be at different ELD levels in listening, speaking, reading, and writing.

Differentiating for Toua and Aung

For assignments 1–4, differentiate the language-based expectations and scaffolding and support needed for level 3 students Toua and Aung. Recall that both are 3rd-grade students at level 3 in listening, speaking, reading, and writing in English. However, Toua is in the SLIFE category and does not read in his home language. Further, Aung has had some schooling in English from the missionaries in his refugee camp.

1. Read the assignment above the template.
2. Read the essential learning and language demands below the template.
3. Review the standards-based topic, language-based expectations for non-ELLs.
4. Complete the template to show the differentiated assignment for Toua and Aung by adding appropriate language-based expectations and scaffolding and support for these students.

After you complete the template, read on for additional insight on how to differentiate this assignment.

Assignment 1: *Write a two-page report*

Standards-Based Content or Topic (from the curriculum)	
About a president	
Non-ELL	**Level 3**
Language-Based Expectations	
■ *Write a two-page report*	■ ■ ■ ■
Scaffolding and Support	
Using	*Using*
■ *A graphic organizer for note taking and library-based resources*	■ *A graphic organizer for note taking and library-based resources* ■ ■ ■

Essential Learning: *Identify main idea and details in informational texts about a president, and, using evidence from the text, present a report.*

Language Demands: *Use oral and written language to identify, summarize, give an opinion, and argue.*

Toua and Aung might be asked to report on the current president to facilitate building on their background knowledge because they are most likely to have some knowledge of current events and the sitting president. Their writing may be shorter than the writing of non-ELLs but should include increasingly complex sentences and academic vocabulary. Books and source materials with extensive visual supports appropriate for readers at level 3 should be provided for both students. Also, a graphic organizer that includes academic sentence frames and visual supports can help them with note taking. The teacher should take care to show examples of successfully completed assignments and to model the use of research materials, graphic organizers, and sentence frames.

Toua and Aung require some assistance with the process of writing to ensure that the final product is comprehensible. Toua needs more support with the reading and writing process than Aung, and his report is likely to be shorter, because Aung's written English has been accelerated by his previous writing instruction.

Assignment 2: *Write and present*

Standards-Based Content or Topic (from the curriculum)	
An original haiku	

Non-ELL	Level 3
Language-Based Expectations	
Recite aloud	▪ ▪ ▪ ▪
Scaffolding and Support	
Using ▪ *Memory only, based on teacher modeling of the writing of a haiku* ▪ *Teacher modeling of poetry reading* ▪ *In-class analysis of the haiku form* ▪ *Choral reading of several haiku poems*	*Using* ▪ *Memory only, based on teacher modeling of the writing of a haiku* ▪ *Teacher modeling of poetry reading* ▪ *In-class analysis of the haiku form* ▪ *Choral reading of several haiku poems* ▪ ▪ ▪

Essential Learning: *Poetry-writing skills; presentation skills, including eye contact, volume, expression, and fluency of speech; memorization skills; developing familiarity with poetic forms.*

Language Demands: *Use the haiku genre orally and in writing.*

Having modeled the writing of a haiku, the teacher models the reading of the poem, emphasizing eye contact, volume, expression, and fluency. The form of the haiku is analyzed with the class using the templates provided. The class then participates in the choral reading of several haikus. Tips for memorization are provided. The teacher works with Toua and Aung individually to assist in writing their haikus, and they practice presenting poems with the ELL teacher or a paraeducator before presenting to the class. Toua and Aung each present a simple original haiku, but their support is individualized according to their particular needs throughout the process. Recall that Toua may need additional support because of his SLIFE status.

Assignment 3: *Complete math story problems*

Standards-Based Content or Topic (from the curriculum):
Math story problems

Non-ELL	Level 3
Language-Based Expectations	
■ *Complete a page of math story problems*	■ ■ ■ ■
Scaffolding and Support	
Using	*Using*
■ *Instruction in the meaning of math phrases (e.g., greater than, in all)* ■ *Learning from teacher modeling of the translation of problems from prose to numbers using manipulatives*	■ *Instruction in the meaning of math phrases (e.g., greater than, in all)* ■ *Learning from teacher modeling of the translation of problems from prose to numbers using manipulatives* ■ ■ ■

Essential Learning: *Convert informational text into a mathematical equation.*
Language Demands: *Use oral and written language to identify main ideas and details in math word problems, compare and contrast, explain math solving problem processes.*

The teacher explicitly teaches the math phrases, such as *greater than* and *in all*, that describe math functions found in the story problems. The teacher then models the translation of several problems from prose to numbers using manipulatives and provides opportunities for guided practice, giving Toua and Aung the extra assistance they need. Because Aung and Toua are at ELP level 3, they may be expected to complete a representative portion of a page of assigned story problems, such as the even- or odd-numbered problems. This allows the student extra time on each problem.

Because of Toua's SLIFE status, his literacy development and math development are likely to follow a different trajectory than Aung's. As such, Toua could benefit from additional one-on-one support in both reading and writing to complete this assignment.

Assignment 4: *Create and present a song, rap, or chant*

Standards-Based Content or Topic (from the curriculum)	
About the moon's phases	

Non-ELL	Level 3
Language-Based Expectations	
■ *Create a song, rap, or chant*	■ ■ ■
Scaffolding and Support	
Using	*Using*
■ *Visually supported instruction on phases of the moon* ■ *Example as a model* ■ *Discussion of rhythm and rhyme* ■ *Discussion and modeling of presentation skills*	■ ■ ■ ■

Essential Learning: *Develop rhythm, rhyme, and presentation skills; explain the moon's phases.*

Language Demands: *Use oral and written language to describe, sequence, and explain using a particular genre (song, rap, or chant).*

The moon's phases are taught with video clips and manipulatives. The teacher models (or shows a video clip of) a song, rap, or chant about some other topic in science. The class analyzes the elements of rhythm and rhyme; presentation skills are explicitly discussed and modeled. Then in a workshop format students begin creating their final products as the teacher circulates throughout the room to help students, giving particular attention to Toua and Aung.

Depending on the context, Toua and Aung might work together on the assignment or with one-on-one support from a bilingual educator or a trained buddy. Toua, because of his SLIFE experience and the various elements of writing, is likely to need additional individualized support for literacy development—though he may be on par with his peers in terms of the understanding of this particular content.

Differentiating for Your Students

For assignment 5, choose an assignment from your curriculum. Differentiate the assignment for a student at ELP level 3 in your class. Consider how student background factors like prior schooling, home language literacy, cultural orientation, and challenging experiences are likely to influence this student's content and language learning in your classroom.

1. Write the assignment at the top of the template.
2. Identify the essential learning and language demands, and write this below the template.
3. Fill in the standards-based topic, language-based expectations for non-ELLs and for your student at ELP level 3.
4. Plan and implement the assignment in your classroom. If possible, videotape the lesson or invite an ELL coordinator or coach to observe the lesson. Focus on the teacher's use of appropriate differentiation strategies for students at level 3 in any domain.

Assignment 5: _____

Standards-Based Content or Topic (from the curriculum)

Non-ELL	Level 3
Language-Based Expectations	
■	■ ■ ■ ■
Scaffolding and Support	
Using ■	*Using* ■ ■ ■

Essential Learning: _____

Language Demands: _____

Chapter 7

Differentiating
for Students at Level 4

*I think what it shows is that everyone can do something and make a
difference in this world. We might not be able to do it all but we can do
something, and isn't there great satisfaction in that? The happiest people
I know are people who are doing things for other people.*

— FORMER GOVERNOR ROBERT D. RAY,
founder of the Iowa Bureau of Refugee Services

This chapter focuses on students at level 4. We begin by describing student
characteristics in the domains of listening, speaking, reading, and writing and
continue with our example differentiated writing assignment, with attention
to students at level 4 in writing. Then we offer level-appropriate assignment/
assessment and instructional strategies for students at level 4 in each domain.
Teachers are reminded to be relentless in their insistence that students continue to advance and develop their facility with listening, speaking, reading,
and writing to achieve higher levels of English language proficiency (ELP).
Only through providing a vision and definition of what comprises social and
academic English for students at this level, appropriate and focused assignments/
assessments and instruction, and consistent targeted feedback, can teachers
support students' continuous development of content and language. Teachers
must be vigilant to prevent stalling at any stage of linguistic development, particularly in the areas of reading and writing, which tend to develop more slowly
than listening and speaking. To avoid such potential stagnation in language
development—which can result from a lack of targeted instruction—teachers are
encouraged to regularly consult all data available to them, including ELP levels,
student work, and portfolios. Along with the guidance in this book, teachers
can use such student-specific information to design appropriate assignments/
assessments and instruction, while maintaining the responsive vigilance needed
to push students to higher levels of academic achievement and language profi-

ciency. This combination supports students at level 4 in continuing to advance along the ELD continuum to level 5. In this way, teachers are able to elicit level 4 production, as well as (through providing and eliciting where deemed appropriate) increasingly refined examples of level 5 language production.

Variation in Students' Backgrounds

Student Scenarios

Mariella, a 5th-grade student, was born in El Salvador and was adopted as a 2nd grader by a monolingual English-speaking family. She now has a sister who is also in 5th grade and a brother in 1st grade. Mariella did not learn to read or write Spanish prior to arriving in the United States because poverty prevented her from attending school. However, she has made quick progress in learning English because her new home environment immerses her in the English language and U.S. culture. In addition, Mariella's sister tutors her in class work. Mariella regularly reads lower-reading-level books to her brother, though she can read some 5th-grade text if it is well supported with visuals and context clues. Her writing has been helped by the fact that her sister and their friends regularly text each other on their cell phones. Her entire family has been very supportive and encouraging of Mariella's ELD, as well as the retention of Spanish language and Salvadoran culture. They have demonstrated consistent patience when her lack of socialization in school has led to a rocky adjustment to classroom routines. Because some of her behavior in 3rd grade was deemed inappropriate at school (e.g., roaming the halls), her teachers referred her for special education, though she was not placed in the program.

Rafael, another 5th-grade student, came to the United States from Mexico with his uncle and two young cousins in 1st grade. Rafael was at grade level in his Mexican elementary school and surpassed many of his peers in reading ability in Spanish. His speedy acquisition of English led his English as a second language teacher to refer him for talented and gifted programming, but he could not earn a high enough score on the standardized test to qualify. While at school, Rafael is an engaged student. He completes scaffolded and supported grade-level assignments when given class time, though not when assignments are given as homework. He happily participates in group work and gets along well with his peers, in the classroom and on the soccer field. Though his English is not perfect, his errors rarely hinder understanding. He wants to play the trumpet, but his uncle cannot afford to purchase an instrument for him.

While both Mariella and Rafael speak Spanish and have experienced the struggles of low socioeconomic status, the rest of their backgrounds are quite dissimilar. Mariella's extreme living situation in El Salvador and limited formal schooling contributed to her adjustment issues in the United States. Such difficulties with classroom socialization, peer relationships, and academic progress, specifically in terms of literacy development, can be more readily understood when teachers apply the lens of previous educational experiences. With appropriate instruction targeting Mariella's specific linguistic and academic needs, as well as the additional cultural and linguistic support from home, she has made excellent progress in 5th grade. She is approaching proficiency in English and in the content areas. The concerns about her behavior that led to the special education referral were deflected by an astute special education teacher. This teacher recognized that Mariella's problematic behaviors and initially low levels of academic achievement were caused by the normal new language development processes and by the need for significant social and cultural adjustments, rather than by a cognitive or behavioral disorder.

Rafael, on the other hand, arrived in his U.S. classroom with strong academic skills already developed in Spanish. This experience positioned him to transfer those skills to English, and as a result, his teachers saw his ELD progress quickly. Unfortunately, as noted, he has been unable to score high enough on the standardized test designed for non-English language learners (ELLs) that his district requires for placement in the talented and gifted program. This mismatch of testing practice does not minimize the fact that Rafael is, indeed, a talented and gifted student. He would be much better served if his district would adopt more culturally and linguistically sensitive identification and testing procedures and then serve him through appropriate talented and gifted programming.

Another issue for consideration is the fact that Rafael does not hand in homework regularly, despite reminders from his teachers. They are confused by his behavior because he attends so well to work done in the classroom and certainly does not lack the skills needed to complete the homework. What his teachers might discover in a home visit is that Rafael's uncle does not speak English and is unable to help him with his homework. Further, his uncle does not see the need to complete the homework because Rafael is doing well in the classroom. Also, there is no dedicated place at home for him to do his homework, and his cousins interrupt any efforts to complete it. Finally, Rafael's uncle expects him to care for his two young cousins and to assume responsibility for completing a number of chores around the house, including preparing simple meals, cleaning, and doing laundry. While his uncle supports Rafael's attendance at school, he also relies on Rafael to take care of essential home duties, as when they lived in Mexico.

In keeping with his desire to learn more, Rafael would like to play the trumpet in the 5th-grade band, but his uncle is unable to afford the monthly instrument fee. Some of his teachers have decided to seek donations of used instruments from former band alumni to share with students who might not otherwise be able to have this opportunity. Rafael can only develop his musical ability and talents if he is afforded parity of access to both academic and extracurricular opportunities. Such resourcefulness on the part of knowledgeable and caring teachers can make all the difference in the successful integration and retention of diverse learners in the school.

Student Descriptors

Students like Mariella and Rafael who performing at level 4 are well on their way to oral and written competence in English for academic purposes. However, like some students at level 3, they could be at risk of stalled language and academic development unless they receive targeted, linguistically differentiated instruction paired with assignments/assessments of the same kind. Readers are reminded that they must consult students' ELP levels in listening, speaking, reading, and writing individually, rather than assuming that a composite score of 4 means that the student scored at level 4 in each language domain. Table 7-1 presents the student descriptors for level 4.

Listening

In terms of listening, students at level 4 can process increasingly complex social and academic input, expanding the ability to understand language about both abstract and concrete topics. In addition, students at this level can derive increased meaning from longer stretches of discourse. While the need for many of the supports and scaffolds for students at earlier levels of listening has diminished, contextualizing and clarifying supports are still needed at times.

Speaking

When speaking, students at level 4 continue to deepen their ability to use oral language in social and academic situations. Their language is growing in com-

Table 7-1   Student Descriptors, Level 4

Listening	Speaking	Reading	Writing
■ Understands social and academic discourse of differing lengths and levels of complexity ■ Comprehends a wide variety of social and general academic and content-specific vocabulary related to both concrete and abstract concepts, particularly with visual or contextual support	■ Generates grammatically varied speech in a wide range of social and academic contexts ■ Uses academic vocabulary related to concrete and abstract concepts ■ Errors do not typically obstruct meaning	■ Comprehends increasingly complex text on known topics ■ Unknown topics continue to require visual or contextual support	■ Produces social and academic texts about concrete and abstract concepts ■ Uses increasingly precise general academic and content-specific vocabulary ■ Uses increasingly complex grammar and mechanics ■ Errors do not typically obstruct meaning

plexity and in lexical (vocabulary) precision. Students at level 4 in speaking likely appear fully proficient in social contexts and approach proficiency in academic contexts. Though errors occur at times, they do not obstruct meaning.

Reading

Students at level 4 in reading make sense of texts of varying complexity as they approach grade-level English language proficiency, as defined in their contexts and including ELP levels from the state ELD system. While these students can comprehend text dealing with familiar topics, unfamiliar topics require the building of background knowledge or creating connections to existing knowledge and experiences. Teachers are reminded to make explicit, persistent efforts to push these students, even though they might appear to be proficient, to higher levels of reading development in English.

Writing

Level 4 writing mirrors level 4 speaking; students at this level are capable of producing increasingly complex communication with greater precision in vocabulary and mechanics. These students are also able to write social and academic texts about abstract concepts using different genres, a wider range of general academic and content-specific vocabulary, and increasingly complex grammar. As with speaking, errors may occur, but they generally do not impede understanding.

A Word about Language Objectives

Once teachers have identified what their students at level 4 can do with English in the domains of listening, speaking, reading, and writing, they need to identify how all students need to use oral and written language to participate in each classroom activity and demonstrate their learning relative to the content objectives and essential learning. These language demands provide the basis for developing language objectives. In our example differentiated assignment, all students need to use language to describe, sequence, and explain. It is important to remember that students at all ELP levels can use writing for these purposes. However, teachers need to differentiate the language objectives to meet students at level 4 in writing where they are.

Teachers can draw on the student descriptors in Table 7-1 to differentiate their language objectives for students at level 4 in writing. With a clear understanding of what students at level 4 can do with listening, speaking, reading, and writing on the one hand and of the language demands of the assignment on the other, teachers can differentiate the language-based objectives for these students. Teachers also need to remember that students may not be at level 4 in all domains and that listening and speaking generally develop before reading and writing. Furthermore, students at level 4 may appear to be at grade-level because they sound like they speak English. However, these students still benefit from differentiation. In fact, without such differentiation these students may get stuck at level 4.

A solid linguistic foundation across all four language domains positions students at level 4 to be able to demonstrate their learning in ways that capitalize on their language development. However, teachers need to remember that students at level 4 have not yet developed the skills needed to meet grade-level expectations.

Example Differentiated Assignment

This example assignment is for a 5th-grade social studies class. Students are asked to write a set of instructions using an introduction; sequential organization; detailed description using appropriate grade-level vocabulary and sentence structures; and a conclusion for a self-selected content-based process. The essential learning for this assignment is clarity in communicating steps in the content-based process, use of transition words, and logical sequencing; it is the same for all students, regardless of their ELP level. The assignment focuses on the domain of writing, and all students need to use writing to *explain* the steps in the content-based process they have chosen, *describe* each step in the process, and *sequence* those steps.

Mariella and Rafael are two level 4 writers in this class. Recall that both Mariella and Rafael speak Spanish, as do a number of the non-ELLs in the class. However, Mariella struggles more in the class than Rafael because she hadn't attended school in El Salvador before being adopted by a U.S. family that speaks only English at home. The teacher of this class should keep these student strengths and needs in mind as he plans for this assignment.

Table 7-2 shows the portion of the example differentiation template that teachers need for students at level 4 in writing. Column 1 includes the language-based expectations and scaffolding and support provided for the non-ELLs in the class. Column 2 presents the language-based expectations and scaffolding and support for Mariella, Rafael, and other students at level 4 in writing, and it represents what these students can do independently. Column 3 presents the language-based expectations and scaffolding and support for students at level 5, the next ELP level. This column is included to remind teachers to teach to students' potential and help them progress along the ELD continuum.

Readers may note that the types of scaffolding and support are the same for students at level 4 and level 5 in this example, though this is but one way to differentiate this particular assignment. Some teachers may elect to provide different types of scaffolding and support for these two levels, depending on the specific language demands of the assignment, while other educators will differentiate their expectations during the grading process.

Numerous collaborative possibilities exist for teachers who want to join forces to facilitate the learning of students at level 4. For instance, teachers might meet weekly to plan assignments/assessments and associated lesson plans. Then the ELD teacher might preteach important aspects of the inter-related content and language and follow up with students to provide further support after the content teacher has taught the material.

Assignment/Assessment Strategies

Even at level 4, large-scale standardized tests and classroom tests designed for non-ELLs tend to be problematic for ELLs. In fact, the scores from such measures must be looked at skeptically because language ability is likely to be confounded with content knowledge and skills in those scores. That is, the results from tests designed for monolingual English speakers likely reflect both ELD and content knowledge for students at level 4, making the scores difficult to interpret. Do they represent language development, content understanding, or both? When a student is performing at an ELP level that does not match the expectations of the content test, he or she is unable, by definition, to fully comprehend unmodified, grade-level questions or produce an appropriate response linguistically, particularly when measured against a field of non-ELLs. Students at level 4, like those at levels 1–3, need assessment procedures that are designed to take into account their current linguistic and cultural realities.

While there is a tension between these needs and the language demands of many tests, students at level 4 must be afforded access to a level playing field where demonstration of learning is concerned. Developing language skills should not and must not relegate these students to failing marks and closed doors in terms of more advanced educational opportunities (e.g., qualifying for talented and gifted programs or Advanced Placement coursework). Using tests that are appropriate for students at level 4 is a critical approach that allows students to demonstrate learning while progressing along the trajectory toward English language proficiency. Further, this approach recognizes the gifts and potential of individual students that are unable to be measured or identified by means of standardized or other testing that expects language mastery.

All Domains

Teachers can use the following strategies with students at level 4 in listening, speaking, reading, and writing.

Table 7-2 Example Writing Assignment Differentiated for Students at Level 4

Standards-Based Content or Topic *(from the curriculum)*		
For a content-based process		
Non-ELL	**Level 4**	**Level 5**
Language-Based Expectations		
Write a set of instructions using	*Write a set of instructions using*	*Write a set of instructions using*
■ *Introduction*	■ *Compound and complex sentences*	■ *Compound and complex sentences*
■ *Sequential organization*	■ *Introduction (two complex sentences)*	■ *Introduction (two complex sentences)*
■ *Detailed description using*	■ *Sequential organization*	■ *Sequential organization*
○ *appropriate grade-level vocabulary*	■ *Greater variety in transition words (e.g., after, as soon as; meanwhile)*	■ *Detailed description using*
○ *grade-level sentence structures*	■ *Increasingly precise descriptions with an increasing use of grade-level content/academic vocabulary*	○ *appropriate grade-level vocabulary*
○ *appropriate and varied transition words*	■ *Conclusion (two complex sentences)*	○ *appropriate and varied transition words*
■ *Conclusion*		■ *Conclusion*

Non-ELL	Level 4	Scaffolding and Support	Level 5
Using	Using		Using
■ Model assignment	■ Level 4 model assignment		■ Level 5 model assignment
■ Teacher demonstration of the task using think-aloud	■ Teacher demonstration of the task using a think-aloud		■ Teacher demonstration of the task using a think-aloud
■ Sequential graphic organizer to plan for writing	■ Sequential graphic organizer with key complex phrases to plan for writing		■ Sequential graphic organizer to plan for writing
■ Language wall with sequencing words and key sentence structures	■ Photographs of relevant content-based processes		■ Language wall with a wide range of sequencing words (color-coded—push students to use more advanced transition words, such as after, as soon as; meanwhile) and complex sentence structures
■ Feedback designed to push students to produce accurate grade-level writing	■ Language wall with a wide range of sequencing words (color-coded—push students to use more advanced transition words, such as after, as soon as; meanwhile) and complex sentence structures		■ Compound and complex academic sentence frames posted in the classroom
	■ Word and picture cards featuring grade-level content/ academic vocabulary		■ Feedback designed to push students to produce accurate grade-level writing
	■ Supplementary think-aloud demonstration of writing smooth transitions between ideas		
	■ Compound and complex academic sentence frames posted in the classroom		
	■ Pictorially supported procedure texts		
	■ Realia related to processes (to use in teaching and writing)		
	■ Additional work on more advanced literacy skills (for SLIFE)		
	■ Additional time to complete the assignment, if needed (for SLIFE)		
	■ Level-appropriate feedback designed to push students to the next level of writing		

Essential Learning: *Clarity in communicating steps in a content-based process, effective use of transition words, and logical sequencing.*

Language Demands: *Use writing to describe each step in a process, sequence those steps, and explain how following these steps leads to the completion of the process.*

Engage Students in Grade-Level Assignments/Assessments with Scaffolding and Support. While students at levels 1–3 may require tasks that take different forms from those designed for their non-ELL peers, students at level 4 have often acquired sufficient oral and written English to participate in grade-level assignments/ assessments, as long as they receive needed scaffolding and support. Such scaffolding and support may include additional explanations about how to complete the task, extra time, peer or teacher tutoring, use of a bilingual dictionary or other differentiated resources, and so on.

However, the fact that students at level 4 can begin to engage in grade-level assignments/assessments should not lead to comparison with their non-ELL peers. Such inappropriate comparison can result in these students' discouragement and despair. Both authors have dealt with students at level 4 who tearfully disparaged themselves and expressed worry that they would never measure up, based on grade-level equivalents for their large-scale standardized content test performance and their understanding of their disparate performance in comparison with non-ELLs on classroom assessments. Students at level 4 often do not fully understand that language development takes place incrementally over time, requiring patience on the part of both the teacher and the learner. As a result, these students' attempts at grade-level assignments/assessments must be met with support and encouragement.

Teachers are also encouraged to take into account students' realities at home when assigning homework because students may not have the time or the resources to complete some assignments. In addition, students need careful, targeted corrections to facilitate higher ELP levels, such as can be provided by differentiated scoring rubrics.

Differentiate Grading by ELP Level. The grading of students at level 4 should highlight what these students can do linguistically, rather than reflect an expectation of grade-level language production. Teachers must be clear about what they are grading. Demystifying and clarifying the assessment process by using a specific and accessible scoring rubric supports students in their understanding of expectations. This rubric can be made sensitive to the needs of students at level 4 by differentiating expectations according to what students at this level can do with listening, speaking, reading, and writing.

Explain Directions for Assignments/Assessments Orally and Provide Visual Support. While students at level 4 may comprehend the directions for many assignments/ assessments, teachers are cautioned to make no assumptions. Rather, teachers should still provide visual support like realia, icons, manipulatives, and models for assignments/assessments. Some routine classroom tasks may be unfamiliar or bewildering to these students—some of whom arrive as newcomers at level 4 with very different school experiences, such as extremely large classes where students rarely talk or where they rely on rote memorization rather than group work. One newcomer that we know, on grade level in his home language, failed an early assessment in math because he was unfamiliar with the true/false testing format. Two weeks later, the student was promoted from Algebra I to Algebra II, illustrating the importance of teaching test-taking skills to students who are still learning English.

Simultaneously Assess Content and Language Development. The growing and increasingly refined language development of students at level 4 allows them to articulate content learning in more precise ways. Further, they can address more abstract content using increasingly complex and accurate language. Thus, it can be appropriate to assess the language and content learning of students at level 4 simultaneously through assignments and performance-based assessment tasks like summarizing, story retelling, questioning and responding, analyzing, and evaluating. Teachers must embrace the responsibility for embedding opportunities into assignments/assessments that provide the forum for students to produce pretaught language to the greatest extent of their ability. This means going beyond questions that warrant one-word responses. Rather, teachers should construct tasks requiring students to respond with increasingly complex discourse and commensurate vocabulary. For instance, when assigning an essay on *Romeo and Juliet*, a teacher might incorporate pretaught language and sentence structures such as, "Analyzing the Montagues and Capulets: predict what might have happened if the families had lived in the 21st century," into the assignment itself. This prompt indicates the kinds of language that the teacher expects. A teacher might further guide students by saying, "Use vocabulary taught in class and complex sentences when constructing your answer."

Table 7-3 presents assignment/assessment strategies that teachers can use with students at level 4 in listening, speaking, reading, and writing. Again, teachers are reminded to look beyond the composite score to identify what students can do with English in each domain.

Listening

Teachers can use the following strategies to create assignments/assessments for students at level 4 in listening.

Increase the Use of Academic and Grammatically Varied Language When Discussing Concrete and Abstract Topics. Because students at level 4 can comprehend longer stretches of discourse for a wider range of academic purposes, teachers need to create assignments/assessments that require this more advanced oral language. For example, all students, particularly students at level 4, need to be able to

Table 7-3   Assignment and Assessment Strategies for Students at Level 4

Listening	Speaking	Reading	Writing
■ Increase the use of academic and grammatically varied language when discussing concrete and abstract topics ■ Use visuals to support comprehension of complex discourse and sentences.	■ Require students to produce complex discourse in a range of genres and an increased use of academic and grammatically varied language about concrete and abstract topics. ■ Expect language to reflect increasingly complex sentence and discourse-level frames used during instruction	■ Use a combination of grade-level texts (with scaffolding) and high-quality, visually supported, age-appropriate reading materials matched to students' reading levels, expecting comprehension of increasingly complex text. ■ Use traditional paper-and-pencil tests wisely, employing visual support and linguistic scaffolding as needed.	■ Elicit writing of increasingly academic and grammatically varied language about both concrete and abstract topics ■ Expect language to reflect discourse-level frames and models used during instruction ■ Use traditional paper-and-pencil tests wisely, employing simplified English, visual support, and linguistic scaffolding.

gain meaning from academic lectures that use expository and persuasive language. They also need to be able to comprehend videos and listen for specific purposes, such as to identify the main idea of a lecture, distinguish the pros and cons of an oral argument, and compare the perspectives of different characters in a narrative that is read aloud. Teachers must include these types of oral language in their assignments/assessments of student comprehension. Teachers should also remember that the language in the assessments needs to mirror that used in the assignments.

Use Visuals to Support Comprehension of Complex Discourse and Sentences. Although students at level 4 in listening can comprehend more complex language, they need additional scaffolds and supports during assignments and on assessments. For example, teachers can use videos that highlight the essential learning of an assignment and they can use note-taking guides with charts, graphs, or photos to help these students see the structure of a narrative, expository, or persuasive piece that is read aloud. Teachers can also fill in parts of the note-taking guide to support students' efforts in identifying the most important information during assessment, assuming these same scaffolds were used during instruction.

Speaking

Teachers can use the following strategies for students at level 4 in speaking to create assignments/assessments.

Require Students to Produce Complex Discourse in a Range of Genres, with an Increasing Use of Academic and Grammatically Varied Language about Concrete and Abstract Topics. As with non-ELLs, students at level 4 must be pushed to produce more advanced language. All teachers must recognize the importance of explicit language instruction for upper-level speakers, and for non-ELLs, to rightfully expect this sort of performance on assignments/assessments. This advanced and precise academic language is not learned in social contexts and, unless explicitly taught, is unlikely to be acquired. Intentional instruction of language takes into account the linguistic developmental levels of non-ELLs and students at level 4, leading to greater linguistic facility that can and should be assessed. For example, a teacher could explicitly teach period language (e.g., "four score and seven years ago") prior to expecting students to give presentations where they take on the identities of famous historical figures.

Expect Spoken Language to Reflect General Academic and Content-Specific Vocabulary and Complex Sentence and Discourse, Used during Instruction. When assessing students at level 4 in speaking, teachers can still expect some errors, especially when students experiment with new vocabulary and sentence structures that they have not explicitly learned. However, teachers are encouraged to hold these students accountable for the oral language used in instruction. For example, if the science assignment asks students to compare and contrast the rainforest before and after deforestation, teachers should assess for content and for the comparative sentence frames used in instruction.

Reading

Teachers can use the following strategies to create assignments/assessments for students at level 4 in reading.

Use a Combination of Grade-Level Texts with Scaffolding and High-Quality, Visually Supported Age-Appropriate Reading Materials Matched to Students' Reading Levels, Expecting Comprehension of Increasingly Complex Text. Students at level 4 are able to process increasingly complex text, including a widening variety of genres, accompanied by related academic vocabulary development. Grade-level text, while sometimes beyond the comprehension level of these students, displays increasingly sophisticated sentence and discourse structures, grammar, mechanics, and vocabulary. Level 4 is the appropriate level at which students can often begin deriving meaning from grade-level texts, provided that scaffolding and support are given when needed. Teachers are reminded that texts used in assignments/assessments, such as reading passages on a social studies test, must be of the same variety as those used during instruction. Only use grade-level text in an assessment if it is targeting grade-level reading; otherwise, the high reading level of the assignment/assessment materials may interfere with students' abilities to demonstrate what they know and can do related to content only.

Use Traditional Paper-and-Pencil Tests Wisely, Employing Visual Support and Linguistic Scaffolding. Traditional paper-and-pencil tests may not be the most appropriate ways to ascertain what students at level 4 in reading know and can do in the content areas. Teachers are reminded that students at level 4 in reading are unable to consistently read at grade level, though informal, ungraded assessments that are formative in nature can inform teachers of these students' instructional needs related to language and content. Once these areas and items are targeted instructionally, they can be assessed through a variety of pretaught means, traditional and nontraditional. Teachers are urged to continue using authentic assessments with students at level 4 in reading rather than relying on more traditional tests and to use visual support like clip art and graphs, as well as linguistic scaffolding. Even though these students' language ability may be sufficient to deal with the individual words on a traditional test, many constructions used in these tests, such as "which of the following" and "all of the following except" may be unfamiliar. It is incumbent on teachers to examine their curriculum for such language and to explicitly teach this test language, which also appears on mandated large-scale standardized tests.

Writing

Teachers can use these strategies to create assignments/assessments for students at level 4 in writing.

Elicit Writing of Increasingly Academic and Grammatically Varied Language When Discussing Concrete and Abstract Topics. At level 4, it is possible to assess content knowledge through writing. Conversely, teachers can assess writing using specific content as the topic. When using writing assessment, teachers must decide what they are trying to assess: Is it content knowledge, or writing ability, or both? Any of these objectives might be acceptable, but teachers must be clear about the goals of the assessment if they are to develop appropriate assessment procedures and score student performance fairly. Ultimately, teachers must ensure that what their assessments measure matches the construct of interest or measurement goal. Figure 7-1 helps to illuminate this relationship.

Teachers should expect students at level 4 to produce writing that is fully representative of the range of level 4 production. In content-testing situations, teachers may not wish to grade writing ability, as is often the case when working with students at levels 1–3. However, many assignments/assessments could offer appropriate opportunities to expect and require level 4 writing, reflecting content knowledge and level 4 writing ability, such as a social studies essay test

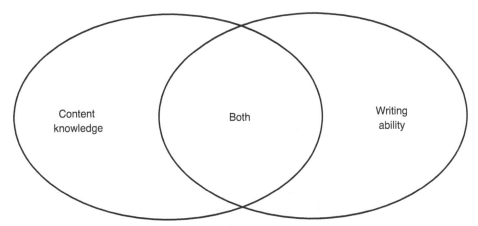

Figure 7-1 Potential construct overlap in assessing content knowledge through writing (and vice versa).

question on the Revolutionary War. Holding all students, ELLs and non-ELLs, accountable for their writing ability in this way fosters authentic opportunities to demonstrate increased learning of content knowledge and the writing ability necessary for success in future endeavors. Of course, teachers should expect students' language use to reflect discourse-level frames and models used during instruction.

Use Traditional Paper-and-Pencil Tests Wisely, Employing Simplified English, Visual Support, and Linguistic Scaffolding. Teachers can begin to expect the writing of students at level 4 to reflect their instruction of increasingly complex and sophisticated language. At this level, students may be expected to produce collateral errors, but these generally do not hinder understanding. As with non-ELLs who inhabit a range of language development levels and may write with frequent errors, students at level 4 in writing can be expected to display similar characteristics across the level 4 range. These students should not be held to a higher standard for writing than their non-ELL peers, nor should teachers allow any less. This is part of what we mean by wise use of traditional assessments like essay tests.

Another aspect of this essential wisdom is recognition that the test format itself may hinder students in demonstrating what they know and can do in the content areas. For instance, the kinds of language found on many multiple-choice tests, such as "All of the following except _____," may be a hindrance for students at level 4 in writing. Teachers are encouraged to routinely examine test questions, end-of-chapter review questions, and the like, searching for grammatical constructions that require explicit instruction. Authentic assessments may be better than traditional paper-and-pencil tests in ascertaining the content knowledge and skills of students at level 4.

Instructional Strategies

The preceding strategies for assessing students at level 4 can only be used effectively if appropriate instruction supports students in demonstrating their learning throughout assignments/assessments. Even with students who have achieved level 4, teachers are cautioned, as with students at levels 1–3, to take the following steps:

1. Examine their assumptions
2. Learn about students' backgrounds
3. Determine students' instructional levels based on content knowledge and skills, and levels of language development
4. Continue to teach essential learning from the curriculum and its associated language in a differentiated manner

As with students at level 3, students at level 4 are at high risk for stalling their progress and never achieving grade-level English skills. Teachers must consistently rely on various measures, such as formative assessments, informal classroom observation, and annual ELP assessments, to inform them of instructional needs. Routinely consulting and applying such information enables teachers to incrementally ratchet up and fine-tune their instruction related to content and language. Having analyzed such assessment data regularly, teachers can explicitly and intentionally provide students with the necessary linguistic knowledge that, unless explicitly taught, is unlikely to be casually absorbed. This preparation allows students to demonstrate their knowledge and skills in an ever-improving linguistic fashion as they increase their mastery of content and language. With such pinpointed expectations consistently maintained across various forms of assessment, students continue to progress on their trajectory toward grade-level language use, supported by differentiated instruction.

All Domains

Teachers can use the following instructional strategies to support students at level 4 in the domains of listening, speaking, reading, and writing.

Provide Sensory Support for Every Lesson. While teachers might suspect that students at level 4 no longer need sensory supports to make meaning from teaching presented in English, teachers should examine their assumptions. Although some students at level 4 might be ready to exhibit more learning independence, other students at this level are likely to have various cultural and linguistic needs that require sensory support, including real objects, pictures, hands-on materials and experiences, nonverbal communication, demonstrations, modeling, and simulations in every lesson. As a result, teachers are encouraged to familiarize themselves with students' backgrounds to make appropriate educational decisions and maximize their instructional impact. Further, because the learning preferences of a majority of students are visual and kinesthetic, rather than auditory, such sensory experiences benefit ELLs and non-ELLs on that front as well. For example, when learning about place value, students may benefit from an activity where different students represent different place values by lining up to represent a number. In other words, to represent 4,395.27, six students would be assigned the six digits in the number and asked to stand in order and explain their individual place values.

Explicitly Teach and Require Students to Use General Academic and Content-Specific Vocabulary and Grammatically Varied Language about Concrete and Abstract Topics, with Diminishing Errors. For students at level 4 to reach grade-level expectations for English language use within the content areas, teachers must explicitly teach this type of academic language. This teaching is meaningful for ELLs and non-ELLs inasmuch as all students are learning to use academic English orally and in writing at school. Furthermore, neither ELLs nor non-ELLs are likely to acquire such academic language unless teachers integrate its modeling and practice into daily classroom activities. Although students at level 4 are likely to continue to make some errors in their language production, teachers are urged to require academic language from these students and to provide targeted error correction as appropriate. For instance, rather than allowing students to use simple words and phrases when answering questions related to a short story, teachers might require students to use complete, complex sentences with pretaught vocabulary.

Provide Scaffolding and Support Needed for Students to Engage in Grade-Level Assignments/Assessments. Although students at level 4 are still officially designated as ELLs, and may sometimes still need assignments/assessments differentiated, they are likely able to engage in many grade-level assignments/assessments. However, when they do participate in these assignments/assessments, extensive scaffolding and support are likely necessary for their success. This support can take the form of additional explanations regarding expectations, supplementary materials for use in completing assignments/assessments, coaching in the completion of assignments/assessments, and so on.

Table 7-4 presents instructional strategies that teachers can use with students at level 4 in the domains of listening, speaking, reading, and writing.

Listening

The following instructional strategies can support students at level 4 in listening and help them comprehend oral language at more advanced levels.

Table 7-4   Appropriate Instructional Strategies for Students at Level 4

Listening	Speaking	Reading	Writing
■ Scaffold language development by modeling and prompting an increasing use of academic and grammatically varied language when discussing concrete and abstract topics ■ Promote higher-order thinking processes during oral teaching by providing students with graphic organizers	■ Provide opportunities for students to produce extended oral discourse, increasingly including abstract concepts ■ Scaffold extended oral language production by providing visually supported discourse-level frames and models for high-quality academic discourse ■ Insist on increasingly correct and precise language	■ Use a combination of grade-level texts with scaffolding and high-quality, visually supported, age-appropriate reading materials ■ Promote higher-order thinking processes during reading by providing students with graphic organizers	■ Use and require an increased level of academic and grammatically varied language when discussing concrete and abstract topics ■ Expect language to reflect increasingly complex sentence and discourse-level frames used during instruction ■ Scaffold extended written language production by providing discourse-level frames and models for high-quality academic discourse ■ Insist on increasingly correct and precise language ■ Provide students with graphic organizers to enhance higher-order thinking ■ Ask students to create and use identity texts

Scaffold Language Development by Modeling and Prompting an Increased Level of Academic and Grammatically Varied Language When Discussing Concrete and Abstract Topics. To set the stage for the full development of the receptive abilities of students at level 4 in listening, teachers should examine their own classroom language production. Educators must ask themselves if their language during instruction is indicative of their ELD goals for their students at level 4, complete with complex sentence structures and sophisticated vocabulary. Is their own language demonstrative of the discourse of academia, such as "When hypothesizing about the outcome of this experiment _____." As teachers are using high-level discourse and encouraging students at level 4 in listening to be daring and try something new with language, they should remember that such opportunities for English language enrichment are the only ones many ELLs and non-ELLs have—and this should motivate teachers to examine their classroom practices even more. For instance, even high school teachers could employ the marble jar activity in their classrooms, awarding classes a marble each time a high-level vocabulary word or sentence structure is used. Once the jar for each class is full, the class has earned some sort of reward.

Promote Higher-Order Thinking Processes during Oral Teaching by Providing Students with Graphic Organizers. When used in conjunction with live and taped lectures, presentations, and stories, as well as movies, podcasts, video clips, and the like, graphic organizers facilitate and support attending to details through listening. Providing such organizers enables students to record information they consider important and, depending on the format of the organizer, to better understand relationships among ideas and concepts. Once students develop note-taking skills using graphic organizers, they are better prepared to gain meaning from auditory input when such support is unavailable.

Speaking

These instructional strategies are recommended for students at level 4 in speaking.

Provide Opportunities for Students to Produce Extended Oral Discourse That Increasingly Includes Abstract Concepts. Students at level 4 in speaking are linguistically prepared to engage in increasingly imaginative and complex activities across domains. Opportunities for speaking might include debate on a current event, guest speaking at a local civic or church group, speaking as a member of a panel at a local conference, or other authentic community-based activities. Such activities, while setting high expectations for students in terms of oral production, develop language across domains. Researching, editing, rewriting, rehearsing, videotaping, refining presentation skills, and so on all contribute to the students' abilities to produce extended academic discourse with increasing ease and credibility. Furthermore, these authentic types of skills develop multiple language domains in rewarding ways for students and can increase their motivation and self-esteem.

Scaffold Extended Oral Language Production by Providing Visually Supported Discourse-Level Frames And Models For High-Quality Academic Discourse. At level 3, teachers have provided sentence-level scaffolding for the production of academic language. To advance speaking abilities at level 4, teachers must now provide discourse-level scaffolding to expand the production of academic language. Discourse-level language includes expanded and well-organized paragraphs of varying length and complexity. Insisting on the refined organizational form of increasing amounts of oral academic language must be intentional and embedded in instruction. For example, classroom instruction could include speech featuring complex processes, persuasion, and opinions that students would, in turn, be expected to produce. During this instruction, teachers must address features of expanded academic discourse, such as how to include more detail, cite data, transition between ideas, and ensure cohesiveness. For example, teachers can provide sentence frames such as, "In accordance with our hypothesis, the results of our experiment demonstrate _____. This outcome means that _____." Targeted discourse features can be posted visually in the form of a language wall for ease of student reference.

An often overlooked aspect of discourse development relates to questioning techniques. The development of precise questioning abilities is key in helping students to articulate what it is that they really want to know. Without this skill, students inquire without precision, accuracy, or appropriateness and may be left wondering, without the means to access essential knowledge. Or students might ask a question such as, "How do we get hail?" Such a simple and basic question should not be considered as representative of the language production capabilities of a student at level 4. Teachers must seize this teachable linguistic moment to scaffold the student's questioning technique to serve the student well in advanced education or in her or his career. For example, teachers might model and then require students at level 4 to produce questions like the following:

What factors contribute to hail formation?
What meteorological conditions lead to the formation of large hail?
What is the difference between graupel and hail?

Teaching students how to present orally and how to generate questions that elicit more complex responses are integral components of instruction as students at level 4 refine their complementary skills of listening and speaking.

Insist on Increasingly Correct and Precise Language. Students at level 4 need teachers to provide focused and pinpointed language instruction and correction. Teachers are remiss if they simply let errors go when they are able to grasp a student's overall meaning, even if the utterance is stated incorrectly or just too simply. For example, when a student states, "The author says _____," she or he might be prompted to use the word *asserts* rather than *says*. The oral production of students at level 4 in speaking is likely far from perfect and relies on teacher input in setting high standards for increasing precision and correctness. While teachers need not pounce on every error, they must continue to provide alternate structures, academic vocabulary, and models for students to adopt as they advance toward grade-level expectation in English, furthering the likelihood of their success in higher education and in the professional world. It should be noted that non-ELLs, as well as students at level 4 in speaking, benefit from this type of explicit insistence on the continued refinement of language.

Reading

The cultural and linguistic issues that might have precluded the rapid acquisition of reading skills for students with limited or interrupted formal education (SLIFE) at levels 1–3 may have dissipated by the time that students achieve level 4. However, teachers are reminded to continue making individually based decisions according to students' biographical profiles and linguistic needs. Also, because students at level 4 in reading are, by definition, reading below grade level, it is incumbent on school districts to ensure that appropriate reading instruction is in place, regardless of the student's age and keeping in mind that simply receiving the same instruction as non-ELLs is not equitable—or enough.

Use a Combination of Grade-Level Texts with Scaffolding, and High-Quality Visually Supported Age-Appropriate Reading Materials. Students at level 4 in reading can begin to independently read grade-level text, though they likely require support because their reading ability is not at grade level. Examples of such support include teacher explanation; preteaching vocabulary; glossaries; advance organizers and outlines; and other topical resources, such as first-person accounts, magazine and newspaper articles, and Internet research. Lower-reading-level materials can also serve as needed supplements to grade-level texts.

Promote Higher-Order Thinking Processes during Reading by Providing Students with Graphic Organizers. In addition to providing graphic organizers for students at level 4 in reading, teachers can ask the students themselves to create organizers that help them to make sense of written text. Teachers might provide a critical question or prompt that would focus students' reading on higher-order thought processes, such as "Analyze the reasons for the Civil War from a Northern perspective." Students then create an organizer that would help them individually accomplish the assigned task. By level 4 reading, most students have been exposed to a variety of organizers, and asking them to create their own is another way teachers can push student thinking to the next level.

Writing

The issues that slowed the writing development of SLIFE learners at levels 1–3 have likely diminished by level 4. Although achieving level 4 in writing likely takes longer for those students than for their peers who arrived in the United States at or near grade level in their home languages, by level 4 the development rate may become more consistent for the two groups. However, level 4 is a very broad designation, and student performance can fall anywhere within that wide range of development. With this in mind, teachers should remember the importance of tailoring instruction to the specific needs of individual students, based on their backgrounds and current instructional needs.

Use and Require an Increased Level of Academic and Grammatically Varied Language When Discussing Concrete and Abstract Topics. Students at level 4 are often able to participate in grade-level written instruction, as long as needed scaffolding is provided. Teachers must ensure that the assignments are meaningful and relevant and that they elicit extended writing reflective of abstract thought. Examples include essays in which students evaluate solutions to a given problem (e.g., pollution), persuade others to take a stand on an issue (e.g., the merits of vegetarianism), or outline the implications of a current event or issue (e.g., health care, nuclear armament).

While this strategy is equally applicable to speaking and writing, teachers must remember that academic writing production, is more formal in style than speaking or texting, and must follow certain conventions. This academic style must be explicitly taught, modeled, and expected of students.

Scaffold Extended Written Language Production by Providing Discourse-Level Frames and Models for High-Quality Academic Language. For writing, as for speaking, posted templates or frames are helpful for guiding students in language production. Templates can offer more complex structures for organization and for expansion from sentence to discourse-level language. For instance, teachers can assist students in analyzing high-quality writing from a variety of sources and authors to better understand discourse features. Then teachers might post a frame for constructing similar writing, such as an argumentative essay, that provides guidance for articulating detailed reasoning, transitioning from idea to idea, enhancing cohesion, and so on. Teachers might also provide sentence frames that model more complex sentences appropriate for particular content areas and genres, such as "In accordance with our hypothesis, the results of our experiment demonstrate _____. This outcome means that _____."

Insist on Increasingly Correct and Precise Language. As with speaking, level 4 writing presents excellent opportunities for teachers to scaffold students' written language production to a higher level. Teachers must insist on students' sustained efforts to continue to develop their writing in English through the production of correct and precise language. Without this much needed push from teachers, students are at risk of permanently remaining at level 4 in writing. For instance, if a student were to write "The liquid in the jar began to boil after one minute," the teacher might prompt the student to use the word *beaker* instead of *jar*.

Provide Students with Graphic Organizers to Enhance Higher-Order Thinking. As with reading, students at level 4 in writing can use graphic organizers provided by the teacher or generate their own graphic organizers to assist in the development of their written products. These graphic organizers can serve as springboards for students to respond to complex prompts eliciting higher-order thinking and advanced discourse. For example, students might be provided with a variety of graphic organizers, such as outlines and concept maps, to help them organize their thoughts as they write a research paper.

Ask Students to Create and Use Identity Texts. These texts focus on students' personal characteristics and experiences across languages and cultures. Projecting their identities by creating products in English allows students to define, reframe, and develop their lives in their new linguistic and cultural environments in meaningful ways. For example, in the Toronto District School Board, ELLs completed projects on grade-level standards-based topics, culminating in a red carpet gala that provided students with a platform to share their individual voices and receive affirmations of self from multiple audiences (Cummins, Hu, Markus, & Montero, 2015).

Instruction That Integrates Language Domains

The integration of language domains within a single activity, assignment, or assessment becomes more straightforward as students reach higher ELP levels across domains. However, teachers must base their instruction on domain-specific data; that is, students may be at different levels in the domains of listening, speaking, reading, and writing, and this must be taken into account. Within the context of appropriately differentiated expectations, the most efficient way to develop language is to attach instruction and assessment to authentic representations of the curriculum, accomplishing simultaneous instruction and assessment of content and language.

Conclusion

Students at level 4 need targeted linguistic differentiation to support their content and language learning. This chapter outlined differentiated strategies for engaging students at level 4 in learning and demonstrating that learning.

Professional Learning Activities

Working individually or with others in professional learning communities, differentiate the first four assignments for Mariella and Rafael. For assignment 5, choose the assignment and differentiate it for at least one of the students at ELP level 4 in your class. When differentiating for students at ELP level 4, remember that they may be at different ELP levels in listening, speaking, reading, and writing.

Differentiating for Mariella and Rafael

For assignments 1–4, differentiate the language-based expectations and the scaffolding and support needed for level 4 students, Mariella and Rafael. Recall that both are 5th-grade students at ELP level 4 in all domains. Mariella reads almost at grade level. Rafael was at grade level in his Mexican elementary school and completes scaffolded and supported assignments when given time in class.

1. Read the assignment above the template.
2. Read the essential learning and language demands below the template.
3. Review the standards-based topic, language-based expectations for non-ELLs.
4. Complete the template to show the differentiated assignment for Mariella and Rafael, by adding appropriate language-based expectations and scaffolding and support for these students.

After you complete the template, read on for additional insight on how to differentiate the assignment.

Assignment 1: *Write a letter to a relative in the voice of a Revolutionary War-era individual*

Standards-Based Content or Topic (from the curriculum)	
In the voice of a Revolutionary War-era individual	

Non-ELL	Level 4
Language-Based Expectations	
Write a letter to a relative	▪ ▪ ▪ ▪
Scaffolding and Support	
Using ▪ *Understanding gained from in-class role plays and teacher modeling*	*Using* ▪ *Understanding gained from in-class role plays and teacher modeling* ▪ ▪ ▪

Essential Learning: *Research a Revolutionary War-era individual. Identify main ideas and details of a significant event; describe and explain perspectives of different groups at the time of the Revolutionary War; write a letter to a relative.*

Language Demands: *Use oral and written language to describe and explain.*

Instruction is designed using sensory support so that the teaching is comprehensible to Mariella and Rafael. Before the assignment is given, students reprise the roles of famous Revolutionary War figures using costumes and role-playing. Both students also need supplementary instruction regarding U.S. history to understand and participate in this assignment. Letter writing is modeled with a template posted on the wall. Students then write their letters in a workshop format, so the teacher can give assistance where needed.

The assignment is adjusted for Mariella and Rafael in terms of the amount and kinds of language required for writing the letter. For example, the teacher may focus on enhancing the use of vocabulary for one student and on expanding the use of varied grammatical structures for another. Because Rafael has difficulty completing assignments at home, he may benefit from additional scaffolding and support, beyond what Mariella receives. Also, he may require extra time in class to complete the assignment, whereas Mariella could complete the assignment at home.

Assignment 2: *Research and develop a group presentation on the merits of recycling*

Standards-Based Content or Topic (from the curriculum)	
Merits of recycling	
Non-ELL	**Level 4**
Language-Based Expectations	
Give a group presentation	▪ ▪ ▪ ▪
Scaffolding and Support	
Using	*Using*
▪ *Information gained from an in-class video and independent research* ▪ *Graphic organizer to guide the presentation* ▪ *Video of an example presentation from last year* ▪ *Peer and teacher feedback during rehearsal*	▪ *Information gained from an in-class video and independent research* ▪ *Graphic organizer to guide the presentation* ▪ *Video of an example presentation from last year* ▪ *Peer and teacher feedback during rehearsal* ▪ ▪ ▪

Essential Learning: *Conduct independent research on the merits of recycling; summarize and synthesize information using evidence from the text; develop presentation and research skills.*

Language Demands: *Use oral and written language to summarize and synthesize; interact with others in group; present group ideas to an audience.*

Because the class is divided into groups for this assignment, it is important to place Mariella and Rafael within an appropriate group to ensure that they can make contributions to the presentation. The teacher shows a video of a presentation from last year, and the class discusses the strong and weak points of that presentation. The class also watches a video about recycling various natural resources, taking notes on a provided graphic organizer. They discuss the information in the video and brainstorm a list of additional information sources. Then, the students access available print and online materials to create their oral presentations, according to a provided graphic organizer. Both Mariella and Rafael need additional guidance in how to access these resources. Each group rehearses its presentation in front of another group to obtain peer feedback; the teacher should also provide feedback during this rehearsal workshop.

Mariella and Rafael should be required to speak during the presentation using level 4 language, with an emphasis on aspects of language that are appropriate for each. For example, one may need to emphasize vocabulary and the other sentence complexity. The scoring of their parts of the presentation must be differentiated according to their language development levels.

Assignment 3: *Collect and present data about consumer preferences*

Standards-Based Content or Topic (from the curriculum)	
About consumer preferences	

Non-ELL	Level 4
Language-Based Expectations	
Collect data through interviews, construct a bar or line graph, and present findings	• • • •
Scaffolding and Support	
Using	*Using*
• *Modeling of the development of interview questions* • *Modeling of the construction of simple graphs* • *Explicit instruction in how to present information to a group* • *A videotape of a practice presentation to use in perfecting presentation skills*	• *Modeling of the development of interview questions* • *Modeling of the construction of simple graphs* • *Explicit instruction in how to present information to a group* • *A videotape of a practice presentation to use in perfecting presentation skills* • • •

Essential Learning: *Collect data, represent data in charts and graphs, and present findings.*

Language Demands: *Use oral and written language to interview, summarize, represent, and explain.*

For this assignment, the class is divided into four groups. Each group must interview 10 people from a certain age group (elementary students, middle school students, high school students, adults) about their preferences as consumers. Students must brainstorm questions, and the teacher should model this process and demonstrate for the class the construction of graphs to display similar data. Students videotape themselves to refine their presentation skills prior to the graded presentation, where they are rated by their peers according to a shared rubric.

Mariella and Rafael can successfully complete this assignment if the language-based expectations for them are appropriate. For instance, the questions that they are expected to ask and the language that they are expected to use during the presentation must align with their current levels of language development and support their continued development in vocabulary, sentence complexity, and length of communication. The practice of this kind of data collection may be less familiar to Mariella and Rafael than to their peers, and instruction should be provided accordingly. Because it is unlikely that Rafael can garner assistance with this assignment at home, he may need additional time and support to complete this work.

Assignment 4: *Demonstrate how to double or halve a recipe*

Standards-Based Content or Topic (from the curriculum)	
Doubling or halving a recipe	

Non-ELL	Level 4
Language-Based Expectations	
Write a summary and make a display about how to double or halve a recipe	■ ■ ■ ■
Scaffolding and Support	
Using ■ *An example assignment provided by the teacher* ■ *Modeling of doubling and halving* ■ *Think-aloud demonstration of summarizing* ■ *Support from the family and consumer science teacher*	*Using* ■ *Example assignment provided by the teacher* ■ *Modeling of doubling and halving* ■ *Think-aloud demonstration of summarizing* ■ *Support from the family and consumer science teacher* ■ ■ ■

Essential Learning: *Converting a math word problem into a fraction and solving the problem; basic cooking skills; presentation skills.*

Language Demands: *Use oral and written language to describe a process; summarize, and explain.*

The teacher begins by showing students a final product in the form of a display board and a batch of jam. The display board components serve as a template for student work and are analyzed by the class. The teacher then models the process of doubling the recipe by adding fractions and writes a summary of the jam-making process through a think-aloud using an overhead projector or document camera. After tasting the jam, students go to work on their own recipes in a workshop format. Families and the consumer science teacher should lend a hand in cooking the recipes.

The language-based expectations for the assignment must be in line with what Rafael and Mariella can do with scaffolding and support. That is, the expectations for them must acknowledge that the language that they are expected to produce is not on par with non-ELLs in their grade. For instance, their summaries might use simpler vocabulary or grammar or may be shorter than those of their peers. Rafael may be able to garner assistance at home, given the nature of this assignment. If this assistance can only be offered on the weekend because of work schedules, extra time should be granted for this valuable family support of his learning.

This is also a perfect opportunity to showcase beloved recipes that these students may have grown up with. ELLs must not be required to share this sort of cultural information, but offering them the option is a simple way to highlight their rich backgrounds.

Differentiating for Your Students

For assignment 5, choose an assignment from your curriculum. Differentiate the assignment for a student at ELP level 4 in your class. Consider how student background factors like prior schooling, home language literacy, cultural orientation, and challenging experiences are likely to influence this student's content and language learning in your classroom.

1. Write the assignment at the top of the template.
2. Identify the essential learning and language demands, and write this below the template.
3. Fill in the standards-based topic, language-based expectations for non-ELLs, and for your student at ELP level 4.
4. Plan and implement the assignment in your classroom. If possible, videotape the lesson or invite an ELL coordinator or coach to observe the lesson. Focus on the teacher's use of appropriate differentiation strategies for students at level 4 in any domain.

Assignment 5: _____

Standards-Based Content or Topic (from the curriculum)	

Non-ELL	Level 4
Language-Based Expectations	
▪	▪ ▪ ▪ ▪
Scaffolding and Support	
Using ▪	*Using* ▪ ▪ ▪ ▪

Essential Learning: _____

Language Demands: _____

Share your template with your colleagues, and explain why you made the choices that you did. When you implement the lesson in your class, reflect on how your focal students use oral and written language in each of the activities you planned. If you videotape the interaction, work with your colleagues to explore the scaffolding and support you provided. In either case, collect evidence of your students' content and language performances, identify your students' strengths, and list possible next steps for instruction.

Chapter 8

Differentiating for Students at Level 5

A good teacher must be able to put himself in the place of those who find learning hard.

—ELIPHAS LEVI

Teachers who are solidly prepared with an understanding of the tenets of language acquisition and content knowledge are best equipped to implement appropriate assignment/assessment and instructional strategies that support the holistic needs of students at level 5 in English language proficiency (ELP). Such teachers are uniquely qualified to scaffold students along the language development continuum toward mastery of content and language. In this chapter, we discuss students at level 5 who perform close to the range of their non-English language learner (ELL) peers by describing their characteristics and providing assignment/assessment and instructional strategies appropriate to this level.

Teachers should remember that phasing out scaffolding efforts at ELP level 5 is premature. As is the case with non-ELLs, students at level 5 continue to benefit from sustained, pinpointed instruction to polish and perfect their English language use across domains. In fact, such continued attention to the language development needs of these students is critical for maximizing post-secondary options, whether in continued education, a professional setting, and enhancing their quality of life.

Variation in Students' Backgrounds

As we have emphasized throughout this book, the category of *English language learner* is not monolithic. Rather than assume that students have reached the same level in listening, speaking, reading, and writing, teachers need to look at what students can do with English in each domain individually. Students who have reached level 5 have likely taken diverse pathways to get to this relatively advanced ELP level and their prior experiences learning English and content are likely to be quite varied. Some students who have been educated in U.S. schools may have reached level 5 in listening or speaking and they may sound like their non-ELL peers. However, many of these students have only reached levels 2 or 3 in reading and writing and really struggle with grade-level written work. Other students may have arrived in U.S. schools at level 4 or 5 in reading and writing because English language instruction in their home countries focused on these domains; however, they may rarely have found opportunities to use oral English. Teachers need to remember that this kind of variation is possible and provide appropriate assignment/assessment and instructional strategies to meet students at the appropriate level and support their efforts to reach grade-level expectations for oral and written English.

Student Scenarios

Minh, a Vietnamese boy who recently arrived as a 9th grader by immigrating with his family, was an excellent student in Vietnam. In fact, he was the top student in math and English at his school in Ho Chi Minh City. However, because Minh's instruction in English focused on reading and writing, he had few opportunities to interact and develop his listening and speaking abilities. His family now lives with his uncle in the United States. Minh is very motivated to study and hopes to attend a state university to major in electrical engineering. At his new high school, Minh has stunned his math teachers with his ability to complete computations that are far beyond his grade level. In writing, Minh produces extended discourse, although he seems to struggle with listening and speaking. His English placement test indicates that he is at level 1 in speaking, level 2 in listening and level 5 in reading and writing.

Pabitra, a 9th-grade girl from Nepal, arrived in the United States in 8th grade. She came with her parents and brother; they had lived in a refugee camp all her life. While her home language is Nepali, the language of instruction by missionaries in the refugee camp school was English. Her English placement test revealed that she is at level 5 in listening, speaking, and reading and at level 4 in writing. However, she has consistently struggled with math since she arrived. Through an interpreter, her parents confirm that Pabitra was unsuccessful in math in the camp school and has always had difficulty wherever mathematical concepts are needed. Her math and ELL teachers suspect that she should be entitled to special education services because of her mathematics difficulties. However, the school principal (incorrectly) believes that ELLs should not be placed in special education programs until they have either exited the ELL program or have been in U.S. schools for three years.

Minh's academic skills are highly developed in his home language. He also possesses very strong English skills, but only in reading and writing. Minh's profile reflects the methods used during his English language instruction in Vietnam and does not follow the general pattern of language development, wherein listening and speaking develop before reading and writing. Minh's written English has developed without the usual benefit of oral language as a foundation. While Minh benefits from having the complex skills of reading and writing already in place, he requires specific and extensive instruction to develop his listening and speaking skills. Another advantage is that he has arrived with his entire family, for whom education is a top priority. As they did in Vietnam, his parents have high expectations for his academic achievement in the United States. Yet another advantage is that Minh is intrinsically motivated to do well in high school because of his clear professional career goals. However, he is frustrated because he is languishing in a math class that is far beneath his skill level because his high school has an unwritten policy that ELLs cannot participate in advanced courses, such as Advanced Placement (AP).

Minh is at an educational crossroads. He is in dire need of a teacher advocate to carefully study his biographical profile, note his strengths, and assist in designing a program of meaningful and challenging instruction. His course work must, as various federal mandates require, afford him equal access to the curriculum. Based on his ELP levels and level of mathematical prowess, it is likely that Minh could be very successful in the AP calculus class with appropriate scaffolding and support.

Pabitra, in contrast, has reached high ELP levels across all domains; her slightly lower development in writing is not unusual because reading and writing typically follow the development of listening and speaking. The main concern with her current educational programming is her lack of math skills coupled with her inability to understand mathematical concepts. Her ELL and math teachers have recognized a potential disability, corroborated by input from Pabitra's parents, regarding her longstanding math struggles. The principal's position that ELLs are not entitled to special education services until after a waiting period is misinformed, at best. Parental and teacher input about students' skills and abilities should be given great consideration because they know the student best. If bona fide disabilities exist, services must not be delayed. The administrator in this case should become more familiar with current ELL and special education legislation to ensure that all students receive the educational programming that they need as soon as possible. Though care must be taken to accurately identify disabilities in students who are still acquiring English, clear guidance on the subject is available (Hamayan et al., 2013).

Student Descriptors

Students at level 5 are approaching grade-level expectations for English language use in listening, speaking, reading, and writing. However, teachers must

Table 8-1   Student Descriptors, Level 5

Listening	Speaking	Reading	Writing
▪ Comprehends a broad spectrum of social and academic discourse ▪ Attends to language with an increasing amount of linguistic complexity ▪ Understands most grade-level content/academic vocabulary ▪ Approaches grade-level performance in English	▪ Produces a broad spectrum of extended discourse with increasing linguistic complexity and vocabulary mastery ▪ Approaches grade-level performance in English	▪ Comprehends text of increasing linguistic complexity and vocabulary related to a variety of grade-appropriate subjects and genres ▪ Approaches grade-level performance in English	▪ Writes text varying in length, complexity, vocabulary mastery, and level of academic discourse ▪ Approaches grade-level performance in English

remember to review students' ELP levels in listening, speaking, reading, and writing individually, rather than assuming that a composite score of 5 means that the student scored at level 5 in each language domain. Table 8-1 presents the students descriptors for level 5 in listening, speaking, reading, and writing.

Listening

In the domain of listening, students at level 5 can attend to most grade-level language across contexts. These students can comprehend a broad spectrum of social and academic discourse. Students at level 5 understand most language that includes grade-level general academic and content-specific vocabulary as well as complex grammar and discourse. Their performance in English is nearly on par with that of their grade-level non-ELL peers.

Speaking

The speech of students at level 5 demonstrates high levels of complexity and vocabulary attainment. These students can communicate using social and academic discourse and are nearing the level of speech production of the non-ELLs in their grade.

Reading

In terms of reading, students at level 5 can read text of increasing linguistic complexity and vocabulary related to a wide range of grade-level-appropriate topics and genres. These students' reading ability is nearly commensurate with that of their non-ELL contemporaries.

Writing

The writing of students at level 5 displays a variety of general academic and content-specific vocabulary, a range of linguistic complexity, and representations of social and academic discourse. While student writing is not perfect at this level, it is similar to the writing of non-ELLs at the student's given grade level.

A Word about Language Objectives

After teachers determine the essential learning of an assignment/assessment and clearly articulate the content objectives for all students, they need to determine how all students need to use oral and written language to participate in all classroom activities and reach all content objectives. With a clear understanding of the language demands of the assignments/assessments and instructional activities in mind, teachers are prepared to write and differentiate language objectives for their students. For example, an assignment/assessment may ask a student to identify the main idea and supporting details of two texts on the same topic, compare and contrast the perspectives taken in the texts, and write a persuasive argument that presents the student's position and that draws on evidence from each text. Teachers can use the student descriptors for students at level 5 to create appropriate language objectives for these students, given what they know about what students at level 5 can do with listening, speaking, reading, and writing. At level 5, students can participate in grade-level assignments/assessments with minimal support.

Example Differentiated Assignment

This example assignment is for a 9th-grade language arts class. Students are to write a set of instructions using an introduction, sequential organization, detailed description using appropriate grade-level vocabulary and sentence structures, and a conclusion for a self-selected task. The essential learning is clarity in communicating steps in a content-based process, use of transition words, and logical sequencing and it is the same for all students, regardless of their ELP level. The language demands ask students to use writing to describe steps in a process, sequence those steps in a logical order, and explain the content-based process. Table 8-2 presents the assignment differentiated for students at level 5 in writing, like Minh and Pabitra. Note that the language-based expectation and the scaffolding and support are the same for students at level 5 and for non-ELLs. However, students at level 5 may still depend on certain types of language-related scaffolding and support more than students who can use oral

Table 8-2   Example Assignment Differentiated for Students at Level 5

Standards-Based Content or Topic (from the curriculum)	
Assignment: *For a content-based process*	
Non-ELL	**Level 5**
Language-Based Expectations	

Write a set of instructions using
 	
 ■ *Introduction*
 ■ *Sequential organization*
 ■ *Detailed description using*
  ○ *appropriate grade-level vocabulary*
  ○ *grade-level sentence structures*
  ○ *appropriate and varied transition words*
 ■ *Conclusion*
	Write a set of instructions using
	
	 ■ *Compound and complex sentences*
	 ■ *Introduction (two complex sentences)*
	 ■ *Sequential organization*
	 ■ *Detailed description using*
	  ○ *appropriate grade-level vocabulary*
	  ○ *appropriate and varied transition words*
	 ■ *Conclusion*

Scaffolding and Support	
Using ■ *Model assignment* ■ *Teacher demonstration of the task using a think-aloud* ■ *Sequential graphic organizer to plan for writing* ■ *Language wall with sequencing words and key sentence structures* ■ *Feedback designed to push students to produce accurate grade-level writing*	*Using* ■ *Level 5 model assignment* ■ *Teacher demonstration of the task using a think-aloud* ■ *Sequential graphic organizer to plan for writing* ■ *Language wall with a wide range of sequencing words (color-coded—push students to use more advanced transition words, such as after, as soon as, meanwhile) and complex sentence structures* ■ *Compound and complex academic sentence frames posted in the classroom* ■ *Feedback designed to push students to produce accurate grade-level writing*

Essential Learning: *Clarity in communicating steps in a content-based process, effective use of transition words, and logical sequencing.*

Language Demands: *Use writing to describe each step in a process, sequence those steps, and explain how following these steps leads to the completion of the process.*

and written English according to grade-level expectations. The differentiation may come at the time of grading these students' work.

To facilitate the success of students at level 5 in achieving the objectives of classroom assignments/assessments, teachers can collaborate in multiple ways. For instance, the ELD teacher and the math teacher might co-plan a unit of instruction for a 9th-grade math class that includes Minh and Pabitra. Recall that Minh has reached level 2 in listening and level 1 in speaking, although he has reached level 5 in reading and writing. Pabitra has reached level 5 in listening, speaking, and reading, and level 4 in writing. Recall also that Pabitra struggles with math and that there has been some concern that she might need a special education teacher. The math and ELD teacher might invite a special education teacher who knows Pabitra to suggest math interventions that could support her. As the ELD and math teacher co-teach the lesson, they are sure to support Minh's speaking development, while providing him with many opportunities to work with comprehensible oral English. After the teachers implement their lesson, they can reflect on their successes and identify what they need to focus on next in their co-teaching.

Assignment/Assessment Strategies

In terms of language ability, students at level 5 can successfully participate in traditional tests, including large-scale standardized tests, though language accommodations may be warranted. However, teachers need to be aware that any assessment designed for non-ELLs may not be entirely appropriate for ELLs because of potential inherent cultural biases, like references to unfamiliar topics (e.g., knights and castles in elementary reading). These kinds of assessments should be carefully screened before they are used for ELLs. If tests deemed to be inappropriate must be used, results must be interpreted accordingly.

All Domains

Engage Students in Grade-Level Assignments/Assessments with Minimal Scaffolding and Support. Students at level 5 may need some scaffolding or support—though it should be minimal—because these students are approaching grade-level expectations in reading, writing, listening, and speaking in English. Such assistance may take the form of additional explanations about how to complete the task, allowing additional time, and so on. However, these students may also be able to complete grade-level tasks without support. Even as their ability increases, their continuing language development may still be reflected in occasional errors.

Simultaneously Assess Content and Language through Grade-Level Assignments/ Assessments. Although students at level 5 are approaching the range of grade-level expectations in oral and written English, teachers are reminded to maintain high expectations for students' continued development of linguistic complexity, precise vocabulary, and conventions of discourse. That is, oral and written language development must continue to be emphasized for students at level 5 across all genres necessary for social and academic success. Non-ELLs who have not fully developed their academic language skills may also exhibit level 5–like skills. As a result, teachers should target both linguistic and content development in their assessments to address the differentiated needs of both ELLs and non-ELLs. This requirement does not mean that all content teachers must assess the English language arts curriculum, rather that teachers should expect grade-level performance in students' language production within their content

Table 8-3   Assignment/Assessment Strategies for Students at Level 5

Listening	Speaking	Reading	Writing
■ Use extended discourse, including precise and grammatically varied language across all grade-level-appropriate topics and contexts	■ Require students to produce extended discourse, including precise and grammatically varied language across all grade-level-appropriate topics and contexts	■ Use grade-level texts, providing scaffolding as needed	■ Use and require extended discourse, including precise and grammatically varied language across all grade-level-appropriate topics and contexts

areas. Table 8-3 presents assignment/assessment strategies that teachers can use with students at level 5 in listening, speaking, reading, and writing.

Listening

Use Extended Discourse, Including Precise and Grammatically Varied Language across All Grade-Level-Appropriate Topics and Contexts for Assignments/Assessments. Students at level 5 in listening should be expected to comprehend grade-level English that is presented orally, for example, during lectures, videos, or academic presentations. Teachers may need to focus students' attention on areas that continue to prove challenging, for example, when following a detailed argument or listening to grade-level content in a new genre.

Speaking

Require Students to Produce Extended Discourse, Including Precise and Grammatically Varied Language across All Grade-Level-Appropriate Topics and Contexts. Students at level 5 in speaking continue to benefit from explicit instruction in the use of correct grade-level English, and they should be expected to produce grade-level English when speaking. Teachers across all content areas must embed the necessary English language instruction to facilitate students' continued language development, even at this level. Without targeted instruction combined with increasingly higher goals, students at level 5 are unlikely to progress further. Even if a district elects to stop providing these students with ELD services, teachers should consider what they would want for their own children as they work to ensure that all students, whether receiving language development support or not, are fully competent with English skills. "Good enough" is simply not sufficient in the globally competitive workplace. For example, teachers might explicitly tell students that they must use a wide variety of connectors when making a persuasive oral argument during assessment; rather than relying on language such as *also* and *in addition*, students might be expected to use *moreover* and *furthermore*.

Reading

Use Grade-Level Texts, Providing Scaffolding as Needed. At level 5, students may be able use stand-alone grade-level texts, though some scaffolding may be required. This may also be the case for non-ELLs who don't meet grade-level expectations in reading. Thus, if teachers elect to use grade-level texts in their assignments/assessments, they must ensure that students (ELLs and non-ELLs alike) can make sense of those texts. Providing assistance to students within the assignment/assessment—for example, by providing a glossary or word bank to accompany a reading selection within a test—can accomplish this goal. The exception to this rule of support would be if the assessment is testing grade-level reading ability; in that case, such supports are unwarranted.

Writing

Use and Require Extended Discourse, Including Precise and Grammatically Varied language across All Grade-Level-Appropriate Topics and Contexts. Teachers must decide exactly what they are assessing in terms of language or content when expecting students to write in response to an assignment/assessment task. If they are, indeed, assessing grade-level production of language within the content area, teachers should expect students to produce language that is representative of level 5 writing. They can then score this writing using a differentiated rubric. If the mastery of language is secondary to concept attainment or content, teachers can devise ways of assessing that are not language dependent, allowing students to demonstrate their content-area knowledge and skills without language mastery.

If the assessment targets language and content, it is necessary to have explicitly taught both. For example, in writing a poem in a language arts class, a teacher may require that students structure their writing using a certain meter and rhyme scheme and use exacting descriptive vocabulary.

Instructional Strategies

At level 5, as with all other levels, the critical action step of greatest significance is to determine students' instructional level based on their language proficiency levels and their content knowledge and skills. Next, teachers must target those instructional levels in terms of content and language development. This focused instruction contributes to the ongoing improvement of content learning and language development. Without these intentional focused actions, ELLs are less likely to reach their full academic potential.

All Domains

Explicitly Teach and Require Students to Use Precise and Grammatically Varied Language across All Grade-Level-Appropriate Topics and Contexts, Expecting and Allowing Minor Errors. For students to make increasingly detailed improvements toward grade-level expectations within the content areas, teachers must continue to explicitly teach and model high-level language during their instruction. Particularly at level 5, where the language development levels of ELLs and non-ELLs can often intersect, continuing and sustaining instructional efforts that aim for high expectations can make a pivotal difference for both groups of students. Teachers can turn to the student descriptors for level 5 and consult the assignment/assessment strategies for this level to target students' instructional needs. This practice affords teachers an authentic way to zero in on instructional gaps related to the curriculum and on overlooked discrete points of language development. This individualized and differentiated instruction is beneficial for both ELLs and non-ELLs. Without it, these students are unlikely to meet grade-level expectations in English that provide entrance to the world of advantage. For instance, students at level 5 should produce language with grammar and mechanics that is nearly at grade level; minimal errors that do not inhibit understanding could be overlooked as appropriate for a given grade level.

Engage Students in the Same Tasks Assigned to non-ELLs, Reducing Scaffolding and Support. The necessity of providing scaffolding and support in assignments/assessments for students at level 5 is likely to be minimal as they approach grade-level expectations in English. Because they are able to engage in most grade-level assignments/assessments with few errors, students at level 5 can, at times, seem "fully English proficient." Teachers are reminded, however, that these students, by definition and in keeping with the results of their English language proficiency assessments, are *not* yet fully English proficient. As a result, they continue to benefit from careful attention from teachers to interpret assessment results to inform instruction. Scaffolding for these students, while minimal, should be tailored to their individual needs.

Table 8-4 presents instructional strategies that teachers can use with students at level 5 in listening, speaking, reading, and writing.

Listening

Scaffold Language Development by Modeling Precise and Grammatically Varied Language across All Grade-Level-Appropriate Topics and Contexts, Expecting and Allowing Minor Errors. Teachers must themselves generate speech worthy of emulation.

Table 8-4   Appropriate Instructional Strategies for Students at Level 5

Listening	Speaking	Reading	Writing
■ Scaffold language development by modeling precise and grammatically varied language across all grade-level-appropriate topics and contexts, expecting and allowing minor errors	■ Provide opportunities for producing extended discourse using precise and grammatically varied language across all grade-level-appropriate topics and contexts ■ Emphasize the use of increasingly complex and precise language	■ Use grade-level texts, providing scaffolding as needed	■ Provide opportunities for producing extended written discourse using precise and grammatically varied language across all grade-level-appropriate topics, contexts, and genres ■ Emphasize the use of increasingly complex and precise language

In so doing, they model ways for students at level 5 (and non-ELLs) to articulate concepts and ideas in a formal register, using complex constructions and precise vocabulary. When such speech becomes the norm in the classroom, students are bound to incorporate it into their own way of speaking. For example, one teacher, when admonishing her students, used the command "Modulate, people!" rather than "Be quiet!" As a result, students were later heard to exhort the class with the same terminology. The authentic use of high-level language then becomes a permanent part of student repertoires.

Speaking

Provide Opportunities to Produce Extended Discourse Using Precise and Grammatically Varied Language across All Grade-Level-Appropriate Topics and Contexts. Students at level 5 need multiple opportunities to use the advanced language that teachers model. Such opportunities may include classroom discussions, debates, role-play, and persuasive speeches within the content areas. Teachers are encouraged to remind students to use the discourse-level frames and models that were the focus of teaching for students at level 4. Teachers must then expect such high-level production of students at level 5.

Emphasize the Use of Increasingly Complex and Precise Language. At level 5, teachers must continue assisting students in refining their language production within and across the content areas. Teachers should create an environment conducive and receptive to error correction because errors at level 5 are minimal. As a result, teachers can take opportunities to help students' polish their spoken language, for example by clarifying the use of the conditional: "I wish that I *were* _____," rather than "I wish that I *was* _____."

Reading

Use Grade-Level Texts, Providing Scaffolding as Needed. Though students at level 5 are not at grade level in terms of reading, they are able to access grade-level texts to a great extent, particularly when scaffolding is provided. As with students at level 4, this scaffolding may take the form of teacher explanation, preteaching vocabulary, glossaries, advance organizers and outlines, and other topical resources, such as first-person accounts, magazine and newspaper articles, and internet research. At level 5, these supports should be gradually withdrawn, as appropriate.

Another way to enhance reading ability is through frequent drop everything and read (DEAR) times, during which *all* students and staff in the K–12 setting can be expected to spend time reading materials of their choice. Sources for reading could include books and other materials in students' home languages, bilingual books, chapter books, novels, comic books, graphic novels, newspapers, and magazines. One school even involved the principal and custodians in this regularly scheduled schoolwide activity for a common 20-minute period. The goal in this sort of initiative is to encourage students to engage with text based on personal interest, as well as to increase their reading performance. Teachers must use a wide lens to determine acceptable reading materials. If students choose to read comic books or anime-style publications, we must celebrate that they are reading, in any language, rather than focusing on the genre.

Writing

Provide Opportunities to Produce Extended Written Discourse Using Precise and Grammatically Varied Language across All Grade-Level–Appropriate Topics, Contexts, and Genres. As with speaking skills, students do not improve their writing skills unless provided opportunities to practice and perfect them. In addition to providing such opportunities, teachers must continue to elucidate their expectations through sharing samples of successful student work, presenting authentic historical examples, and modeling and supporting the writing process. The fact that students are at level 5 does not take into consideration their familiarity (or lack of familiarity) with the various topics, contexts, and genres of writing at a given grade level. As a result, teachers must always remember to build and activate background knowledge and experiences that contribute to enhanced writing. In the same way, students must be schooled in the formal style of written academic text (e.g., using third person for academic writing), in contrast with the more casual style of spoken language. Attentive feedback regarding levels of formality can improve students' academic language and enhance access to professional and higher educational opportunities.

Emphasize the Use of Increasingly Complex and Precise Language. Students at level 5 can express meaning through writing, but it is incumbent on teachers to assist them in refining their writing to reflect more nuanced and precise language. At times, the ability to express ideas in grammatically complex ways is an integral part of communicating such shades of meaning. Consider the following examples:

Teachers must help students to be clearer.

versus

It is incumbent on teachers to assist students in refining their writing to reflect more nuanced and precise language.

While the objective of both sentences is the same, the second sentence uses language that is likely to have more influence in higher education and in professional contexts. This sentence also conveys the speakers' language proficiency to the listener. The second sentence uses a more formal style and includes grammatical complexity, as well as a frozen phrase ("it is incumbent upon") and sophisticated vocabulary. These techniques must all be explicitly taught.

As with students at levels 1–4, students at level 5 need to pay more attention to vocabulary than their non-ELL peers. As demonstrated by the preceding example, targeted vocabulary instruction continues to be essential for explicitly developing and expanding student vocabularies.

Instruction That Integrates Language Domains

Grade-level classroom activities designed for non-ELLs likely require the integrated use of listening, speaking, reading, and writing. In employing such activities with students at level 5, teachers must be vigilant in attending to issues of language development. Because these students are able to perform, albeit below grade level, they often fall between the cracks and do not receive the critical instruction that would lift them to the next ELP level. Particularly at level 5, teachers must not reduce their efforts or expectations regarding continuing language development; teachers must not settle for "good enough."

Conclusion

In this chapter, we emphasized that ELLs can demonstrate different ELP levels across the language domains, such as we saw with Minh who is at level 5 in reading and writing and level 1 in speaking. Further, ELLs, like their non-ELL peers, can potentially benefit from talented and gifted programming and special education services, if appropriate. Care needs to be taken so that there is neither over—nor under-representation of ELLs in these programs.

Professional Learning Activities

Working individually or with others in professional learning communities, differentiate the first four assignments for Minh and Pabitra. For assignment 5, choose the assignment and differentiate it for at least one of the level 5 ELP students in your class. When differentiating for students at level 5, remember that they may be at different ELP levels in listening, speaking, reading, and writing.

Differentiating for Minh and Pabitra

For assignments 1–4, differentiate the language-based expectations and the scaffolding and support needed for level 5 students, Minh and Pabitra. Recall that Minh is at level 5 for reading and writing, level 1 in speaking, and level 2 in listening. Pabitra lived in a refugee camp before coming to the United States, where her schooling was in English. She is at level 5 in listening, speaking, and reading and level 4 in writing.

1. Read the assignment above the template.
2. Read the essential learning and language demands below the template.
3. Review the standards-based topic, language-based expectations for non-ELLs.
4. Complete the template to show the differentiated assignment for Minh and Pabitra, by adding appropriate language-based expectations and scaffolding and support for these students.

After you complete the template, read on for additional insight on how to differentiate the assignment.

Assignment 1: *Write a research paper on a global issue as experienced in a country other than the United States*

Standards-Based Content or Topic (from the curriculum)	

On a global issue as experienced in a country other than the United States

Non-ELL	Level 5
Language-Based Expectations	
Write a research paper	<ul><li></li><li></li><li></li><li></li></ul>
Scaffolding and Support	
Using<ul><li>*Lecture on global issues*</li><li>*Example paper as a model*</li><li>*Library and internet resources*</li></ul>	*Using*<ul><li>*Lecture on global issues*</li><li>*Example paper as a model*</li><li>*Library and internet resources*</li><li></li><li></li><li></li></ul>

Essential Learning: *Research paper writing, development of world citizenship awareness, recognition of global issues.*

Language Demands: *Use language to read, summarize, compare, and contrast informational text; write a research paper; cite evidence from a range of informational texts; include citations in written report.*

It is unnecessary to adjust this assignment for either Minh or Pabitra because the assignment can focus on his or her country of origin and, hopefully, address a familiar topic. Because Minh's listening and speaking ability is far below his reading and writing ability, he should be provided with supplementary reading materials to compensate for the difficulties he may have understanding the lecture on global issues. He can also benefit from the support of a bilingual staff member who could clearly explain the serious expectations and ramifications of plagiarism and how to avoid it. The staff member could also help Minh with the conventions and formatting for his research paper. Perhaps Minh could be required to listen to a podcast, a television show, or a webinar on a global issue or to take notes and prepare an oral presentation in addition to his research paper. For Pabitra, this assignment is also focused on her weakest domain and, therefore, provides an excellent avenue for targeting corrections to her writing that can propel her to the next level of written English proficiency. She may also likely need assistance in understanding the format and conventions required for the research paper and information about the seriousness of plagiarism and how to avoid it. Both students can benefit from a visually supported lecture on global issues and guidance on how to best utilize library and internet resources.

Assignment 2: *Create a map or chart of a park showing plant and animal life*

Standards-Based Content or Topic (from the curriculum):	
A park showing plant and animal life	

Non-ELL	Level 5
Language-Based Expectations	
Create a map that includes notes about indigenous plant and animal life, and chart a food chain	▪ ▪ ▪ ▪
Scaffolding and Support	
Using	*Using*
▪ *Advance organizer that outlines animals and plants in a food chain* ▪ *Means of identifying new vocabulary needed for the assignment* ▪ *Example assignment* ▪ *Teacher modeling of map making and food chain construction*	▪ *Advance organizer that outlines animals and plants in a food chain* ▪ *Means of identifying new vocabulary needed for the assignment,* ▪ *Example assignment* ▪ *Teacher modeling of map making and food chain* ▪ ▪ ▪ ▪

Essential Learning: *Map making and chart-making skills; characteristics of local plants and animals and their ecosystems; sequencing events.*
Language Demands: *Use oral and written language to describe, sequence, and explain.*

Neither of these newcomers is likely to be familiar with the names of indigenous plants, and some animal names may also be unfamiliar. The teacher should provide Minh and Pabitra an advance organizer that outlines the unit and identifies the new vocabulary necessary for the assignment. Examples of completed assignments are shown, and map making and food chain construction are modeled.

Because map making might be a new skill for both students, Minh and Pabitra might work with more proficient partners to complete the assignment. Such pairing would also promote interaction, thereby developing Minh's speaking and listening abilities, which, at levels 1 and 2, respectively, require considerable focused attention and sustained development opportunities. Minh's partner needs explicit guidance in how to work with a student with advanced reading and writing skills and beginning listening and speaking skills. Using his advanced reading and writing skills, Minh can prepare himself to engage in instruction using the advance organizer. Minh may need assistance with general mapping skills because of his educational background experiences.

Assignment 3: *Translate and perform a scene from Romeo and Juliet*

Standards-Based Content or Topic (from the curriculum)	
From Romeo and Juliet	

Non-ELL	Level 5
Language-Based Expectations	
Act out a scene (from a modern vantage point)	■ ■ ■ ■
Scaffolding and Support	
Using ■ *Explicit instruction for interpreting Elizabethan English to understand the plot*	*Using* ■ *Explicit instruction for interpreting Elizabethan English to understand the plot* ■ ■ ■

Essential Learning: *Universal literary themes, theater acting skills, basic comprehension of Elizabethan English, translation of Elizabethan English to modern English.*
Language Demands: *Use oral and written English to recount, translate, and perform.*

This is a challenging assignment for Minh and Pabitra, so it is prudent to think about how useful the assignment is in terms of developing the students' weaker language domains and enhancing content knowledge and skills. In the case of this assignment, can these students produce the extended discourse required? Could additional activities focusing on developing listening and speaking be integrated to make this assignment beneficial and productive for Minh and Pabitra?

At level 1 in speaking and level 2 in listening, Minh is ill equipped to successfully complete this assignment without intentional differentiation based on the skills he has and can reasonably be expected to perform. Teachers should focus on the content standard using a modern-day English version that Minh can comprehend. He could benefit from listening to this version while reading along and then practice reciting the modern-day version at home to develop his spoken fluency. Minh could read aloud with a partner, a peer tutor, or a paraeducator. In this way he would be prepared to take a small role in the class assignment. Alternatively, Minh could be excused from learning Elizabethan English (because learning basic English is a prerequisite to learning Elizabethan English) so that he can focus on plot comprehension. With this differentiation for his listening and speaking levels, Minh can be expected to participate in the role-playing activity and focus on his speaking and listening skills. Because of his educational background, however, role-playing may be an unfamiliar activity, so limited instruction in basic acting techniques may be warranted.

Given that Pabitra is at level 5 in listening, speaking, and reading and level 4 in writing, she is fairly well equipped to cope with this assignment. However, teachers must remember that reading Shakespeare is often very difficult, even for non-ELL students. Furthermore, ELLs may lack the critical background knowledge and schema. This assignment could be differentiated for Pabitra to incorporate more writing, based on formative assessment data that clarify the gaps in her writing skills. The teacher could remind Pabitra of specific types of errors that the two are trying to eliminate, so that Pabitra understands the targeted nature of the corrections and pays particular attention to self-correction and using increasingly complex structures and vocabulary. Pabitra is also likely to benefit from instruction in basic acting techniques. She needs explicit guidance in how to make sense of Elizabethan English and how to translate it to modern English (as does the entire class, though Pabitra may need more support in this area).

Assignment 4: *Create a one-month budget for the first month after high school*

Standards-Based Content or Topic (from the curriculum)	
Fact-based one-month budget for life after high school	
Non-ELL	**Level 5**
Language-Based Expectations	
Create a poster presenting and explaining a budget	▪ ▪ ▪ ▪
Scaffolding and Support	
Using ▪ *Lecture on budgeting* ▪ *Model assignment* ▪ *Resources related to cost of living (e.g., apartment ads, grocery fliers)*	*Using* ▪ *Lecture on budgeting* ▪ *Model assignment* ▪ *Resources related to cost of living (e.g., apartment ads, grocery fliers)* ▪ ▪ ▪

Essential Learning: *Living within one's means; budgeting; research skills; setting goals; and preparing for future events.*

Language Demands: *Use oral and written language to describe, explain, argue, and defend.*

Both Minh and Pabitra can benefit from a visually supported lecture on budgeting, a model assignment, and guidance in where to find and how to use resources related to the cost of apartments and groceries. Given Pabitra's seeming disability with math concepts, teachers might consider consulting with special education teachers about ways to make this assignment more achievable for her.

This assignment should be appropriate for Minh, but he would benefit from giving an oral presentation about what he creates to improve his spoken English. His presentation may be made for the teacher or in his ELL class, rather than in front of the entire class. To develop Minh's level 2 listening skills, teachers should provide him with advance organizers to outline what is addressed in the lecture leading up to the assignment. Graphic organizers should be provided to scaffold note taking, with academic sentence frames and examples to scaffold his presentation and explicit teaching in phonemic awareness and pronunciation.

Pabitra's need for tutoring in math activities extends to this assignment. A paraeducator, bilingual staff member, more proficient peer, or a volunteer must assist her in developing the budget to ensure that the math is done correctly. For example, the task might be broken down for her so that numbers are added incrementally instead of all at once. Because Pabitra is at level 5 in listening and speaking, her need for graphic organizers is no greater than that of the non-ELL students. That being said, if all students would benefit from such supports, Pabitra would most certainly as well.

Differentiating for Your Students

For assignment 5, choose an assignment from your curriculum. Differentiate the assignment for a student at ELP level 5 in your class. Consider how student background factors like prior schooling, home language literacy, cultural orientation, and challenging experiences are likely to influence this student's content and language learning in your classroom.

1. Write the assignment above the template.
2. Identify the essential learning and language demands and write these below the template.
3. Fill in the standards-based topic, language-based expectations for non-ELLs, and for your student at ELP level 5.
4. Plan and implement the assignment in your classroom. If possible, video-tape the lesson or invite an ELL coordinator or coach to observe the lesson. Focus on the teacher's use of appropriate differentiation strategies for students at level 5 in any domain.

Assignment 5: _____

Standards-Based Content or Topic (from the curriculum)	

_____

Non-ELL	Level 5
Language-Based Expectations	
▪	▪
	▪
	▪
	▪
Scaffolding and Support	
Using	*Using*
▪	▪
	▪
	▪
	▪

Essential Learning: _____

Language Demands: _____

Share your template with your colleagues and explain why you made the choices that you did. When you implement the lesson in your class, reflect on how your focal students use oral and written language in each of the activities you planned. If you videotape the interaction, work with your colleagues to explore the scaffolding and support you provided. In any case, collect evidence of your students' content and language performances, identify your students' strengths, and list possible next steps for instruction.

Chapter 9

Bringing It All Together in Elementary, Middle, and High School Classrooms

*We can, whenever and wherever we choose, successfully teach all children
. . . we already know more than we need to know in order to do that.*

— RON EDWARDS

In practice, teachers generally do not find themselves neatly assigned to classrooms with students who function at uniform levels of English language proficiency (ELP). Rather, English language learners (ELLs) in a given classroom may be operating at different ELP levels and individual student's ELP levels can vary across domains, as discussed in previous student scenarios. For example, we have met a student who functions at level 5 in reading and writing but level 2 in listening and level 1 in speaking. This chapter examines how teachers can differentiate for the range of ELLs they find in their classes.

To accomplish this purpose, we describe three hypothetical classrooms—elementary, middle, and high school—of heterogeneous students. Each classroom includes five ELLs from a variety of cultural and linguistic backgrounds who are functioning at a range of ELP levels across domains, and we have incorporated several situations that can present significant challenges to teachers. The scenarios in this chapter should not be interpreted as representative of the proportion of challenging cases related to serving ELLs because our proportion is intentionally (but unnaturally) high. That is, these particular scenarios have been deliberately selected to provide teachers with a broader range of reference when searching for guidance as they face similarly challenging situations.

The chapter begins with a general discussion of how teachers at any grade level can differentiate assignments/assessments and instruction for students functioning across all five ELP levels. We also include specific guidance regarding teacher collaboration. The majority of the chapter provides concrete examples of differentiation for ELLs in practice at the elementary, middle, and high school levels. In each example, we look closely at student scenarios, answer frequently asked questions about issues raised by these scenarios, and show teachers how to differentiate assignments/assessments for the ELLs in these classes.

Thinking about All Five Levels Simultaneously

Classroom Scenarios

Mrs. Davis serves five ELLs in her 3rd grade classroom: Hanna from China, Hiroshi from Japan, Minji from Korea, Myriam from Haiti, and Mutaz from Syria. These students range from beginning to advanced ELP levels. Mrs. Davis wonders how to teach writing to such a diverse group of students.

In his 7th-grade classroom, **Mr. Clark** is working to meet the needs of five very diverse ELLs: Martha from Sudan, Irina from Russia, Jesús from Mexico, Claudia from California, and Karol from Poland. While Karol has reached advanced ELP levels, Irina and Jesús are closer to the beginning of their journey to English language proficiency (ELP). Mr. Clark is stumped about how to facilitate the effective participation of all these students in an upcoming unit on giving speeches.

Ms. Moore has welcomed five ELLs into the 6th-period section of her 10th-grade Cultural Issues class: Mercy from Liberia, Kumar from Nepal, Manivone from Laos, Yasir from Afghanistan, and Victor from El Salvador. While Victor is nearly proficient in English, Kumar and Yasir both score at level 1 in all four language domains. Ms. Moore is wondering how to prepare all five of these students for their group presentation to the school board, a service learning project selected for their group through a random drawing.

Differentiation is essential if students with diverse backgrounds and skills are to be successful academically. For students who are learning English, the obvious impetus for differentiation is their ELP levels. However, related literacy issues, differences in cultural norms and expectations—including those related to school-based learning, and differing sets of background knowledge pertinent to content learning—all validate the need for differentiation according to individual needs. All of these factors, but particularly students' ELP levels, require differentiation that is tailored to specific needs, rather than a one-size-fits-all approach for all ELLs. If diverse learners do not receive instruction that closes gaps in their knowledge and skills, they cannot meet standards for which teachers are held accountable. Further, such underserved students fall short of reaching their full potential.

Teachers should routinely prepare their assignments/assessments and instruction to address the range of linguistic capabilities of students in their classrooms and to effectively engage each student in every lesson. Such effective planning can be accomplished using any lesson planning template that teachers prefer, assuming the template builds incremental scaffolding that targets student needs. This process also allows teachers to address the same content standards and essential learning implemented for non-ELLs, while differentiating language objectives as needed. Using the principle of learning language through content and, therefore, teaching both simultaneously, allows teachers to meet district and state expectations for addressing content standards while respecting the learning needs of students at various ELP levels.

Supporting Collaboration through Reciprocal Mentoring

Teachers of culturally and linguistically diverse students can effectively expand their knowledge and expertise by reaching out to colleagues for support and collaboration. To this end, it is essential that content teachers and ELD teachers understand one another's roles. Content teachers focus on teaching standards-based content in a way that is comprehensible, meaningful, and engaging for all students. Guidance in this book clarifies key ways to accomplish this goal. However, preparing all teachers to teach content to students at different ELP levels is not meant to replace the expertise of the ELD teacher. That individual is to teach ELLs the oral and written English that they need to be successful inside and outside of school. The ELD teacher also assists content teachers in understanding how to best serve the ELLs in their classes.

Given the large student–teacher ratios that are increasingly common in U.S. schools and the large range of needs that each ELL brings to bear—including issues related to busing, scheduling, and parent communication—ELD teachers cannot be held solely responsible for teaching all of the language that ELLs need to learn. Instead, content and ELD teachers must collaborate to determine how to best meet student needs. This cooperation may take many forms, including co-teaching, collaboration on lesson planning, intensive language instruction on certain content topics by ELD teachers, and so on. Different contexts likely call for different forms of shared responsibility. However, the differentiation template and strategies presented in this book can ground both content and language teachers, providing a common understanding, language, and starting point in their work to serve ELLs well.

Together, teams of educators—including content and language teachers, but also "specials" teachers, talented and gifted teachers, special education teachers, paraeducators, and administrators—can work collaboratively to fill in gaps about shared student needs, content and background knowledge, and useful strategies to more effectively meet students' needs. Such reciprocal mentoring (Jones-Vo et al., 2007) empowers educators from different areas of expertise to assume equal instructional roles that, when combined, effectively meet the needs of the range of students in today's classrooms.

To support this highly beneficial collaboration, we provide a blank template for communication among educators in the Appendix. This ELL Differentiation Communiqué can be used to share content and language objectives and appropriate differentiation strategies among content teachers, ELD teachers, paraeducators, and others. For example, a science teacher could fill in the content objectives for the week, including targeted vocabulary and differentiated assignment/assessment expectations and then hand the Communiqué to the ELD teacher. The ELD teacher could then, if needed, help to refine the content teacher's plans for differentiated expectations. She or he could also suggest strategies or co-teach using appropriate instructional strategies, accessible materials, and other cultural and linguistic insights. The Communiqué acts as a living document between educators to support the instruction and assessment of each ELL according to his or her ELP levels.

Through collaboration and recognition that ELP levels are not static, teachers are better equipped to support language learners and propel them to the next ELP level by targeting their current developmental stages and characteristics and setting higher expectations. This repetitive and cyclical process spirals upward in a way that fosters language development and the attainment of content knowledge and skills.

Differentiating Lessons for Students at All Five Levels

To meet the need for comprehensive lesson planning that considers all the different language development levels of students in a given classroom, we provide a template for the development of differentiated assignments/assessments across all five ELP levels. This tool allows educators to do the following:

- Ensure that students at all ELP levels target the same content standards
- Consider and differentiate the language-based expectations of assignments/ assessments for students at different ELP levels
- Guarantee that adequate scaffolding and support are provided for students at each ELP level
- Maintain awareness of "next steps" for students at all five ELP levels by considering the expectations at subsequent ELP levels

This blank Differentiated Assignment Template that teachers can use when planning for the diverse ELLs in their classes is in the Appendix.

The Differentiated Assignment Template assists teachers in creating assignments/assessments that are consistent in terms of content—thus avoiding the watering down of standards—and attainable for students at differing ELP levels. Differentiated assignments are made accessible for students by deriving language-based expectations for each level from the student descriptors at each level, and by providing scaffolding and supports drawn from instructional strategies for each ELP level. Notice that the column for non-ELL grade-level expectations appears on the right, rather than on the left as in the preceding chapters. This placement denotes the progression of language development from level 1 to fully proficient in English, as defined by state ELD standards. This placement also assists teachers in recognizing the trends across levels in terms of increasing language-based expectations and decreasing scaffolding and support.

Teachers are encouraged to begin using the template for differentiating across all five ELP levels by first outlining the language-based expectations for assignments/assessments and the scaffolding and support for non-ELLs in the class. Next, teachers can use the student descriptors and the assignment/assessment and instructional strategies presented according to ELP level in this book to differentiate the assignment for all of the ELLs in their classes, starting with level 5 and working step by step backward to level 1. Many teachers have found it easier to work in this step-wise fashion, rather than jumping from the language-based expectations for non-ELLs immediately to level 1. Teachers should find that the scaffolding and support section of the Differentiated Assignment Template increases for students at lower ELP levels, while the language-based expectations diminish at higher ELP levels. The language-based expectations clarify how learning is assessed for students at each ELP level, while the scaffolding and support section clarifies how to use instructional strategies to support students at each of the five ELP levels.

In the spirit of backward lesson design (Wiggins & McTighe, 2006), teachers can use the template to design assignments/assessments prior to designing instruction. Teachers first identify the goals and outcomes of instruction for students at different ELP levels using the student descriptors for each ELP level; this information goes in the row for language-based expectations for assignments/assessments on the template. Next teachers select instructional strategies for students at different ELP levels; this information goes in the row for scaffolding and support on the template. This approach enables all students to produce desired standards-based products and performances, given consideration of their ELP levels in listening, speaking, reading, and writing, as well as any other important background information about the students' readiness to learn.

Elementary School Examples

When explicitly considering lesson design to meet the needs of a variety of ELLs functioning at different ELP levels across all four language domains in the classroom (listening, speaking, reading, and writing), teachers are reminded to integrate meaningful instruction, productive interaction, and appropriate assessment strategies based on students' ELP levels; their content knowledge and skills; and, importantly, knowledge gained from individual student background profiles.

As mentioned in the classroom scenario, our hypothetical 3rd-grade class includes the following five English language learners. Their individual ELP levels in the language domains of listening, speaking, reading, and writing are noted using L, S, R, and W.

Elementary School Student Scenarios

Hanna experiences hearing impairment, lack of interaction with others, and is confined to a wheelchair. She was adopted this year by her U.S. family, from an orphanage in China. Hanna has not learned to read and write in Chinese. She now lives with her adoptive parents and two English-speaking siblings and has begun 3rd grade. Hanna's parents have embarked on a series of surgeries to support her future ability to walk. They have also hired a tutor to work with her English development, and they have very high expectations for her achievement. Hanna's ELP levels are L = 2, S = 2, R = 1, and W = 1.

There are several unknown factors, particularly the unknown conditions she experienced, that may affect Hanna's ELD and could help or hinder her language development. Some children from orphanages can fail to receive the stimulation and interaction they need; some have physical or mental disabilities at birth; and others manifest the effects of fetal alcohol syndrome. With international adoption, health records can be unclear or ambiguous. As a result, teachers must be strong advocates for children when sorting out issues of language development and disability. Teachers must recognize that neither lack of exposure to education nor differences in language and culture are intrinsic indicators for special education. Further, teachers must be cognizant that students who qualify for both special education and ELD services are entitled to both streams of service. In that case, reciprocal mentoring (Jones-Vo et al., 2007) can be a useful strategy for bringing the expertise of both fields to bear for the benefit of students.

Hiroshi is a second-generation language learner born in the United States to parents originally from Japan. The family immigrated to take research positions with U.S. companies. Hiroshi spent his early years benefiting from his parents' bilingualism; his parents speak and read both Japanese and English to him and encourage his growing bilingualism. Hiroshi sometimes struggles with pronunciation, but his enthusiasm for speaking is not dampened. His ELP levels are L = proficient (according to state ELP tests), S = 5, R = 4, and W = 4.

Hiroshi is like many of his non-ELL classmates in terms of language development; nevertheless, he could benefit from sustained, targeted instruction and assessment. As a second-generation ELL, Hiroshi seems proficient in English in many ways, so it is premature to abandon instruction to scaffold his weaker areas until he reaches full proficiency in all four domains of language.

Minji has been living with her mother and her aunt, a graduate student, in a small apartment for two years. Korean is spoken exclusively in the home because her mother has not been able to study English. As a result, Minji's ELD depends mostly on her school exposure and experiences. However, her spoken and written Korean is excellent because her mother and her aunt work with her to maintain their language and culture. Minji's ELP levels are L = 4, S = 3, R = 3, and W = 2.

Minji's family models the importance of taking advantage of educational opportunities for her, even to the extent of leaving her father behind in Korea, to achieve long-term goals for the betterment of the family. Minji's scores reflect strong listening skills, yet girls in her culture are often expected to be soft-spoken. This cultural norm could explain Minji's lower speaking score because she tends not to initiate interactions and is a quiet student in class. The fact that her Korean writing is developed and maintained is a strong support for her continuing English literacy development.

Myriam was adopted through a church organization one year ago. An under-resourced student who was living on the streets of Haiti at one time, Myriam was suffering from malnutrition and attachment issues. She was also unable to read or write in her home language of Haitian Creole. One year later, Myriam is learning about U.S. culture and adjusting to her new family and school—after some significant initial behavior issues. She has gained two years growth in reading in one year, thanks to intensive instruction by a volunteer retired reading teacher. Myriam's ELP levels are L = 3, S = 3, R = 3, and W = 2.

Thank goodness for school volunteers! Teachers are reminded that the potential involvement provided by civic groups, church organizations, businesses, and the like offers a vast network of possibilities for supporting educational programs. In this case, a retired reading teacher intervened to make all the difference for a culturally and linguistically diverse student by regularly providing targeted literacy instruction for this struggling learner. Further, by understanding that Myriam's behavior at school resulted from her childhood experience of living without supervision, and after trying various interventions to ascertain that her learning was progressing, teachers were better able to sort out the fact that Myriam was not a candidate for special education. Rather, Myriam is an ELL with limited formal schooling. This background calls for powerful instruction that emphasizes building her literacy skills so that she can have a chance at achieving school success.

Mutaz, a child from Syria, has recently arrived in the United States with his mother and father after living for two years in Jordan. Prior to arriving in his 3rd-grade U.S. classroom, Mutaz lived in an area overcrowded with other refugees fleeing bombings and surprise attacks; he has spent time without adequate food, water, shelter, or clothing. Mutaz was not afforded any schooling opportunities in Jordan and is well below grade level in his home language of Arabic. On the playground, Mutaz's behavior has occasionally become violent, causing teachers, on one occasion, to call the police. After it was explained to his mother (in English because there are no Arabic interpreters in the school district) that Mutaz should not come to school the following day, the student, nevertheless, appeared. There are as yet no other Syrian members of the community resettled in the city. Mutaz's ELP levels are L = 1, S = 1, R = 1, and W = 1.

Because Mutaz is the first student representing Syria in this school district, the teachers should proactively assume the role of cultural brokers by researching and informing others about the cultural and linguistic factors related to this new student and his family. This goal can be accomplished by collaborating with community organizations, such as universities and local civic organizations, to gain relevant insights. Such useful information could be communicated widely to stakeholders, including teachers and community sponsors, by means of electronic messages, in-service meetings, or informal conversation. Useful information about the newcomers might include background information about their cultural needs, name pronunciation, previous education, and other relevant characteristics, to ensure respectful interaction and to meet their basic needs at the outset. The lack of Syrian-Arabic–speaking interpreters should be compensated for by seeking interpreters from another Arabic-speaking country. They can be valuable cultural brokers, using Arabic to assist in the communication of events and expectations and answering questions from the newcomers. The importance of this essential communication cannot be overstated. Further, it is important to build an ongoing relationship between school and home to include parent–teacher conferences, parent updates on student progress by phone (these calls should focus on the positive whenever possible), invitations and reminders to parents to attend school events such as student concerts and Family Math Night, and so on.

In this case, knowing that Mutaz is currently unable to read or write in his home language, has experienced untold trauma, and has had to struggle for his very existence, teachers could anticipate that he might exhibit behavior that differs from his peers. Further, such behavior could predictably appear aggressive or offensive. Expecting such a student to follow traditional U.S. school guidelines from his first day of enrollment might be unrealistic for a variety of reasons. Such students likely have little background knowledge to apply to their new school setting behavior. Teachers should realize that some survival behaviors that might be considered aggressive in U.S. schools are the very behaviors that enabled this student to prevail when others did not survive. Teaching new behaviors and appropriate socialization should be a high priority for such students, as should a concern for mental health issues related to trauma.

Teacher Questions, Concerns, and Responses

These students' 3rd-grade teacher has several questions regarding the students themselves and how to best address their linguistic and academic needs.

Since Hanna and Myriam are living in English-speaking homes, do they need any ELD services?

Although the benefit of an English-speaking home environment is certainly significant, these students are still eligible for ELD programming, based on their ELP scores. They should be given the same services as ELLs who come from homes where English is not spoken at the same development levels. It can be anticipated, however, that the language development of Hanna and Myriam will likely progress more quickly than that of students who do not use English at home.

Why isn't Hiroshi already fluent in English because his parents are? Why do they insist on using Japanese at home? Likewise, in Minji's case, why aren't they using English at home because her aunt speaks English?

Hiroshi's and Minji's families are to be commended for facilitating the students' home language abilities by using those languages in their homes. Recall that we, as educators, want to support this right for two important reasons: (1) the skills learned in the home language transfer to the new language; and (2) the home language and culture of any student is and should be an important part of her or his identity development. Students whose parents are bilingual can benefit from their parents' abilities to assist them with school work and clarify the meaning of various English terms and expressions, as well as engage their children in practicing and manipulating English orally. As a result, these students may acquire English a bit more quickly than students whose parents are not bilingual. However, this result does not always occur.

How can volunteers assist Myriam in my classroom?

Because the volunteer has been so successful in teaching Myriam to read, it is recommended that this work continue. After providing an early emphasis on the development of oral English to ensure that the student can derive meaning from sentence-level text, the teacher can then provide high-quality, age-appropriate, lower-reading-level books that offer extensive visual support and are aligned with content curriculum for these sessions. This type of intentional alignment of supplementary materials improves the connection between the tutoring and classroom activities and ensures the student access to the curriculum. The tutoring sessions might also focus on writing development because that is Myriam's weakest domain. Again, when this work addresses curricular content topics, all the better.

In Mutaz's case, how can teachers support him and his family, given his recent immigration and resettlement?

As illustrated by Maslow's hierarchy, which describes the necessary order of needs being met, the first step is to ensure that the family has its material and safety needs fulfilled. For example, does the family have beds to sleep on and is there food in the cupboard? Is everyone physically well and up to date in terms of medical needs? A home visit to welcome and get to know the family is an excellent opportunity to set the tone for future visits and to establish an ongoing relationship. When these needs are addressed, the student is likely to feel more comfortable and supported. He is therefore better positioned to begin learning at school.

Differentiating an Elementary Lesson

A unit focusing on the rain forest is ripe with opportunities for content and language development at the elementary level. By first determining what ELP levels are represented in the classroom, teachers can design assignments/assessments according to students' ELP levels using the differentiated template. The completed template lists appropriate student scaffolding and supports for various ELP levels and includes instructional strategies. such as building appropriate background, preteaching vocabulary, gathering realia and pictorially supported texts, creating graphic organizers, and so on. Using a variety of interactive strategies, teachers can embed opportunities to use language across domains according to student needs. In this way, students at different ELP levels have access to rigorous content-area instruction. Ultimately, using the leveled recommendations on the template, teachers can differentiate instruction and assessment to ensure student engagement and facilitate successful learning.

Table 9-1 illustrates how one assignment on the topic of the rain forest might be differentiated. The essential learning for this assignment is for students to explain, describe, and compare and contrast features of the rain forest before and after deforestation using appropriate language in a text that is organized logically. The language demands are for students to write a three paragraph essay that describes, explains, compares, and contrasts. After creating the assignment for non-ELLs, identify the language-based expectations and the scaffolding and support, first for level 5, then level 4, working back to level 1. It should be noted that this same assignment could be differentiated in other ways, according to instructional needs; there is no single correct differentiation of an assignment.

We have filled out the template with general guidance for students at each of the ELP levels. Given that the students in this hypothetical 3rd-grade class—as in many real classrooms—exhibit different ELP levels in different language

Table 9-1   Example Assignment Differentiated for Elementary School Students

Assignment: *Describe, compare, and explain features of the rain forest before and after deforestation*

Standards-Based Content or Topic (from the curriculum)				
Features of the rain forest before and after deforestation				

Level 1	Level 2	Level 3	Level 4	Level 5	Non-ELL
		Language-Based Expectations			
Copy three words or phrases that describe, compare, and explain	Write three simple sentences using occasional content/academic vocabulary that describe, compare, and explain	Write three short paragraphs using some content/ academic vocabulary and simple/complex sentence structures that describe, compare, and explain.	Write a three-paragraph essay using some content/academic vocabulary and complex sentence structures that describe, compare, and explain	Write a three-paragraph essay using some content/academic vocabulary and complex sentence structures that describe, compare, and explain	Write a three-paragraph essay using grade-level vocabulary and sentence structures that describe, compare, and explain

Level 1	Level 2	Level 3	Level 4	Level 5	Non-ELL
		Scaffolding and Support			
Using	Using	Using	Using	Using	Using
■ Experiences gained during a botanical center field trip	■ Experiences gained during a botanical center field trip	■ Experiences gained during a botanical center field trip	■ Experiences gained during a botanical center field trip	■ Experiences gained during a botanical center field trip	■ Experiences gained during a botanical center field trip
■ Word-and-picture cards featuring pretaught vocabulary (to be used when labeling a Venn diagram)	■ Pretaught vocabulary,	■ Pretaught vocabulary	■ Pretaught vocabulary	■ Pretaught vocabulary	■ A Venn diagram to guide writing
■ A chant to assist students in remembering key phrases and vocabulary	■ A chant to assist students in remembering key phrases and vocabulary	■ A Venn diagram	■ A Venn diagram	■ A Venn diagram	
■ A Venn diagram,	■ A Venn diagram	■ A chant to assist students in remembering key phrases and vocabulary	■ Academic sentence and discourse frames posted in the classroom	■ Academic sentence and discourse frames posted in the classroom	
■ A think-aloud demonstration of labeling	■ A think-aloud demonstration of labeling	■ A think-aloud demonstration of labeling	■ Pictorially supported rain forest texts	■ Pictorially supported rain forest texts	
■ Pictorially supported rain forest texts	■ Pictorially supported rain forest texts	■ Academic sentence frames posted in the classroom	■ Photographs of forestation and deforestation to guide writing	■ Photographs of forestation and deforestation to guide writing	
■ Realia related to rain forest products (e.g., fruit, medicinal plants, wood carvings)	■ Realia related to rain forest products (e.g., fruit, medicinal plants, wood carvings)	■ Pictorially supported rain forest texts			
■ Photographs of forestation and deforestation to guide writing	■ Photographs of forestation and deforestation to guide writing	■ Photographs of forestation and deforestation to guide writing			

Essential Learning: *Describe, explain, compare, and contrast the features of the rain forest before and after deforestation.*

Language Demands: *Write a three paragraph essay that describes, explains, compares, and contrasts.*

domains, teachers may pull strategies from more than one column for a given student. This is an opportunity for educators to engage in reciprocal mentoring by sharing and combining their individual areas of expertise for the benefit of their students. However, the most critical consideration for the writing assignment is to match the expectations to each student's writing level, as indicated by students' ELD levels in writing. Teachers are urged to push students to higher levels of performance, so that students move along the ELD continuum.

Of course, language is not the only topic that informs teachers about appropriate instruction and assessment of the ELLs in their classes. Information from students' background profiles should always be considered when designing instruction and assessment. Here we offer some additional guidance regarding the individual ELLs who are a part of this elementary classroom:

Hanna

- Ensure that she is positioned in the classroom so that she can hear.
- Make sure that every aspect of the field trip is wheelchair accessible.
- Share assignments with her parents and tutor.

Hanna, Myriam, and Mutaz

- Bear in mind that this assignment is more demanding for these students, who cannot read or write in their home languages, than for students who can transfer home language literacy skills to English.

Hiroshi and Minji

- Because these students' home languages are very distinct from English, it is more difficult for them to learn English than it is for other students who have home languages closer to English.
- Because these students are literate in their home languages, the teacher could ask them to brainstorm ideas in their home languages before writing in English.
- Another option would be to have them write about the field trip in their home language. Remember that ELLs should not be expected to do more work than their non-ELL peers. However, teachers should encourage the use of the home language whenever it can be used to support the learning of English.
- Because these students come from more collective cultures, they may feel more comfortable with a collaborative approach to the assignment.

Mutaz

- Because this student is completely new to formal schooling, teaching may need to initially focus on school survival skills, including how to hold a pencil and how to negotiate the lunch line. A paraeducator or trained volunteer could help with this.

- Mutaz's refugee experiences have undoubtedly affected him, and teachers need to make allowances while he adjusts to his new homeland.

When elementary school teachers get to know their students, in terms of ELP levels and other background factors, they can apply the differentiation strategies to engage all students, particularly ELLs.

Middle School Examples

Developing middle school units of instruction follows the same process as for elementary schools. When planning lessons that meet the needs of middle school ELLs at different ELP levels, teachers should integrate meaningful instruction, interactive activities, and appropriate assessment strategies based on students' ELP levels in listening, speaking, reading, and writing; students' content knowledge and skills; and, importantly, students' individual background profiles.

Our middle school class includes the following 7th-grade students.

Middle School Student Scenarios

> **Martha** arrived in the United States as a refugee from Sudan three years ago through the United Nations High Commissioner for Refugees. A speaker of Dinka and English, Martha is often called on to translate for her grandmother. Martha never attended school in Sudan and is not literate in her home language. After fleeing the war to Kenya, she lived in a crowded refugee camp. Martha now lives with her grandmother, a respected elder in the African community. She is quickly becoming westernized by pop culture and developing a taste for fast food through the influence of her peers. Martha is trying out her new independence and exhibits behaviors in school that cause her teachers to think she might need special education services. Martha's ELP levels are L = 4, S = 4, R = 3, and W = 2.

Martha's teachers may be fooled into thinking that she is proficient in English and that any lack of academic success can be attributed to laziness. In fact, while Martha scores well in listening and speaking because of her social language ability, the development of her academic reading and writing skills depends on insightful and targeted instruction at school to scaffold her toward proficiency. Martha does not receive supplementary instruction at home because only Dinka is spoken there. As for her experimental behavior, teachers, counselors, and others can provide opportunities to talk about typical teen issues in safe settings, perhaps in a girls' discussion group. It is not unusual for ELLs to try out the behaviors, attitudes, language, and styles of others. In so doing, they may exhibit behaviors that are atypical of their heritage cultures.

> **Irina** is a recent adoptee through a program that pairs Russian children with potential families during a summer exchange program. Irina is fluent and literate in Russian and her

new U.S. family includes three other siblings. She reads well in Russian and is rapidly expanding her verbal communication skills in English. Irina's ELP levels are L = 3, S = 3, R = 2, and W = 1.

On grade level at her Russian school, Irina is poised for success in acquiring English relatively quickly by readily transferring her knowledge of content and concepts to English. In addition, Irina can benefit greatly from interactions with her three English-speaking siblings, which should hasten her oral language development. Irina's beginning level of writing in English is not surprising, given that she initially learned to write in another alphabet and that she has been enrolled in U.S. schools for only a short time.

Regardless of the status of language speakers in the home, internationally adopted students should always be considered for potential participation in ELD programming, based on their home language. While the student's new home is exclusively English speaking, Irina's original language, which was not English, can have long-term effects on her language learning. As a result, it is important for teachers to know not only what language is currently spoken in the home, but also what language the student first heard and used.

Jesús's Mexican family owns a successful local restaurant that employs extended family members. Though his sister came to the United States with her father five years ago, Jesús and his mother arrived in the United States last year when, after interrupted schooling, he started to attend middle school. Jesús's ELP levels are L = 3, S = 2, R = 2, and W = 2.

Because Jesús had stopped attending school in his rural Mexican hometown, he arrived at his U.S. middle school with unique learning needs. The interruption in his schooling resulted in gaps in content, literacy, and academic language development. Therefore, Jesús is not prepared to fully engage with the middle school curriculum. Because of his limited prior schooling, Jesús struggles to get motivated to participate in school. He also seems to put a lot of energy into finding ways to avoid engaging in activities and assignments/assessments. Unsavory influences also provide temptations for Jesús.

Knowing that Jesús needs to experience success in school to become motivated to participate, his teachers must work to facilitate this process in a variety of ways, including the following:

- Implementing instructional and assessment strategies appropriate to his language development levels across domains
- Using an engaging reading program
- Providing a trained volunteer or paraeducator (under the direction of a teacher) dedicated to literacy instruction
- Embedding reading and writing topics that include personal interests

- Incorporating service learning at venues relevant to the student
- Including opportunities for student choice
- Partnering the student with a mentor

As Jesús comes to see himself as a successful student at school, teachers can expect him to engage more fully with classroom assignments and achieve.

> **Claudia** is a migrant student from California. Her family moves frequently, so while she always starts the school year in the same community, she may move away after only two months. Claudia is a good student who enjoys school. Her parents have not learned to read or write very well in Spanish, their home language, and they rely on Claudia for translation, after-school care of younger siblings, and household responsibilities. Claudia's ELP levels are L = 4, S = 4, R = 3, and W = 3.

Because Claudia and her family return annually to this community, along with other migrant families, community organizers now anticipate their arrival by hosting a welcome picnic in the city park, collecting furniture and clothing, donating food pantry items, and encouraging community residents to rent housing to the migrant families. Claudia's teachers should welcome her return enthusiastically and assure her that they can help her build critical skills by working hard together.

> **Karol's** family immigrated to the United States two years ago to reunite with his grandmother. On grade level in Poland, Karol exhibits signs of giftedness and has learned English extremely quickly. Karol has also quickly adopted U.S. culture, styles, and music. Karol's father is a long-distance truck driver and is often gone for extended periods. Karol has been testing his mother's patience during his father's absences by associating with a group of students who negatively influence his behavior. Karol's ELP levels are L = proficient, S = proficient, R = proficient, and W = 5.

Academically, Karol is positioned to perform very well. This school district has developed assessments and checklists that identify ELLs for participation in gifted and talented (GT) programming without requiring standardized test scores that tend to preclude ELL participation. As a result, Karol has already been participating in the GT program for a year. Karol scores proficient in three language domains; his only area of weakness is writing, where he scores a 5. It is not unusual for ELLs to achieve proficiency in writing last. Because his score may be similar to a non-ELL's score on the ELP test, some districts exercising local control might elect to stop providing Karol with ELD services, but Karol—and students with a similar profile—still benefit from targeted ELD instruction in writing.

Karol, like all ELLs, benefits from explicit information and counseling about long-range planning, college options, goal-setting, financial aid, and so on.

Teacher Questions, Concerns, and Responses

The 7th-grade teacher who serves these students in his language arts/social studies class has several questions regarding how to best meet the needs of these diverse learners.

Is it okay for me, as the teacher, to be a cultural informant to clarify what may be helpful for school success?

Definitely! Sometimes ELLs display behavior that may not be in their best interests. The reason for this behavior could be that they are emulating other students, are unaware of cultural norms followed in the school, or for other reasons. It is certainly appropriate for any teacher to provide guidance to ELLs regarding what constitutes appropriate behavior in the school setting.

Should Irina be exempted from writing activities since she's at level 1?

No. She likely cannot move to level 2 or higher in writing if she is not engaged in writing activities that are matched to her current ELP level and that scaffold her toward the next higher level. Though it may take a bit of creative thinking to differentiate writing assignments/assessments for her, such scaffolding is a must. The completed templates at the end of this section offer guidance in this regard.

Since Jesús has gaps in his educational background, why is he placed in 7th grade?

It is important to place students in a grade that is within two years of their age-appropriate grade. Even if Jesús were to be placed in 5th grade, he might still have gaps, particularly (and obviously) in U.S. history. Further, putting him in a grade below his same-age peers might alienate him at an age when peer interaction is a priority. Teachers must address ELLs' educational gaps in the same way that they would address content gaps for non-ELLs—through differentiated instruction. It may be that a paraeducator or trained volunteer could assist in this endeavor for Jesús.

Why do migrant workers, such as Claudia's family, come to our community for such a short period of time and then leave? Because I can't accomplish much with her in the short period of time that she's here, why invest my time and energy into catching her up, especially when I have so many other students who need help and are here all year?

Claudia needs an advocate, a teacher to help her to be successful so she can maintain her interest in and enjoyment of school. Claudia, like any other student, deserves to benefit from high-quality instruction and teacher concern. For many ELLs, one special teacher who recognizes their value can make all the difference. Every teacher can be that encouraging and welcoming teacher who helps students to value themselves, set goals, and reach their full potential.

Again, a paraeducator or trained volunteer—possibly a classroom peer or a student from the high school—whom the teacher takes the time to find may make school success possible for students like Claudia. Another potential resource would be education majors from a local college who might need practicum hours or want to gain experience to add to their résumés.

On a practical note, school districts receive federal funds for each ELL in their district at a fall cutoff date in the following school year, whether the student remains a full school year or not. Such funding helps districts to provide services and materials for families that do seasonal work for U.S. companies. Migrant funds and programs should be explored by districts with migrant students.

How can Karol's language skills be better than those of some non-ELLs in the class? Why should he receive any additional support in writing when many students who grew up speaking English don't write as well as he does?

This is an excellent question. However, if Karol is still entitled to ELD services, he should receive them. Further, if his ELP level indicates that accommodations are necessary, they should be provided. ELP tests and the criteria that determine when ELLs are no longer provided with ELD services may need to be revisited if a large number of entitled ELLs are outperforming their non-ELL peers.

Differentiating a Middle School Assignment

The example middle school assignment asks students to create and present speeches about different countries and cultures using multimedia software. The essential learning for this assignment is to summarize key features of a given country orally and in writing, present information using multimedia technology, and speak clearly to communicate information. To complete this assignment, students need to use oral and written language that describes and explains. Drawing on the authentic and motivating aspect of this assignment allows students to learn more about their own backgrounds and to share with peers. This assignment also provides teachers with many opportunities for facilitating language development in listening, speaking, reading, and writing. Thus, this language-rich assignment offers an ideal format for a range of imaginative differentiation possibilities.

In terms of scaffolding to support students, teachers can choose from the variety of suggestions listed in Table 9-2 and in the quick-reference chart. Strategies such as making connections to previous experiences and learning, providing new experiences, creating a word or language wall supported by pictures, and posting academic sentence and discourse frames are just a few of the possibilities. As always, teachers must intentionally embed multiple interactive opportunities for students to manipulate and practice language.

Table 9-2 is a completed Differentiated Assignment Template for this speech-making assignment. The essential learning for this assignment is to summa-

Table 9-2   Example Assignment for Middle School Students

Assignment: *Create and present a speech describing an assigned country using multimedia technology*

Standards-Based Content or Topic (from the curriculum)

About an assigned country

Level 1	Level 2	Level 3	Level 4	Level 5	Non-ELL
		Language-Based Expectations			
Create a 3–4 slide speech using provided content/academic words and phrases that describe and explain	*Create and present a 5–6 slide speech using occasionally provided content/academic vocabulary and simple sentences that describe and explain*	*Create and present a 6–8 slide speech using some content/academic vocabulary and simple/complex sentence structures that describe and explain*	*Create and present a 10-slide speech using some content/academic vocabulary and simple/complex sentence structures that describe and explain*	*Create and present a 10-slide speech using a variety of content/academic vocabulary and simple/complex sentence structures that describe and explain*	*Create and present a 10-slide speech using grade-level vocabulary and simple/complex sentence structures that describe and explain*
		Scaffolding and Support			
▪ 3–4 sample PowerPoint slides on the United States (picture or clip art plus key word[s]) ▪ Videos describing various countries ▪ Think-aloud review and demonstration about making a PowerPoint presentation	▪ Outline of required speech components ▪ Videos describing various countries ▪ Think-aloud review about making a PowerPoint presentation ▪ Teacher-selected websites for clip art and pictures ▪ PowerPoint technology	▪ Outline of required speech components ▪ Videos describing various countries ▪ Think-aloud review about making a PowerPoint presentation ▪ Teacher-selected websites ▪ PowerPoint technology	▪ Outline of required speech components ▪ Videos describing various countries ▪ Think-aloud review of making a PowerPoint presentation ▪ Teacher-selected websites ▪ PowerPoint technology ▪ Academic sentence frames posted	▪ An outline of required speech components ▪ Videos describing various countries ▪ Think-aloud review about making a PowerPoint presentation ▪ Teacher-selected websites ▪ PowerPoint technology	▪ Outline of required speech components ▪ Videos describing various countries ▪ Think-aloud review about making a PowerPoint presentation ▪ Teacher-selected websites ▪ PowerPoint technology

Level 1	Level 2	Level 3	Level 4	Level 5	Non-ELL
■ Teacher-selected websites for clip art and pictures ■ PowerPoint technology ■ Assistance from a prepared and skilled buddy ■ Assistance from the teacher or a bilingual paraeducator ■ Student's own culture as a topic ■ Terminology in English and the student's home language ■ Word and picture cards featuring pretaught vocabulary ■ Pictorially supported texts ■ Cultural artifacts ■ Photographs of native country ■ Presentation made to buddy, teacher, or small group (ELL class), if possible	■ Assistance from a prepared and skilled buddy, (as needed) ■ Assistance from the teacher or a bilingual paraeducator, ■ Student's own culture as a topic ■ Photographs of native country ■ Word and picture cards featuring pretaught vocabulary ■ Pictorially supported texts ■ Cultural artifacts ■ Photographs of native country, ■ Presentation made to buddy, teacher, or small group (ELL class), if possible	■ Student's own culture as a topic ■ Academic sentence frames posted ■ Cultural artifacts ■ Photographs of native country			

Essential Learning: Summarize key features of a given country orally and in writing, present information using multimedia technology, and speak clearly to communicate information.

Language Demands: Use oral and written language to describe and explain.

rize key features of a given country orally and in writing, present information using multimedia technology, and to speak clearly to communicate information. The language demands are to use oral and written language to describe and explain. Readers are reminded that individual assignments can be differentiated in a myriad of ways; this is simply one example with many ideas for support and scaffolding. Again, the key to successful differentiation is the alignment of expectations with the descriptors and strategies outlined in this book and presented on the quick-reference chart.

This template includes the language-based expectations for students at the five different ELP levels, and it focuses on the domains of writing and speaking. Following the language-based expectations, we see the scaffolding and support that students at each of the different ELP levels need to create and present their speeches. Individual students may be at different levels in writing and speaking, the two language domains required in the speech assignment. Therefore, guidance for different ELP levels in writing and speaking may be drawn on to support each student. Further, teachers are also reminded to push students within a given ELP level toward the next level. The expectations outlined in the table are appropriate for each ELP level, according to the student descriptors presented on the quick-reference chart. However, educators must remember that these levels are broad and that a student whose test data list one level may be on the cusp of the next level and should be pushed toward that level. Alternately, a given student may be at the lower end of the continuum for his or her ELP level and may struggle to meet the assignment/assessment demands for that level.

In addition to the linguistic abilities of one's students, other student factors inform the teaching and learning process of individual students. The following discussion serves as guidance for some of the ELLs in this hypothetical class.

Martha

- Because this student has not developed literacy skills in her home language, it can take her longer to learn write in English than level 2 writers who have had the opportunity to learn to read and write in their home languages. This fact must be kept in mind as students are given time to work.
- This student's desire to be like "American" students can be used to help with her motivation to complete the assignment.

Irina

- If necessary, Irina can be supported by her family in the labor-intensive process of writing the outline for the speech.
- The teacher should provide needed scaffolding during in-class work times.
- A paraeducator or trained volunteer could be an excellent source of support for Irina.

Irina, Jesús, and Karol

- This may be an appropriate time to allow Irina, Jesús, and Karol to do the assignment in their home languages. This is not recommended as a daily course of action because improved English is the goal, but allowing students to use their home languages in the classroom is encouraged. It would be a pity if any of these students were to lose her or his home language, a particular concern with Irina because she was adopted by an English-speaking family.

- All three of the students could give the speech in their home languages, allowing the rest of the class to understand what it feels like to sit in a classroom where the language is unfamiliar.

- These students' home languages and cultural insights would be honored if they were to present about their countries of origin in their home languages. This opportunity could also serve as a motivating factor for Jesús, who has struggled because of gaps in his schooling.

When teachers think creatively about what their students can do with oral and written language, any language, and when they draw on students' home languages and cultures as resources for learning, many possibilities emerge for engaging ELLs from any background.

High School Examples

Differentiating for high school students follows the same process as that used at elementary and middle school levels. When planning lessons to meet the needs of a variety of students functioning at a range of ELP levels across the four domains of listening, speaking, reading, and writing in the classroom, teachers are reminded to integrate meaningful instruction, student interaction, and appropriate assessment strategies based on students' content knowledge and skills, ELP levels, and, importantly, individual background profiles.

This example assignment is for a sophomore Cultural Issues class that includes the following students.

High School Student Scenarios

Mercy is a Liberian student who arrived with her cousin five years ago. She witnessed atrocities against her family and experienced violence herself. She has been plagued by mental health issues, including post-traumatic stress disorder. Though her home language is English, the variety of language and the cultural differences combine to qualify her for ELD programming services. As a student, Mercy has difficulty with long-term projects and she tends to isolate herself. Mercy's ELP levels are L = 5, S = proficient, R = 3, and W = 3.

Mercy needs a very caring approach because of her background. Teachers who work with refugee students must be aware of the psychological effects of violence, torture, and rape on victims. They also need to be familiar with community resources available to assist students in dealing with the aftermath of trauma. Cultural sensitivity must always be exercised when dealing with such issues.

Mercy's teachers should assign buddies to ensure that she is not isolated in the classroom or during lunch. Buddies, paraeducators, or trained volunteers might also work with her on breaking down long-term projects to make them easier to complete. While Mercy scores as proficient in speaking on the test used by her district, she still needs targeted instruction and assessment, particularly in the areas of reading and writing.

Mercy's high level of speaking ability is not entirely surprising, given that a form of English is her home language. Special focus must be given to developing her academic English skills, particularly in reading and writing.

> **Kumar** is a 15-year-old student from Nepal. He suffered from polio as a child and depends on a crutch for his mobility. Because of this disability, he was never allowed to attend school, although his older brother was. Kumar's immature behavior since arriving only a short time ago has shocked teachers who are not sure how to proceed. Kumar's ELP levels are L = 1, S = 1, R = 1, and W = 1.

In some countries, children with disabilities are not afforded educational access and are instead kept at home. This lack of formal schooling may result from a variety of factors, depending on the culture. These reasons may include the unavailability of appropriate services and resources to serve potential special education students or cultural attitudes about disabilities that cause family embarrassment. Regardless of the reason for limited formal schooling, such children must be afforded the same access to educational opportunities as their non-ELL peers. It is critical to enact immediate meaningful early literacy instruction, even though this student is older than students who usually receive literacy instruction at an introductory level. Enrolling students who have not been afforded the opportunity to develop literacy skills, particularly in advanced grades, presents challenges. School districts need to energetically embrace their responsibility to afford equal access to the curriculum to all students and ensure that appropriate literacy development instruction is available to ELLs with limited or underdeveloped literacy skills. This undeniable mandate must be seized and acted on in an intentionally goal-oriented long-range plan; such students depend on it for their survival and future quality of life.

> **Manivone** is the 16-year-old daughter of a Laotian woman and her Vietnamese-American husband. Vietnamese is spoken in their home. Before marrying her husband last year when he made a return visit to Vietnam, Manivone's mother was living in a small Vietnamese village where she worked farming rice. Manivone's mother only completed 3rd grade and could not afford to send Manivone to school in Vietnam. However, she has taken

steps to ensure her daughter receives educational opportunities since they arrived a year ago as a new family of three. Manivone's ELP levels are L = 3, S = 2, R = 1, and W = 1.

Never is the need for explicit and rich literacy instruction more imperative or crucial than it is now, at the high school level, for a student like Manivone whose literacy skills in the home language are at beginning levels. As is the case with Kumar, Manivone's teachers must devise a comprehensive program to support her in acquiring literacy in English that is at grade level and age appropriate. If such instruction does not happen, Manivone is likely to add to the alarming dropout statistics related to female ELLs in the United States.

Manivone would likely benefit from a variety of social supports, such as assigned buddies, a peer tutor, a counselor, a mentor, or a bilingual advocate.

Yasir is a recent refugee student from Afghanistan. He arrived with his widowed mother and four siblings to enroll in school three months ago. Yasir's father was a high-ranking dignitary before his untimely death in Afghanistan. Through an interpreter, Yasir's mother shares that he is "different" from her other children and that she did not send him to school with his siblings. He is unable to remember facts or concentrate on tasks for an extended period. Yasir's ELP levels are L = 1, S = 1, R = 1, and W = 1.

One of the most important pieces of data regarding Yasir is his mother's input that he is "different." Obviously an ELL, Yasir must be evaluated carefully to determine the extent of his seeming disabilities. This process does not need to be postponed until he is proficient in English. Rather, it should be initiated immediately. Excellent guidance for this process is provided by Hamayan et al. (2013).

In the meantime, teachers must enlist the assistance of paraeducators, trained volunteers, peer mentors, or others who can help Yasir with appropriate instruction. Note that these individuals may require very explicit guidance from ELD and special education teachers in how to work with this student.

Victor came to the United States from El Salvador three years ago. After working odd jobs for six months, he was informed that he could attend school. He immediately enrolled in high school and applied himself with uncommon energy while continuing to work full-time. Victor is on track to graduate in the top 3% of his class. Victor's ELP levels are L = proficient, S = proficient, R = 5, and W = 5.

Victor is a highly motivated and self-directed student who regards his access to education as a privilege. Because his parents still live in rural El Salvador, Victor is driven by the desire to make his parents proud of him and help support his family. In class, Victor often appears to be dozing, but he works the night shift and comes to school with only a few hours of sleep. He would benefit from a discreet application for free or reduced-cost breakfast and lunch and information about free health clinics and other services in the community. Because Victor is proficient in listening and speaking, his language-based instructional and assessment needs focus on reading and writing. Although he is a senior, he is only now taking this sophomore-level Cultural Issues class because of scheduling concerns that relate, in part, to his arrival at this high school only three years ago. In a partnership with a local medical school, medical student tutors have volunteered to spend time mentoring high school ELLs in chemistry and math. This program has benefitted Victor greatly, both academically and socially.

Teacher Questions, Concerns, and Responses

The Cultural Issues teacher has many questions about appropriately serving these unique students.

If Mercy's home language is English, why does she qualify for ELD services?

Although English is Mercy's home language, the form of English that she learned in Liberia is not standard U.S. English. As a result, Mercy's ELP test scores qualified her for ELD services. Further, Mercy's unfamiliarity with U.S. schools and culture indicate that she needs the guidance in negotiating the intricacies of U.S. academic settings that ELD programs optimally address. As such, this type of support is entirely appropriate for Mercy.

Why shouldn't Kumar and Yasir immediately be put in a special education classroom?

Never experiencing formal schooling does not indicate a cognitive disability. However, given the information provided by Yasir's mother, he may, in fact, possess a cognitive disability. Evaluation may be appropriate for Yasir, though a very thoughtful approach is required because that he does not yet speak English. Again, *Special Education Considerations for English Language Learners* (Hamayan et al., 2013) is recommended for its clear guidance.

Why is Manivone placed in a high school Cultural Issues class, given her limited school experience and literacy skills?

When ELLs enroll in high school, they cannot typically spend the entire day in a program designed to teach them English. As a result, these students must enter content classes even at beginning ELP levels; this is the case with students in elementary and middle school as well. Given that ELLs represent many cultures from around the globe, a cultural issues class is a good starting point for their matriculation. High school teachers who have ELLs in their classrooms can use the guidance from this book and quick-reference chart to differentiate their expectations for ELLs at all ELP levels, thereby sheltering their instruction and teaching English through content. Further, the opportunities for interaction with classmates supports oral language development.

Why is Victor enrolled in the ELD program, given that he is performing above many of his non-ELL peers?

This issue was also raised with Karol in the last section. According to the school, district, and state guidelines, Victor is apparently still entitled to participate in ELD programming. However, the criteria for entitlement may need to be revisited if Victor's involvement in this programming seems unnecessary.

What are Victor's educational options after high school? Should I be helping him fill out college applications?

Victor is an undocumented student, and, as such, is ineligible for any federal financial aid. His unauthorized status basically precludes his attending college unless he can pay for it himself. Even if he can somehow afford to pay for college, obtaining an appropriate job following graduation could be problematic because of documentation requirements for employment. Teachers are reminded that such impossible outcomes begin to dawn on some ELLs at early ages, particularly at the middle and high school levels, and can have a negative impact on motivation for academic achievement or staying enrolled in school.

Educators should be aware that all students in the United States are entitled to K–12 public education, regardless of immigration status (*Plyler v. Doe*, 1982). While it is inappropriate to inquire about immigration or citizenship status, teachers may learn about their students' situations and they may be asked for advice. Teachers should be prepared to refer students to the appropriate resources.

Differentiating a High School Assignment

Nothing facilitates speedier language acquisition than engaging students in authentic, real-life applications that contribute to enhanced student motivation. In keeping with this observation, the differentiated high-school lesson plan focuses on developing panels of students to present information on relevant cultural issues to local civic groups, the school board, and other schools as part of a school-wide service learning initiative. The ELLs in this class concentrate their efforts on their own experiences as students in a new country, highlighting their academic accomplishments and extracurricular activities.

The focus of the presentation was developed through a collaboration of the Cultural Issues class and ELD teachers as a way for high school ELLs to inform the school board of their progress and show gratitude for the support that they have been given by the district, which has been working to improve services to diverse learners. The essential learning for this assignment is to describe and explain students' academic accomplishments and extracurricular activities

Table 9-3 Example Assignment Template for High School Students

Assignment: Make an oral panel presentation to the school board that describes and explains students' academic and extracurricular experience in a new country, with attention to cross-cultural issues.

Standards-Based Content or Topic (from the curriculum):

Academic and extracurricular accomplishments of students in a new country with attention to cross-cultural issues

Level 1	Level 2	Level 3	Level 4	Level 5	Non-ELL
Language-Based Expectations					
Introduce self and other presenters using appropriate conventions of public speaking, talking very briefly (e.g., eye contact, volume, content, expression, body language). Develop and deliver a 3–4 slide presentations using provided content/academic words and phrases to describe and explain	Develop and deliver a mini-presentation using occasional content/academic vocabulary and simple sentences and using appropriate conventions of public speaking (e.g., eye contact, volume, content, expression, body language) to describe and explain	Develop and deliver a brief oral presentation using some content/academic vocabulary and simple/complex sentence structures and using appropriate conventions of public speaking (e.g., eye contact, volume, content, expression, body language) to describe and explain	Develop and deliver a short oral presentation using some content/academic vocabulary and complex sentence structures and using appropriate conventions of public speaking (e.g., eye contact, volume, content, expression, body language) to describe and explain	Develop and deliver a short oral presentation using some content/academic vocabulary and complex sentence structures and using appropriate conventions of public speaking (e.g., eye contact, volume, content, expression, body language) to describe and explain	Develop and deliver a short oral presentation using grade-level vocabulary and sentence structures and using appropriate conventions of public speaking (e.g., eye contact, volume, content, expression, body language) to describe and explain
Scaffolding and Support					
▪ information gleaned from a visit to the location where school board meetings are held ▪ a Post-it note brainstorm strategy (students write ideas about their academic and extracurricular experiences in a new country with attention to cross-cultural issues on Post-it notes)	▪ information gleaned from a visit to the location where school board meetings are held ▪ a Post-it note brainstorm strategy (students write ideas about their academic and extracurricular experiences in a new country with attention to cross-cultural issues on Post-it notes)	▪ information gleaned from a visit to the location where school board meetings are held ▪ a Post-it note brainstorm strategy (students write ideas about their academic and extracurricular experiences in a new country with attention to cross-cultural issues on Post-it notes)	▪ information gleaned from a visit to the location where school board meetings are held ▪ a Post-it note brainstorm strategy (students write ideas about their academic and extracurricular experiences in a new country with attention to cross-cultural issues on Post-it notes)	▪ information gleaned from a visit to the location where school board meetings are held ▪ a Post-it note brainstorm strategy (students write ideas about their academic and extracurricular experiences in a new country with attention to cross-cultural issues on Post-it notes)	▪ information gleaned from a visit to the location where school board meetings are held ▪ a Post-it note brainstorm strategy (students write ideas about their academic and extracurricular experiences in a new country with attention to cross-cultural issues on Post-it notes)

Level 1	Level 2	Level 3	Level 4	Level 5	Non-ELL
■ a categorization activity wherein students organize the Post-it notes on a T-chart graphic organizer according to academic and extracurricular accomplishments with attention to cross-cultural issues	■ a categorization activity wherein students organize the Post-it notes on a T-chart graphic organizer according to academic and extracurricular accomplishments with attention to cross-cultural issues	■ a categorization activity wherein students organize the Post-it notes on a T-chart graphic organizer according to academic and extracurricular accomplishments with attention to cross-cultural issues	■ a categorization activity wherein students organize the Post-it notes on a T-chart graphic organizer according to academic and extracurricular accomplishments, with attention to cross-cultural issues	■ a categorization activity wherein students organize the Post-it notes on a T-chart graphic organizer according to academic and extracurricular accomplishments, with attention to cross-cultural issues	■ a categorization activity wherein students organize the Post-it notes on a T-chart graphic organizer according to academic and extracurricular accomplishments, with attention to cross-cultural issues
■ the T-chart as a springboard in order to generate language to describe and explain their accomplishments and activities with attention to cross-cultural issues	■ the T-chart as a springboard in order to generate sentences to describe and explain their accomplishments	■ the T-chart as a springboard in order to generate sentences to describe and explain their accomplishments	■ the T-chart as a springboard in order to generate sentences to describe and explain their accomplishments	■ the T-chart as a springboard in order to generate sentences to describe and explain their accomplishments	■ the T-chart as a springboard in order to generate sentences to describe and explain their accomplishments
■ videos of school board meetings, diagrams, and pictures (to build background)	■ videos of school board meetings, diagrams, and pictures (to build background)	■ videos of school board meetings, diagrams, and pictures (to build background)	■ videos of school board meetings, diagrams, and pictures (to build background), as needed	■ notes, if needed; and	■ notes, if needed; and
■ pretaught vocabulary	■ pretaught vocabulary	■ pretaught vocabulary	■ pretaught and modeled conventions of public speaking, as needed	■ practice.	■ practice.
■ pretaught and modeled conventions of public speaking	■ pretaught and modeled conventions of public speaking	■ pretaught and modeled conventions of public speaking	■ provided academic sentence frames for describing and explaining as needed		
■ provided language frames for describing and explaining	■ provided academic sentence frames for describing and explaining	■ provided academic sentence frames for describing and explaining	■ notes, if needed; and		
■ pictorial notes	■ notes; and	■ notes; and	■ practice.		
■ assistance of a paraeducator or trained volunteer; and	■ practice.	■ practice.			
■ practice.					

Essential Learning: *Describe and explain students' academic accomplishments and extracurricular activities in a new country with attention to cross-cultural issues; present information about oneself to an audience, and use appropriate conventions of public speaking to communicate information.*

Language Demands: *Use oral and written language to describe and explain.*

in a new country with attention to cross-cultural issues, present information about oneself to a live audience, and use appropriate conventions of public speaking to communicate information. Requiring preparation, organization, and practice, this assignment easily incorporates the development of all four language domains. The language demands require students to use oral and written language to describe and explain. Further, the final product—the public presentation—incorporates authentic skills needed beyond school settings. This assignment, like the previous two examples at the elementary and middle school levels, serves double duty as an ideal assessment when accompanied by an accurate and well-thought-out scoring rubric.

The Differentiated Assignment Template presented in Table 9-3 outlines expectations for this assignment tailored to all five ELP levels. Teachers are reminded that this is simply one example and are encouraged to differentiate in their own innovative ways, remembering that the key to successful differentiation is the alignment of expectations with the student descriptors and strategies provided on the quick-reference chart and throughout this book.

Because the ELLs in this class represent different ELP levels in different domains, teachers may need to think broadly when offering scaffolding and support. That is, a given student may have skills in one domain, such as speaking, that enable him or her to easily address the core assignment. However, this same student is not necessarily able to take advantage of all of the scaffolding unless it is differentiated for a lower ELP level in another domain, such as writing. Fortunately, the example template provides ideas regarding different levels of scaffolding that can be applied to any student. This assignment offers an example where reciprocal mentoring, in its various forms, would be very useful; content and language teachers and paraeducators could collaborate to ensure the successful completion of the assignment by all students.

In addition to issues of language, other relevant student factors must also be considered to support the students in successfully completing the differentiated assignment. Some guidance for the individual students in this hypothetical high school class is offered in the following section.

Mercy

- Because Mercy struggles with long-term projects, this assignment needs to be broken down into parts. This strategy can support all the students, but it is critical for her.
- Mercy's tendency to isolate herself means that the teacher may need to continually encourage her to participate with other group members in preparing the panel presentation.
- Perhaps Mercy could be encouraged to develop her part of the panel presentation in concert with Manivone, with the two of them sharing their stories as a team.

Kumar and Yasir

- Because these two students are new to school, extra guidance regarding how to work as part of the group on this academic task needs to be provided.
- These students likely come from more collective cultural backgrounds and may feel very nervous about being singled out to introduce the group. Allowing them to work as a team may help ease this nervousness.
- Remembering all the information needed to make introductions may be a challenge, given that traditional note taking would not work for either of these students. In addition to pictorial notes, teacher prompts during the presentation may be needed.

Manivone

- This student may be very soft spoken, in accordance with cultural expectations. Extra support and guidance are needed to help her feel comfortable in speaking to a large group with sufficient volume to be heard.
- Manivone's culture is also more collective in nature. Thus, she may want to work with Mercy to prepare and tell her story.
- Perhaps Manivone and Mercy could share ideas in a back-and-forth team effort. That is, each student first explains when she arrived in the school district, then discusses her relevant academic accomplishments, and finally each student speaks to the issue of extracurricular activities.

Victor

- With his linguistic strengths, Victor seems to be in the position to take on a leadership role in the panel presentation.
- Victor's high level of motivation and academic accomplishment supports this view.

All Five Students

- These students may need assistance in understanding and obtaining appropriate attire for this event.

Conclusion

Teachers who incorporate differentiation according to student ELP levels support ELLs in essential ways. These teachers recognize that their ELLs bring rich resources to the classroom and that bilingualism, or multilingualism, is a cognitive asset. When supported by appropriate instruction, students demonstrating ability in more than one language are well positioned for academic and professional success. Teachers who collaborate and differentiate according to what students can do with oral and written English—as well as students' home languages—clearly embrace their shared responsibility to provide academic parity through access to the curriculum for every student in the classroom. They recognize that language imposes an obstacle that can be surmounted. These teachers understand that learning language is an incremental process and that students continue to advance along the continuum of language development only with appropriate instruction. They take steps to remove barriers and validate students for what they do know, building opportunities to allow all students to demonstrate their knowledge and skills, even without language mastery. Like teaching a child to ride a bicycle using training wheels, these teachers provide supports and scaffolds for learning, gradually reducing them until the student achieves full proficiency in content and language. In the end, such teachers are uniquely positioned to make a world of difference in ELLs' lives. It is to that worthy goal that they, and we, dedicate our efforts.

Professional Learning Activities

1. **Apply the Differentiated Assignment Template to students in the book.**

   - First, select five ELLs from the scenarios that open chapters 4–8, changing their ages to those represented by students in your classroom. Choose students that represent a range of ELP levels and backgrounds similar to your students.

   - Second, turn to the assignment, which states: *Read a short story and draw personal connections using textual evidence from the story.*

   - Third, write the essential learning and the language demands at the bottom of the template.

   - Fourth, write the language-based expectations that correspond to the ELP levels of your focal students.

   - Fifth, write the scaffolding and support that correspond to the ELP levels of each of your focal students.

   - Sixth, consider the individual needs of your students based the following factors:

     - Educational history
     - Immigrant and refugee status
     - Cultural background
     - Prior difficult experiences
     - Age
     - Language distance
     - Social distance
     - Psychological distance

     Write guidelines that teachers should consider when tailoring the assignment for the selected students on a separate piece of paper.

   - Finally, complete the Differentiated Assignment Template for the students that you selected. Look at the example template on page 280 for suggested ways to adapt this assignment. Note that this completed template represents only one way to differentiate this assignment. The key is to align teacher expectations for use with what students at particular ELP levels can do with language.

Assignment 1: *Read a short story and draw personal connections, using textual evidence from the story*

Standards-Based Content or Topic (from the curriculum)

Personal connections with a short story

Level 1	Level 2	Level 3	Level 4	Level 5	Non-ELL
		Language-Based Expectations			
					Read and explain orally in a group using grade-level vocabulary and sentence structures and evidence from the text to make text-to-world connections
		Scaffolding and Support			
					Use strategies explained by the teacher.

Essential Learning: _____

Language Demands: _____

Suggested Ways to Differentiate the Assignment

Assignment: *Read a short story and draw personal connections, using textual evidence to discuss connections*

	Standards-Based Content or Topic (from the curriculum)			

Personal connections with a short story

Level 1	Level 2	Level 3	Level 4	Level 5	Non-ELL
		Language-Based Expectations			
Read and explain using provided words and phrases, and evidence from the text to make text-to-world connections	Read and explain using occasional content/academic vocabulary, simple sentences, and evidence from the text to make text-to-world connections	Read and explain using some content/academic vocabulary, simple and complex sentence structures, and evidence from the text to make text-to-world connections	Read and explain using some content vocabulary, complex sentence structures, and evidence from the text to make text-to-world connections	Read and explain using a variety of content/academic vocabulary, complex sentence structures, and evidence from the text to make text-to-world connections	Read and explain orally in a group using grade-level vocabulary and sentence structures, and evidence from the text to make text-to-world connections

Level 1	Level 2	Level 3	Level 4	Level 5	Non-ELL
		Scaffolding and Support			
For reading	*For reading*	*For reading*	*For reading*	*For reading*	*Using strategies explained by the teacher*
▪ Using minimal language and visual support, and focused on a familiar topic	▪ Using simplified language, visual support, and focused on a familiar topic	▪ Using simplified language, visual support, and focused on a familiar topic	▪ On grade level but includes visual support	▪ On grade level	
▪ Using strategies explained by the teacher	▪ Using strategies explained by the teacher	▪ Using strategies explained by the teacher	▪ Using strategies explained by the teacher	▪ Using strategies explained by the teacher	
▪ With reading assistance from a paraeducator or trained volunteer	▪ With reading assistance from a paraeducator or trained volunteer	▪ With reading assistance from a paraeducator or trained volunteer	*For discussion*	*For discussion*	
For discussion	*For discussion*	*For discussion*	▪ Using pretaught academic language that is part of environmental print (e.g., on a language wall)	▪ Using pretaught academic language that is part of environmental print (e.g., on a language wall)	
▪ Using pretaught words and phrases	▪ Using pretaught language that is part of environmental print (e.g., on a language wall)	▪ Using pretaught language, including some content/academic language that is part of environmental print (e.g., on a language wall)			
▪ Using everyday language	▪ Using everyday language				
▪ Where appropriate, repeating teacher cues					

Essential learning: Make text-to-world connections; consider how background knowledge influences connections and learning

Language demands: Use oral and written language to describe, explain, compare, and contrast.

2. **Apply the Differentiated Assignment Template to your own classroom.**

- First, select a group of students from your classroom that spans all five ELP levels. (If you do not have students at all five levels, that is fine. Further, you may have more than one student at a given level.) List your focal students on a separate piece of paper.
- Second, write the assignment above the blank template.
- Third, write the essential learning and the language demands at the bottom of the template.
- Fourth, write the language-based expectations that correspond to the ELP levels of your focal students.
- Fifth, write the scaffolding and support that correspond to the ELP levels of each of your focal students.
- Sixth, consider the individual needs of the students that you selected based on the following factors:

  - Educational background
  - Immigrant and refugee status
  - Cultural background
  - Prior difficult experiences
  - Age
  - Language distance
  - Social distance
  - Psychological distance

Write guidelines that teachers should consider when tailoring the assignment/assessment to your students.

Differentiated Assignment Template

Assignment 2: _____

	Level 1	Level 2	Level 3	Level 4	Level 5	Non-ELL
Standards-Based Content or Topic *(from the curriculum)*						
Language-Based Expectations						
Scaffolding and Support						

Essential Learning: _____

Language Demands: _____

Differentiation Communiqué for Teachers
· ·

Educators' names: _____   _____   _____

Class: _____

For the week of: _____

ELLs' names and ELP levels:

_____ L = _____ S = _____ R = _____ W = _____

_____ L = _____ S = _____ R = _____ W = _____

_____ L = _____ S = _____ R = _____ W = _____

_____ L = _____ S = _____ R = _____ W = _____

_____ L = _____ S = _____ R = _____ W = _____

_____ L = _____ S = _____ R = _____ W = _____

Content objectives (to be completed by content teacher):

Language objectives (to be completed by ELD teacher and/or content teacher):

Targeted vocabulary (to be completed by content teacher and/or ELD teacher):
Content vocabulary: Cross-curricular academic vocabulary:

Activities/assignments/assessments (to be listed by classroom/content teacher):

Differentiation ideas based on the quick-reference chart (to be completed by ELD teacher and/or content teacher). Write the names of your students under the appropriate level.

Student Names →	Level 1	Level 2	Level 3	Level 4	Level 5
Connections to prior experience and learning					
Instructional strategies					
Supplementary materials					
Assessment strategies					

Differentiated Assignment Template

Assignment: _____

	Standards-Based Content or Topic *(from the curriculum)*				
	Level 2	Level 3	Level 4	Level 5	Non-ELL
Level 1	Language-Based Expectations				
	Scaffolding and Support				

Essential Learning: _____

Language Demands: _____

Glossary

academic discourse. General and content-specific vocabulary, specialized or complex grammatical structures, and language functions and discourse structures used by members of an academic discourse community (e.g., scientists, mathematicians, poets) to acquire new knowledge and skills, communicate about a topic, or impart information to others.

academic language. The oral and written language used for school success, which is developed primarily through reading academic texts and participating in academic discourse communities.

acculturation model. Describes, interprets, explains, and predicts how the language, social, or psychological distance between a language learner's home (e.g., Spanish, Arabic) and new language and culture (e.g., English) influences that language learner's acquisition of the new language and culture.

affective filter. Introduced by Krashen (1982) to account for the influence of affective factors such as motivation, self-confidence, and anxiety on second language acquisition.

alphabetic principle. The understanding that there are systematic and predictable relationships between written letters and spoken sounds.

balanced literacy approach. An approach to literacy instruction that balances attention to reading and writing and includes modeled, shared, and guided reading and writing instruction prior to expectations of independent reading and writing.

co-teaching. A teaching model in which two experts with different backgrounds, such as an English language development teacher and a general content teacher, teach a class together.

cognate languages. Languages that descend from the same language, such as Spanish and French that descend from Latin.

collaborative lesson planning. Regularly-scheduled meetings during which general education and English language development teachers collectively choose assignments, set clear goals, develop content and language objectives, select important vocabulary, and identify differentiated instruction and assessment strategies that meet learner needs.

collectivistic. Quality of cultural groups that tend to emphasize group-based identity, rights, and needs, and privilege the interests of the group over the individual.

comprehensible input. Introduced by Krashen (1982) to refer to oral and written language that language learners can understand and that is necessary for second language acquisition.

concepts of print. Important early reading skills that include book holding, understanding print directionality, one-to-one matching of spoken and written words, making connections between illustrations and graphics and print, and recognizing punctuation marks.

content assessment. Authentic evidence of what a student knows and can do with content. For an English language learner, content assessment should seek to separate conceptual understanding from language development as long as the language of the content area is not part of what is being assessed.

content objectives. Lesson plan targets relating to the big ideas or essential learning. Content objectives are more or less the same for all students.

conversational fluency. The language people use in everyday communication, or social language, developed primarily through conversation.

cross-training. Professional learning opportunities in which teachers with one type of expertise (e.g., content teachers) gain skills in another area (e.g., language learning and teaching).

cultural competence. The ability to maintain one's own cultural stance while respecting the perspectives of another.

culturally responsive teachers. Teachers who provide instruction that relates to students' cultural backgrounds in terms of content and learning orientation and style while preparing them to participate in new cultural practices.

culture shock. A stressful transitional period when individuals move from a familiar cultural environment to an unfamiliar one, and the individual feels disoriented and threatened.

culture stress. Refers to the long-term impact of dealing with cultural differences.

differentiated assessment. The use of different assessments for diverse student populations to ensure all students can demonstrate what they know and can do.

ELPA21. A consortium of states that designed and developed an assessment system for English language learners. The system is based on the ELPA21 English Language Proficiency Standards and addresses the language demands needed to reach college and career readiness standards.

English as a second language (ESL). The teaching and learning of English as a new language to students who come from homes that do not use English. This term is also used to refer to teachers, curricula, instruction, assessment, and programming for students who are new to English.

English language development (ELD). The process of acquiring English as a new language. This term is also used to refer to the WIDA English language development standards and is also increasingly used to refer to the English component of an English language learners' instruction or program.

English language development continuum. A framework that illustrates the incremental process of English language development, taking place over time and in somewhat predictable stages. Individual states (e.g., California, New York, Texas) and consortia of states (e.g., WIDA, ELPA21) may use different terms to refer to these stages and may include different numbers of stages.

English language proficiency. Skill or ability in using the English language at a particular moment in time. This term is used to refer to English language proficiency (ELP) levels, scores, and assessments.

essential learnings. Big ideas that have enduring value beyond the classroom and are a prerequisite to future classroom-based learning. This term is also used to refer to the desired results of instruction that all students should know and be able to do.

formative assessment. A type of assessment used to document and measure student learning and provide information to the teacher that can guide instruction.

fund of knowledge. Knowledge and skills that people have learned through their lives and that vary depending on their experiences. This term is attributed to Luis Moll, Norma Gonzalez, and colleagues.

general education teacher. The teacher who is responsible for teaching content to K-12 students in the English-medium academic mainstream. General education teachers today can expect to have linguistically and culturally diverse learners in their classrooms, and they need to know how to differentiate instruction and assessment for all students.

graphic organizers. An excellent springboard for instruction because they help students articulate ideas and relationships that they already know or are learning about but need scaffolding and modeling to express.

guided reading. A literacy teaching approach in which the teacher guides small groups of students in reading a common text that is at their instructional (rather than their frustration) level.

heterogeneous grouping. Grouping students with diverse expertise together to support learning. Stands in contrast to groupings of students according to shared expertise (e.g., home language, level of English language development).

higher-order thinking. Cognitive skills required for tasks that involve application, analysis, synthesis, creation, and evaluation.

home language. The language(s) used at home and possibly in other key community contexts.

home language literacy. The ability to read and write in a language used regularly for communication outside of school.

identity. A social construct that is understood as dynamic and multiple, rather than static and unitary. A dynamic notion of identity sees intersections among different aspects of identity including language, gender, race, ethnicity, religion, and socioeconomic status, to name a few.

identity texts. The product of students' creative work or performance in which their identities are reflected in a positive light (Cummins & Early, 2011, p. 3). The text may be spoken, signed, visual, musical, dramatic, or combinations in multimodal form.

imagined communities. Places that can open new positions, roles, and possibilities for all community members. Ideally, new identities, empowering narratives, and imagined communities make space for linguistically and culturally diverse students to have equal access to learning opportunities at school (Norton, 2013).

immigrant. Refers to individuals who have permanently relocated to a new country of their own accord.

independent level. That which students can do with language independently, or without scaffolding or instructional support.

individualistic. Quality of privileging the identities, interests, rights, and needs of the individual over the group.

instrumental motivation. The desire to learn a new language for personal gains, such as getting a job or earning a degree (Schuman, 1978).

integrative motivation. The desire to get to know speakers of a new language, and this desire motivates them to learn the new language (Schumann, 1978).

investment. Norton's notion of investment (2016) goes beyond the traditional idea of "motivation" in acculturation theory and second language acquisition (Schuman, 1978) and accentuates the role of human agency and choice. According to Norton, language learners who choose to invest in their own language learning actively seek or create opportunities to use language for the purposes they need, and they take ownership of and responsibility for their learning.

language distance. The extent to which languages differ from each other.

language domain. Listening, speaking, reading, and writing.

language objectives. Lesson plan targets that focus on the oral and written language that students need to engage with and achieve in content-area instruction; may focus on vocabulary as well as sentence and discourse structures and functions.

language shock. Associated with feelings of discomfort stemming from the inability to conceptualize and use the new language, as well as fear of appearing ignorant.

language-based expectations. What students can be expected to do with language in a particular activity or task. Teachers differentiate language-based expectations according to students' ELD and home language levels in listening, speaking, reading, and writing.

language experience approach (LEA). Allows teachers to use students' own words as texts for teaching reading. Following a shared experience, such as conducting a science experiement, students collaboratively dictate stories while the teacher, or another student, acts as the scribe. These nonfiction stories are then used as material for teaching reading.

linguistically differentiated instruction. Teaching practices that begin with what students know and can do with languages and literacies, including ELD and home language levels in listening, speaking, reading, and writing.

linguistically responsive assessment practices. Recognize the continuum of language development while seeking to ascertain student learning in the content areas.

non-ELLs. Students who are not officially designated as English language learners. There is a wide range of variation in the category of non-ELLs or so-called English speakers.

print-rich environment. Students regularly see reading and writing used in real-life contexts, in keeping with recommendations found in the educational literature (e.g., Peregoy & Boyle, 2016).

psychological distance. The reasons and ways a person responds to new learning situations.

pull-out. A program model in which English language learners are pulled out of the general education classroom for dedicated ELD instruction.

push-in. A program model in which a trained professional joins the general education teacher in the classroom and provides support for the English language learners in the class.

reciprocal mentoring. Collaborative relationships among teachers who bring together different types of professional expertise and learn from each other (coined by Jones-Vo et al., 2007).

refugee. Defined by the United Nations High Commissioner for Refugees (UNHCR) as "a person who is outside his or her country of nationality or habitual residence; has a well-founded fear of persecution because of his or her race, religion, nationality, membership of a particular social group or political opinion; and is unable or unwilling to avail

himself or herself of the protection of that country, or to return there, for fear of persecution." (UNHCR, 2007, p. 6.)

scaffolding. The temporary instructional support that teachers and other more competent peers provide to students throughout the learning process. This support is tailored to student needs and enables students to achieve higher learning goals than they would be able to without such support.

sensory anchor. An experiential foundation to which students connect new vocabulary, concepts, and facts.

shared reading. A literacy instruction approach in which the teacher and students read a text together, discussing various points throughout the reading. The students then read this same text on their own, repeatedly, developing increasing fluency.

shelter instruction. Making complex content-area instruction comprehensible to English language learners while teaching these students how to use language for academic purposes.

silent period. An early stage of second language acquisition that occurs before language learners produce oral language. During the "silent period" (Krashen, 1982), students absorb and process new input in preparation for future language production. The length of this silent period is variable; some students may not produce spoken language for days, weeks, or months.

SIOP Model (Sheltered Instruction Observation Protocol). A lesson planning framework designed by Echevarria, Vogt, and Short (2016) that teachers can use to make complex content comprehensible to English language learners, promote academic language development in a new language, and integrate ELLs into content-area classes. The model consists of eight components. preparation, building background, comprehensible input, strategies, interaction, practice/application, lesson delivery, and review/assessment.

SLIFE (student with limited or interrupted former education). An acronym used by educators that refers to students with limited or interrupted former education. These students need intensive and comprehensive support for literacy and numeracy development with attention to the cultural norms of U.S. schools and society (DeCapua & Marshall, 2011).

social distance. The distance between cultural groups. A small social distance reflects social similarities, and a large social distance reflects social differences (Schumann, 1978).

teacher leader. A classroom teacher who takes on additional leadership responsibilities, works with other teachers, and provides demonstration lessons, coaching, and mentoring.

think-aloud. A strategy in which the teacher talks through his or her thinking process as the teacher demonstrates or models a process (e.g., how to write a text; how to conduct an experiment) for the benefit of students. Students' attention is drawn to the steps taken, and they are provided the opportunity to replicate these steps for themselves.

total physical response (TPR). This technique allows students to participate in classroom activities during the earliest stage of language acquisition. For example, teachers might state and demonstrate basic classroom commands such as "Please sit down" or "Take out your pencil," a few times, having newcomers mirror the teacher's actions. After several repetitions, students should be able to respond to teacher commands without teacher modeling.

transfer. Concepts, knowledge, skills, and practices learned in one language can be transferred to another language.

understanding by design. The three-stage framework and process that Wiggins & McTighe (2005) propose, also known as "backward design." Teachers begin their lesson planning with the end or outcome in mind, select appropriate assessments/assignments that allow students to demonstrate those outcomes, and then plan the instructional activities/tasks that lead to those outcomes.

universal design. An approach to planning that guides teachers to create classroom environments and activities that are accessible to diverse learners. Rather than attempt to retrofit unsuitable instructional design for diverse learners, the universal design for learning begins with the needs of diverse learners in mind.

WIDA Consortium. A consortium of 39 states and U.S. territories that use the English language development (ELD) standards system developed by WIDA. WIDA provides professional development for consortium members, and administers the ACCESS for ELLs—the standardized English language proficiency (ELP) assessment that all ELLs must take annually. The ACCESS for ELLs yields information on students' ELP levels in the domains of listening, speaking, reading, and writing.

word calling. The act of reading aloud without comprehension. Students who are able to read and write in their home language may draw on that prior knowledge and appear to be reading full passages in their second language without comprehending the meaning of the text.

zone of proximal development (ZPD). The difference between what a learner can do without help (i.e., independently) and the next level of development. The concept was introduced, but not fully developed, by psychologist Lev Vygotsky (1896–1934) during the last ten years of his life to explain learning as a social activity.

References

American Educational Research Association (AERA), American Psychological Association (APA), & National Council on Measurement in Education (NCME). (2014). *Standards for educational and psychological testing.* Washington, DC: American Educational Research Association.

Anderson, N. (1999). *Exploring second language reading: Issues and strategies.* Boston: Heinle & Heinle.

August, D., & Shanahan, T. (Eds.). (2006). *Executive summary–Developing literacy in second language learners: Report of the national literacy panel on language-minority children and youth.* Mahwah, NJ: Lawrence Erlbaum. Retrieved March 6, 2010, from http://www.cal.org/projects/archive/nlpreports/executive _summary.pdf

Axtell, R. (1997). *Gestures: The do's and taboos of body language around the world.* New York: Wiley & Sons.

Bachman, L. F., & Palmer, A. S. (1996). *Language testing in practice.* Oxford, UK: Oxford University Press.

Bailey, A. L. (2007). Introduction: Teaching and assessment students learning English in school. In A. L. Bailey (Ed.), *The language demands of school: Putting academic English to the test* (pp. 1–26). New Haven, CT: Yale University Press.

Bernhardt, E. B. (1991). A psycholinguistic perspective on second language literacy. In J. H. Hulstijn & J. F. Matter (Eds.), *AILA Review,* 8 (pp. 31–44).

Blankstein, A.M. & Noguera, P. (2016). *Excellence through equity: Five principles of courageous leadership to guide achievement for every student.* Alexandria, VA: Association for Supervision and Curriculum Development (ASCD).

Bonfils, N. (2009, February). *Reaching out to ESL families.* Session presented at the Iowa Culture and Language Conference, Des Moines, IA.

Bunch, G., Kibler, A., & Pimentel, S. (2012). Realizing opportunities for English learners in the Common Core English Language Arts and Disciplinary Literacy Standards. Stanford, CA: Understanding Language Initiative. Retrieved March 25, 2013, from http://ell.stanford.edu/publication/realizing -opportunities-ells-common-core-english-language -arts-and-disciplinary-literacy.

Capps, R., Fix, M., Murray, J., Ost, J., Passel, J., & Herwantoro, S. (2005). *The new demography of America's schools: Immigration and the No Child Left Behind Act.* Washington, DC: Urban Institute.

CAST. (2008). *Universal design for learning guidelines version 1.0.* Wakefield, MA: Author.

Castellano, J. A., & Diaz, E. (2001). *Reading new horizons: Gifted and talented education for culturally and linguistically diverse students.* Boston: Allyn & Bacon.

Chamot, A. U., & O'Malley, J. M. (1994). *The CALLA handbook: Implementing the cognitive academic language learning approach.* White Plains, NY: Longman.

Chiswick, B. R., & Miller, P. W. (2005). Linguistic distance: A quantitative measure of the distance between English and other languages. *Journal of Multilingual and Multicultural Development, 26*(1), 1–11.

Cloud, N. Genesee, F. & Hamayan, E. (2009). *Literacy Instruction for English Language Learners: A Teacher's Guide to Research-Based Practices.* Portsmouth, NH: Heinemann.

Cook, H. G. (2008, June). *Effects of native language and context factors on the learning trajectory of English language learners: A growth model approach.* Paper presented at the CCSSO Student Assessment Conference, Orlando, FL. Retrieved December 11, 2009, from http://www.ccsso.org/content/PDFs/106 _Cook.pdf

Cummins, J. (2001). The entry and exit fallacy in bilingual education. In C. Baker & N. H. Hornberger (Eds.), *An introductory reader to the writings of Jim Cummins* (pp. 110–138). Buffalo, NY: Multilingual Matters.

Cummins, J. (2012). How long does it take for an English language learner to become proficient in a second language? In Hamayan, E. & Freeman Field, R. (Eds.). *English language learners at school: A guide for administrators* (2nd ed., pp. 37–39). Philadelphia: Caslon.

Cummins, J., & Early, M. (Eds.) (2011). *Identity texts: The collaborative creation of power in multilingual schools.* London: Institute of Education Press.

Curtis, J. L. (2006). *Is there really a human race?* New York: Joanna Cotler Books, an imprint of Harper-Collins Books.

DeCapua, A., & Marshall, H. W. (2011). Reaching ELLs at risk: instruction for students with limited or interrupted formal education. *Preventing School Failure, 55*(1), 35–41.

Delpit, L. (2006). *Other people's children: Cultural conflict in the classroom* (2nd ed.). New York: New Press.

deOliviera, L. C., & Athanases, S. Z. (2007). Graduates' reports of advocating for English language learners. *Journal of Teacher Education, 58*(3), 202–215.

Dresser, N. (2005). *Multicultural manners: Essential rules of etiquette for the 21st century* (rev. ed.). Hoboken, NJ: Wiley & Sons.

Developing Literacy in Second-Language Learners: Report of the National Literacy Panel on Language-Minority Children and Youth (pp. 197–238). Mahweh, NJ: Lawrence Erlbaum.

Dual Language Showcase (2001). Retrieved from http://thornwoodps.ca/dual/index2.htm

Echevarria, J., Vogt, M., & Short, D. (2016). *Making content comprehensible for English learners: The SIOP model* (5th ed.). Boston: Pearson Education.

Education Week. (2009, January 8). Teaching ELL students. [Electronic version.] *Education Week, 28*(17), 26.

Elliott, D. (2004). *And here's to you!* Cambridge, MA: Candlewick Press.

Escamilla, K., Hopewell, S., Butvilofsky, S., Sparrow, W., Soltero-González, L., Ruiz-Figueroa, L., & Escamilla, M. (2014). *Biliteracy from the Start: Literacy Squared in Action.* Philadelphia: Caslon.

Everson, M. E., & Kuriya, Y. (1998). An exploratory study into the reading strategies of learners of Japanese as a foreign language. *Journal of the Association of Teachers of Japanese, 32*(1), 1–21.

Fairbairn, S. (2006). English language learners' performance on modified science test item formats: A pilot study. *Dissertation Abstracts International*, DAI-A 68/01. (Publication No. AAT 3248008.)

Fairbairn, S. (2007). Facilitating greater test success for English language learners. *Practical Assessment, Research & Evaluation, 12*(11). Available online: http://pareonline.net/getvn.asp?v=12&n=11

Fairbairn, S. B., & Fox, J. (2009). Inclusive achievement testing for linguistically and culturally diverse test takers: Essential considerations for test developers and decision makers. *Educational Measurement: Issues and Practice, 28*(1), 10–24.

Field, R. (2015). What kinds of variation do we find in the category "ELL"? In Valdés, Menken, & Castro, (Eds.), *Common Core, Bilingual, and English Language Learners: A Resource for Educators.* Philadelphia: Caslon.

Fitzgerald, J., & Graves, M. (2004). Reading supports for all. *Educational Leadership, 62*(4), 68–71.

Flaitz, J. (2006). *Understanding your refugee and immigrant students: An educational, cultural, and linguistic guide.* Ann Arbor: University of Michigan Press.

Fountas, G. S., & Pinnell, I. (2016). *Guided reading, 2nd Edition: Responsive Teaching across the Grades.* Portsmouth, NH: Heinemann.

Fox, M. (1997). *Whoever you are.* San Diego: Voyager Books, Harcourt.

Franco, L. (2005, June). *What's different about teaching reading to English language learners?* Workshop presented for Heartland Area Education Agency, Des Moines, IA.

Freeman, D. E., & Freeman, Y. S. (2000). *Teaching reading in multilingual classrooms.* Portsmouth, NH: Heinemann.

Freeman, Y. S., & Freeman, D. E. (2002). *Closing the achievement gap: How to reach limited-formal-schooling and long-term English learners.* Portsmouth, NH: Heinemann.

Freeman, Y. S., & Freeman, D. E. (2009). *Academic language for English language learners and struggling readers: How to help students succeed across content areas.* Portsmouth, NH: Heinemann.

García, O., Ibarra Johnson, S., & Seltzer, K. (2016). *The Translanguaging Classroom: Leveraging Student Bilingualism for Learning.* Philadelphia: Caslon.

Garcia, S. B. (2008, February). *A culturally and linguistically responsive approach to implementing response-to-intervention (RTI) models: Realizing the promise for all students.* Workshop presented for Heartland Area Education Agency, Johnston, IA.

Gibbons, P. (2015). *Scaffolding Language, Scaffolding Learning: Teaching English Language Learners in the Mainstream Classroom, 2nd edition.* Portsmouth, NH: Heinemann.

Goldenberg, C. (2006). Improving Achievement for English Learners: What the Research Tells Us. *Education Week*, July 26, pp. 34–36.

González, N., Moll, L. & Amanti, C. (2005). *Funds of Knowledge: Theorizing Practices in Households, Classrooms, & Communities.* NY: Routledge.

Goodman, K. (1994). Reading, writing, and written texts: A transactional sociopsycholinguistic view. In R.B. Ruddell, M.R. Ruddell, & H. Singer (Eds.), *Theoretical models and processes of reading* (4th ed.) (pp. 1093–1130). Newark, DE: International Reading Association.

Gottlieb, M., Carnuccio, L., Ernst-Slavit, G., Katz, A., & Snow, M. A. (2006). *PreK–12 English language proficiency standards.* Alexandria, VA: Teachers of English to Speakers of Other Languages (TESOL).

Graham, S. (winter 2009–2010). Want to improve children's writing? Don't neglect their handwriting, *American Educator.*

Grognet, A., Jameson, J., Franco, L., & Derrick-Mescua, M. (2000). *Enhancing English language learning in elementary classrooms: Trainer's manual.* McHenry, IL: Delta.

Hamayan, E., Marler, B., Sanchez-Lopez, C., & Damico, J. (2013). *Special education considerations for English language learners: Delivering a continuum of services* (2nd ed.). Philadelphia: Caslon.

Harper, C., & de Jong, E. (2004). Misconceptions about teaching English-language learners. *Journal of Adolescent & Adult Literacy, 48*, 152–162.

Herrero, S. (2016). *Biography-driven culturally-responsive teaching* 2nd ed.). New York: Teachers College.

Hindley, J. (1996). *In the company of children.* York, ME: Stenhouse.

Hinkel, E., & Fotos, S. (2002). From theory to practice: A teacher's view. In E. Hinkel, & S. Fotos (Eds.), *New perspectives on grammar teaching in second language classrooms* (pp. 1–15). Mahwah, NJ: Lawrence Erlbaum.

Hoffelt, J. E. (n.d.). *We share one world.* Bellvue, WA: Illumination Arts.

Hofstede, G. (2010). *Cultures and organizations: Software of the mind* (3rd ed.). London: McGraw-Hill.

Honigsfeld, A.M. & Dove, M.G. (2017). *Co-Teaching for English Learners: A Guide to Collaborative Planning, Instruction, Assessment, and Reflection.* Thousand Oaks, CA: Corwin.

Iowa Department of Education. (2007). *Educating Iowa's English language learners: A handbook for administrators and teachers.* Des Moines: Author.

Iowa Department of Education, & the Connie Belin and Jacqueline N. Blank International Center for Gifted Education and Talent Development. (2008). *Identifying gifted and talented English language learners: Grades K–12.* Des Moines: Iowa Department of Education.

Jones-Vo, S., Fairbairn, S., Hiatt, J., Simmons, M., Looker, J., & Kinley, J. (2007). Increasing ELL achievement through reciprocal mentoring. *Journal of Content Area Reading, 6*(1), 21–44.

Kauffman, D. (2007a). *What's different about teaching reading to students learning English? Study guide.* McHenry, IL: Delta.

Kauffman, D. (2007b). *What's different about teaching reading to students learning English? Trainer's Manual.* McHenry, IL: Delta.

Kinsella, K. (2007, May). *Rigorous academic vocabulary development to bolster language and literacy for protracted adolescent English learners.* Workshop presented at the International Reading Association Annual Convention, Toronto, Canada.

Knox, C., & Amador-Watson, C. (2000). *Responsive instruction for success in English (RISE): Participant's resource notebook.* Crystal Lake, IL: Rigby.

Koda, K. (1996). L2 word recognition research: A critical review. *Modern Language Journal, 80*(iv), 450–460.

Kouritzin, S. G. (2004). Programs, plans, and practices in schools with reputations for ESL student success. *Canadian Modern Language Review, 60*, 481–499.

Krashen, S. (1982). *Principles and practice in second language acquisition.* Oxford: Pergamon Press.

Krashen, S., & Terrell, T. (1983). *The natural approach: Language acquisition in the classroom.* Hayward, CA: Alemany Press.

Lapp, D., Fisher, D., Flood, J., & Cabello, A. (2001). An integrated approach to the teaching and assessment of language arts. In S. R. Hurley & J. V. Tinajero (Eds.), *Literacy assessment of English language learners* (pp.1–26). Boston: Allyn & Bacon.

Lau v. Nichols, No. 72–6520, Supreme Court of the United States 414 U.S. 563 (1974).

Lenski, S. D., & Ehlers-Zavala, F. (2004). *Reading strategies for Spanish speakers.* Dubuque, IA: Kendall/Hunt.

Lightbown, P. M., & Spada, N. (2013). *How languages are learned* (3rd ed.). Oxford, UK: Oxford University Press.

Menken, K. & Kleyn, T. (2010). The long-term impact of subtractive schooling in the educational experiences of secondary English language learners. *International Journal of Bilingual Education and Bilingualism, 13*(4), 399–417.

Moule, Jean (2012). Cultural Competence: A Primer for Educators, 2nd edition. Belmont, CA: Cengage.

National Center for Education Statistics. (n.d.). Language minority school-age children. In *Participation in education: Elementary/secondary education.* Retrieved December 24, 2009, from http://nces.ed.gov/pro- grams/coe/2009/section1/indicator08.asp

National Clearinghouse for English Language Acquisition and Language Instruction Educational Programs (NCELA). (2007, Oct. 19). What are the most common language groups for ELLs? In *NCELA FAQ.* Retrieved March 18, 2009, from http://www.ncela.gwu.edu/ex- pert/faq/05toplangs.html

Norton, B. (2013). *Language and Identity: Extending the Conversation* (2nd ed.). Bristol, UK: Multilingual Matters.

Office of English Language Acquisition, Language Enhancement, and Academic Achievement for Limited English Proficient Students (OELA). (2007). *The growing numbers of limited English proficient students: 1995/96–2005/06.* Retrieved June 13, 2009, from http://www.ncela.gwu.edu/files/uploads/4/Growing LEP_0506.pdf

Ontario Education. (2007). *English language learners ELD and ESL programs and services: Policies and procedures for Ontario elementary and secondary schools, kindergarten to grade 12.* Retrieved March 19, 2018, from http://www.edu.gov.on.ca/eng/document/esleldprograms/esleldprograms.pdf

Ormrod, J. (2008). *Educational psychology: Developing learners* (6th ed.). Upper Saddle River, NJ: Merrill Prentice Hall.

Patrick, E. (2004). US in focus: The US refugee resettlement program. In *Migration information source: Fresh thought, authoritative data, global reach.* Retrieved June 29, 2009, from http://www.igrationinformation.org/USfocus/display.cfm?ID=229

Payne, R. (2008). Nine powerful practices. [Electronic version.] *Educational Leadership, 65*(7), 48–52

Peregoy, S. F., & Boyle, O. F. (2016). *Reading, writing, and learning in ESL: A resource book for K–12 teachers* (7th ed.). Boston: Allyn & Bacon.

Plyler v. Doe, No. 80–1538, United States Court of Appeals for the Fifth Circuit. 457 U.S. 202 (1982).

Schumann, J. H. (1978). *The pidginization process: A model for second language acquisition.* Rowley, MA: Newbury House.

Snow, C., Burns, M. S., & Griffin, P. (Eds.). (1998). *Preventing reading difficulties in young children.* Washington, DC: National Academy Press.

Solano-Flores, G. & Trumbull, E. (2003). Examining language in context: The need for new research and practices paradigms in the testing of English-language learners. *Educational Researcher, 32*(2), 3–13.

Ting-Toomey, S. (1999). *Communicating across cultures.* New York: Guilford Press.

Ting-Toomey, S. & Chung, L.C. (2012). *Understanding Intercultural Communication.* New York, NY: Oxford University Press.

Tomlinson, C. A. (2014). *How to Differentiate Instruction in Academically Diverse Classrooms, 2nd Edition.* Alexandria, VA: Association for Supervision and Curriculum Development (ASCD).

Trumbull, E., Rothstein-Fisch, C., Greenfield, P. M., & Quiroz, B. (2001). *Bridging cultures between home and school: A guide for teachers.* Mahwah, NJ: Lawrence Erlbaum.

UNHCR. (2007). *The 1951 refugee convention: Questions and answers.* Geneva, Switzerland: Author. Retrieved February 9, 2009, from http://www.unhcr.org/basics /BASICS/3c0f495f4.pdf

United States Office of Civil Rights (US OCR) and the Department of Justice (DOJ), Jan. 7, 2015, Dear Colleague Letter issued jointly by US OCR and DOJ (pp. 26 & 27).

Uribe, M., & Nathenson-Mejia, S. (2008). *Literacy essentials for English language learners: Essential transitions.* New York, NY: Teachers College Press.

Valdés, G., Menken, K., & Castro, M., editors (2015). *Common Core, Bilingual and English Language Learners: A Resource for All Educators.* Philadelphia: Caslon.

Van Lier, L. and Walqui, A. (2010). *Scaffolding the Success of Adolescent English Language Learners: A Pedagogy of Promise.* San Francisco: West Ed.

Vann, R. J., & Fairbairn, S. B. (2003). Linking our worlds: A collaborative academic literacy project. *TESOL Journal, 12*(3), pp. 11–16.

Vygotsky, L. S. (1978). *Mind in Society: The Development of Higher Psychological Processes.* Boston, MA: President and Fellows of Harvard College.

Wardhaugh, R. and Fuller, J.M (2015). *An Introduction to Sociolinguists,* seventh edition. Oxford: John Wiley & Sons.

WIDA (2014). *The 2012 Amplification of the English Language Development Standards: Kindergarten – 12.* Madison, WI: Board of Regents of the University of Wisconsin.

Wiggins,G., & McTighe, J. (2006). *Understanding by design* (expanded 2nd ed.) Upper Saddle River, NJ: Pear- son Education.

Wong-Fillmore, L. (2000). Loss of family languages: Should educators be concerned? *Theory into Practice, 39*(4), 203–210.

Zweirs, J. (2011). *Academic Conversations: Classroom Talk that Fosters Critical Thinking and Content Understandings.* Portland, ME: Stenhouses.